D1015080

The Lost City of
SOLOMON & SHEBA

An African Mystery

ROBIN BROWN-LOWE

SUTTON PUBLISHING

First published in the United Kingdom in 2003 by
Sutton Publishing Limited · Phoenix Mill
Thrupp · Stroud · Gloucestershire · GL5 2BU

British Library Cataloguing in Publication Data
A catalogue record for this book is available from the British
Library.

ISBN 0-7509-3033-0

For Heather . . .
and recalling a seminal weekend in the Great Karoo
with Pauline and John Pank, Lin Mehmel and
John Rudd when the light suddenly dawned.

Typeset in 11/14.5 pt Sabon.
Typesetting and origination by
Sutton Publishing Limited.
Printed and bound in England by
J.H. Haynes & Co. Ltd, Sparkford.

Contents

The King Solomon's mines I have dreamed of have been discovered and are putting out their gold once more. . . .

H. Rider Haggard, Ditchingham, 15 July 1905

. . . and they came to Ophir, and fetched from thence gold, four hundred and twenty talents, and brought it to King Solomon.

I Kings 9:28

. . . Then shalt thou lay up gold as dust, and the gold of Ophir as the stones of the brooks.

Job 22:24

Far land of Ophir, mined for gold
By lordly Solomon of old,
Who, sailing northward to Perim,
Took all the gold away with him

Hilaire Belloc, *The Modern Traveller*

Foreword

In 1909 when my father took up his duties as Consul-General and British Minister at Addis Ababa's British Legation, he brought with him a number of books on the country, its inhabitants and its history. Only with some background knowledge could he have hoped to deal with this singular people who believed that their emperors were descended directly from Solomon and Sheba. It is to these books that I owe much of what I learned about the early history of Abyssinia (now Ethiopia) where I was born and brought up.

Today, Ethiopians of traditional faith still believe that the Queen of Sheba visited Solomon, King of the Israelites, in Jerusalem, was seduced by him and bore him a son named Menelik, who founded the Abyssinian royal line. Many also believe that Menelik visited his father, Solomon, and on his departure contrived to substitute a copy of the Ark of the Covenant that his father had given him for the original, which he eventually brought back to Aksum.

Robin Brown-Lowe's fascinating quest for *The Lost City of Solomon and Sheba* explores this legend and investigates how refugees from ancient Abyssinia may have gone south to establish stone monuments bearing certain features of buildings they had left; and to mine for gold as they had done previously in their homeland. He also studies the Falashas, sometimes called the 'Black Jews' of Ethiopia, and examines their connection with other ancient religious cults found elsewhere in the Middle East.

Robin Brown-Lowe's vivid account has reminded me of a journey I made, on foot, with mules, through northern Ethiopia, over forty years ago. I passed Gondar and Dabat, where I sold two of my mules and bought three others. Here I encountered a Protestant mission to the Falashas. The Falashas, who now claimed to be Jews, held pre-Talmudic beliefs different from orthodox Judaism. An industrious people, skilled iron-workers, they had been disliked by the Ethiopians who believed they possessed supernatural powers and could turn themselves into hyenas or wolves. As so-called Abyssinian Jews, the Falashas were superficially indistinguishable from their Christian neighbours, among whom, I was told, they lived amicably.

Wilfred Thesiger
Surrey, 2002

Wilfred Thesiger, 1987.
(Heather Lowe)

Introduction

It is a matter of fact that in the very heart of Africa there is a 'lost' civilisation whose people built some 20,000 stone temples, forts, and an irrigation system covering hundreds of square miles. It has been estimated that as much stone was used here as went into the building of the Egyptian Pyramids. A century after this ruined empire was first scientifically investigated by the Royal Geographical Society, however, it remains all but unknown to the general public even though the country in which it is located is lately much in the news. Its origins are also still the subject of intense speculation, even though they could hardly be more exotic – with the suggestion that this realm is the work of the legendary Solomon and Sheba.

My interest in the place began half a century ago as an English boy aged nine, when my family trekked overland to south central Africa, lured by my father's promise that we would start a new life among the gold mines of King Solomon and visit the temple of his lover, the Queen of Sheba. These wonders were to be found, my father assured me, in an African kingdom, Mashonaland, then part of the British Empire as a result of its occupation by the richest man in Africa, Cecil John Rhodes.

Reaching King Solomon's mines would involve a long and dangerous drive to the south of the Mountains of the Moon where my favourite author, H. Rider Haggard, had located the mines in his book of the same name. We had already covered more than half of Africa by then and my intrepid father relished the challenge. As refugees from the austerity of postwar Britain we were – well, he was – more than ready to risk our lives if at the end of it all was a land of milk and honey populated by the benign descendants of the most advanced race in southern Africa.

Today, half a century later, there is still nothing from that wonderful journey that I remember more vividly than my father delivering on his promise and taking us to see Sheba's palace in a ruined city built with the treasure from King Solomon's nearby mines. The city housing the temple and a massive phallic conical tower, where he posed me and my little brother for the official photograph, nestled in an odd jungle of exceptionally dense vegetation rising from savannah grassland against a background of bare stone hills – *kopjes*. Monkey ropes, for which I was always on the lookout in the hope that Tarzan might come attached to one, hung from huge trees, some of which grew out of the granite walls. The undergrowth was dominated by bushes sporting terrible thorns, long white barbs with black tips which I later learned were actually called 'wait-a-minute' (*wag 'n bietjie*) thorns.

We had set out that morning from the nearest town, Fort Victoria. Even though this was dry, high summer, everywhere a strong wind blew from the south-east and a thin rain – *guti* – misted our windscreen. We passed a number of broken stone walls no more impressive than those which divide fields in England, then suddenly the whole view ahead filled with a massive curving flank of stone walling, a monolith sprung whole from the surrounding grass and trees.

My mother, Edith, was nervous of Africa after our traumatic overland journey and would have turned back there and then had not I, totally enthused for the first time in what was already quite an adventurous life, clambered down from our Willy's shooting-brake. Thus my father, Leonard, and I gingerly entered the misty passages of the temple on our own.

Eventually, discretion got the better of even his considerable nerve because while the walls were high and solid, soaring over my head to heights which made it impossible to see their tops, the passage we had entered was peculiarly narrow, hardly wide enough even for a man and a boy to walk side by side. Moreover, it curved away like the scaly, glistening body of a monstrous snake so that there was no way of telling who, or what, lay ahead. Ten minutes of this, and the stones underfoot growing slippery, my father turned back announcing that we needed to get 'get help with this place'.

Even though we had penetrated no more than a hundred yards we quickly got slightly lost retracing our steps. One of the abiding enigmas of the temple is the extraordinary quality of the masonry. Early explorers described them as bricks. In fact they are almost perfectly sculptured granite blocks of such similar shape and size they require no mortar. One section of grand wall looks very like another and, in the deepening guti mist the labyrinth had taken us in. At an unfamiliar junction I was told to wait while Leonard explored the way ahead.

While he was gone, the walls began to talk!

I can hear them to this day, whispering and moaning. I called my father back and drew his attention to the 'voices'. He made a nervous joke about Solomon calling for Sheba, but raised no further objection to our beating a hasty retreat.

Intriguingly, those voices have turned out not to be that much of a fantasy. An intense enquiry into the origins of these ruins has been going on for more than a hundred years and one aspect of the research has revealed that the walls do indeed make eerie sounds, and for good reason. In the more massive structures cunning spaces were constructed by the ancient masons to allow the prevailing winds to pass through the walls. There is also a cave with very peculiar sound characteristics in the ruined acropolis overlooking the temple. It so amplifies any sound made inside it, be it a blast of wind or the human voice, it can be heard in the temple half a mile away. As extensive 'religious' artefacts have also been found in this cave it is now the consensus of opinion that it was used by Monomatapa and Rozvi priests acting as spirit mediums to their gods.

After our adventure in the temple maze we stuck to the high ground. Hundreds of well-made steps led upwards between narrow flanking walls of smooth natural granite until, after many pauses for rest, we arrived within the spectacular acropolis. Here, surrounded by mountainous piles of ancient worked stones the like of which we had seen nowhere else in Africa, Edith laid out on a large flat rock our lunch of avocado sandwiches and Mazoe orange squash. My father gleefully identified the stone from the guide book as a 'sacrificial' altar stone but my mother, after inspecting its surface (for dried blood?), insisted it would do very well.

The hilltop sported a crest of cut stones – stelae – rising from the walls above a sheer cliff, and inexplicable little round towers like pepper pots on the fortress buttresses of an enclosure to the west. In the valley the huge doughnut of the temple some 800 feet long was clearly visible.

Whereupon it began to disappear!

At first it just wobbled when the stones found they could take up no more of the midday heat. These mirages then became so dense and plastic, whole sections of wall, especially the tops of the higher walls and towers, broke down to shifting battlements. By the time we had finished our sandwiches the stone city in the valley below was a shifting miasma of grey, drizzled with blacks and greens. Lost!

My mother checked that we were all wearing our hats and began to ask nervous questions of Leonard as to how long he thought it would take us to return to the rest huts in Fort Victoria. I was spellbound, and protested at this early departure, pointing out that I had yet to see a single one of King Solomon's mines! But Edith observed that they would probably be too dangerous given the way the whole place had been 'let go' and we were on our way by mid-afternoon.

Over the next twenty years, until Rhodesia's white regime decided I had dangerously over-liberal views and forced me to become a political refugee, I went back to the ruins several times. Ever more sanitised, they remained a popular picnic stop on the way to South Africa where, each year, we drove on our summer holidays.

Archaeologists, mainly from Britain, worked away behind the scenes, exorcising the ghosts of Solomon and Sheba and relabelling the ruins with scientifically correct names. The acropolis became the Western Enclosure on the Hill, the temple the Elliptical Building and the various ruins in the valley were cleansed of the names of pioneers, like Baden-Powell of scouting fame, and became numbered Enclosures. Doubts were cast on the popular theory of a Phoenician origin. Admittedly, the general public still preferred to climb to 'the acropolis' and enjoy a barbecue with a view of 'the temple'.

Dark political currents – a ghostly caucasian Queen of Sheba is worshipped by an obeisant black subject in this white-ruled Rhodesia publicity poster for Great Zimbabwe.

The Rhodesian Tourist Board continued to display its famous poster of a ghostly Sheba emerging from her temple with its spectacular conical tower. Today, of course, even the poster has been judged politically incorrect and has gone the same way as its ghostly queen, even though few of the 'riddles' it advertises have been solved. In those days, and now, what little tourism there was paid for the basic preservation of the ruins, and the relegation of Solomon and Sheba to romantic myth did material damage to Great Zimbabwe's image as an international tourist attraction. It is income that cash-strapped modern Zimbabwe can ill-afford to lose.

To return to that naïve ten-year-old, however, here we were driving away, perhaps never to see again the greatest mystery southern Africa had to offer. Little did I know then that this act of deprivation would plant the seed of a fifty-year obsession with the origins of the city and its thousands of associated works. Many years later, when I checked the details of our day's outing with my father, he reminded me that I had been preoccupied by its origins even then and had subjected him to a barrage of questions, not least about its age.

'I told you that nobody could say for sure,' he recalled, 'which was what we thought at the time. A lot of overseas boffins had looked at the place but opinion was completely split.'

'What about the local black people?'

There was not much point in talking to them either, apparently. The first scientific expedition to come here from Britain at the turn of the century had interviewed all the local Africans and established that they knew nothing about the ancient ruins. Nor did they build stone houses themselves and they certainly did not mine gold. And there the matter rested for most of the first half of the twentieth century.

My father, otherwise a compassionate man, was of a generation of Rhodesians who preferred to leave a great many important questions unanswered – in particular the morality of white supremacist rule and its justifications. By our very presence we were 'raising civilised standards'. African culture was decadent, evidence the ruins of Zimbabwe. It well suited the proponents of such views to find that the black people living in mud huts above Great

Zimbabwe knew nothing of an earlier culture. So for all my early years in Rhodesia I shared the popular view that there had to be some kind of ancient classical explanation for this culture skilled in the building of stone monuments and the deep-mining of gold. Even our schoolteachers avoided rocking this comfortable boat.

Eventually, this placebo even became entrenched in white law. When the Rhodesian regime had its back to the wall in the face of African demands for equality and political power, Ian Smith's government banned the Historical Monuments Commission from promoting an African origin for Great Zimbabwe. The Minister of Internal Affairs declared officially (and ordered the preparation of a new guidebook to reflect his views) that there was no *irrefutable* evidence of the origins of the ruins 'at the present time'. Academically he was right – there were at least three learned books refuting an exclusive Shona authorship competing with the three archaeological treatises supporting one. Truth, however, had very little to do with this ban because by then Great Zimbabwe had become a political pawn. It has remained so to the present day; indeed, all that has changed is the skin colour of the protagonists.

Today's Great Zimbabwe guidebooks (this quotation was taken from the Internet) offer an origin theory along these lines: 'Controversy regarding the ruins' origins has persisted for years and is even now not completely dispelled. It has taken years of careful archaeological study to arrive at the answers to these questions. They are now known and they are unequivocal, the original structures were built by indigenous African people, the ancestors of modern Zimbabweans.' Perhaps – but Africa is a big place, with one of its coastlines on the Mediterranean. It is here, says one school of thought (branded the 'Romantics'), that we should look for Africans skilled in monumental stone-building.

Who, indeed, were the ancestors of modern Zimbabweans and who were their ancestors? To imply, as these guidebooks do, that the Zimbabwe culture sprang unaided, uninfluenced and exclusively from Shona soil is to distort both the archaeological evidence and the volumes of comparative and ethnographic information produced by the opponents of a Shona genesis.

There is, for example, little hard evidence that a sufficiently large Bantu population to build several mighty *zimbabwes*, temples, stone forts and irrigation terracing had migrated this far south by the time the Carbon-14 datings say the stone-building began in earnest. I am not, however, disputing the key claim of the Shona school that the ancestors of the modern Shona, a people known as the Karanga, largely assembled these stones. Certainly when the grand *zimbabwes* were raised and improved no other large workforce existed here. But this book will seriously question the modern myth that no other influences and no other nationalities were involved in ancient times.

It took many years for it to be recognised that Great Zimbabwe is actually the largest stone city in Africa south of the Pyramids – indeed, this astonishing statistic is, in my experience, largely unknown to the general public. Yet there is no precedent for monument-sized stone-building this far south in Africa when the Great Zimbabwe complex is believed to have been started, and little or no stone-building has gone on here since the Zimbabwe culture proper ended some 500 years ago.

Today's rural Karanga mostly live in thatched mud huts just as their ancestors did when the first European explorers came to the ruins. Moreover, the granite walls were by then already *ancient* ruins in process of being broken up by aged trees such as the baobab and *spirostachys africana* which take hundreds of years to reach maturity.

Where did the ancient Karanga, born and raised as cattle-herders on this central African savannah, acquire a sophisticated knowledge of architectural geometry, the mathematics of load and stress-bearing structures, and the measuring devices to service the architects, not to mention the function of drains and foundations, the graded battering of rising cones, and the beautiful arts and crafts which went on inside these walls? I shall also be examining a similar set of unanswered questions for the widespread deep gold-mining and crafting industry which paid for it all.

Finally – the greatest riddle of them all – having evolved all these skills, why has not a whisper of it been passed down to the descendants of these architects, skilled masons, sculptors and miners? Even the name of their magnificent temple-city is utterly lost. 'Zimbabwe' translates to nothing more than 'stone building'.

All this defies credibility, yet you must believe in it as an act of faith if you are to be a card-carrying member of the Shona school, just as in Mr Smith's time you had to believe in a classical Semite origin and an émigré architectural elite to stay on message.

I find both these assaults on the truth offensive, even if in the context of the region's recent history they are understandable. None of the rulers of the land on which Great Zimbabwe stands, past and present, have dared properly to investigate its enigmatic origins for fear of the impact it would have on their political claims. We have been saddled with two racially tainted Zimbabwe myths and the truth of this marvellous place has become even more lost in the process. This is a genuine tragedy because even a quick glance at the evidence suggests that the Zimbabwe culture was the product of a number of complex multi-racial associations or partnerships, with Great Zimbabwe arguably the most important ancient monument to cultural partnership on the planet.

I see my task, therefore, as a process of unravelling perhaps 3,000 years of apocryphal legend, myth, science good and bad, passions that have blinded good men to the truth, disinformation by evil men, and downright propaganda.

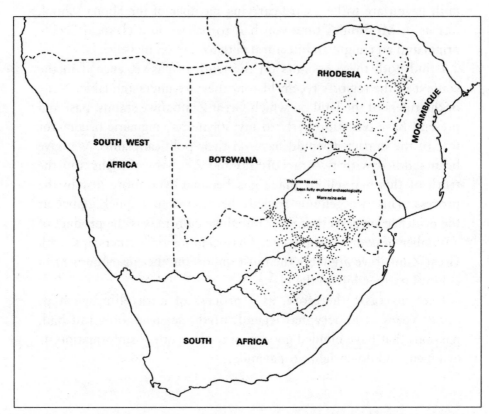

RHODESIA

MOCAMBIQUE

SOUTH WEST
AFRICA

BOTSWANA

This area has not
been fully explored archaeologically
More ruins exist

SOUTH   AFRICA

The dots on this map, dating from the 1970s, show just some of the thousands of *zimbabwe*-type structures that have been discovered across the whole of south-central Africa.

ONE

To Ophir Direct

R umours were rife a century and a half ago that the unexplored hinterland of Africa hid a fabulous eldorado, a place that had provided the Queen of Sheba with the gold to seduce Solomon. The tale has been immortalised as fiction by that most exotic of African adventure writters, H. Rider Haggard, in his novel *King Solomon's Mines*. Actually, Rider Haggard had intimate personal experience of the territory we are about to explore. When in 1886 a small army of intrepid treasure hunters went in search of Solomon's mines this master of derring-do would be up there with the best of them. The rest of the best included Indian fighters from the American frontier wars and Baden-Powell who would go on to found the Boy Scout movement.

It is, I think, the most intriguing aspect of this story that the facts are always stranger than the fiction. For example, it is a fact that King Solomon must have acquired the gold he accumulated in vast quantities from somewhere, and it is also fact that the Queen of Sheba was a major gold dealer. Time and the explorations of people like H. Rider Haggard have revealed that the closest country to both of them where huge quantities of gold had been mined was Mashonaland.

It is agreed by all the schools of thought that this gold, sold through foreign traders, paid for the construction of at least five grand cities with massive walls of stone, one of which, a temple-city, is the largest stone structure south of the Pyramids. Aerial surveys carried out in recent times suggest lesser towns and villages of stone number more than 15,000, not counting a mountain 'kingdom' which incorporates one of the largest stone-terraced irrigation systems on our planet.

1

But the history of this lost Zimbabwe culture – even that part of its history of which we can be sure – is a good deal stranger than the fiction which has been based upon it.

The first classical mention we have of King Solomon's eldorado is a guarded reference in the Bible to a place called 'Ophir', somewhere in Africa. Ophir's exact location is never defined. It would have been surprising if it had been because Ophir, according to the Bible, was the source of the gold which Phoenician mariners, hired by Solomon through Hiram of Tyre, brought home from three-year trips round Africa in their new deep-hulled ships. These ships allowed the Phoenicians to navigate oceans of variable tides, winds and currents. They made extraordinary voyages as far afield as England and India. They went to Africa – Phoenician wrecks have been found on the African coasts – but the location of Ophir remained a well-kept secret, probably because it was the Phoenicians' most valuable piece of information regarding trade.

Advance some thousands of years to the rough frontiers of pioneer South Africa where the Dutch have established a garden in the Cape of Good Hope to victual the ships passing round it in the service of the East India trade. In a few years they will push out from these protected gardens into coastal mountains sparsely populated by a strange Asian-looking race of miniature aboriginals, the Khoi. They move these 'Chinese Hottentots' on, plant vineyards, build villages, every one with a church. They read their Bibles every day and believe every word they read, not least of the riches of Solomon and of his seduction by the voluptuous Sheba. It is an interest focused by the possibility that Solomon and Sheba's fabulous fortunes have been mined in their new wilderness homeland. But where?

A century on and these Europeans have become a deeply religious farming community, the Boers. But Britain takes over the now-thriving Cape Colony and the Boers make another break for freedom, this time trekking in their ox wagons in search of 'free' land deep in the hinterland. In Africa by now, 'free' land means land not within the 'sphere of influence' of other Europeans. Well-watered arable land is the Boers' prime objective and this they find alongside the Vaal and the Orange rivers, but the Bible is still their guidebook and Ophir has yet to be discovered. They set up the Boer states of the Transvaal and the Orange Free State and in a few years will discover beds of diamonds and reefs of gold beyond even the dreams of Solomon and Sheba. But the Transvaal cannot be Ophir either because these deposits are found under virgin land. Even so, the Boers sense they are getting warm.

The first real clue that such a place as Ophir – gold mining in the context of an ancient culture – might actually exist reaches them and soon thereafter, the British, through an unlikely source – the German pastor of the so-called Berlin Mission in the Soutspanberg, a mountain area in the Transvaal. Here resided in rather ambivalent circumstances a pioneering missionary, the Revd Alex Merensky (1837–1918) who, like other missionaries of his time, in particular the better known Robert Moffat and his son-in-law David Livingstone, shared the promotion of the Gospel with the advancement of imperialism.

The scramble for the whole of Africa – essentially a scramble for the natural resources of the dark continent – was well advanced by this time. There was a flush of British pink across the far north (Egypt), the north-east and central areas (Kenya and, soon, Uganda and the Sudan) and across all of the south as far north as the Boer republics. The French sphere of influence extended across most of north-west Africa, although there were solid smudges of British pink here as well (Sierra Leone, the Gold Coast and Nigeria). The Belgians controlled Conrad's heart of darkness (the Congo). The Portuguese had substantial domains on the east and west coasts (Angola and Portuguese East Africa). The Germans under Bismarck had interests on both the east and west coasts (South West Africa and Tanganyika) and there was still an east coast outpost of Arabs on Zanzibar island. But the south-central median of Africa – the place where all held the eldorado of Ophir to be – was ruled by a despotic regiment of refugee Zulus, the Matabele, who now stood in the way of any further exploration of the hinterland from the south.

The European powers all realised that if they could join up their territories or spheres of influence by taking over the middle ground, they would control the continent and its resources – which might include Ophir. Efforts to keep each other out often verged on the ridiculous. The British, for example, would build a railway, dubbed 'the Lunatic Line' all the way from the East African coast to the central great lakes and declare a protectorate over Uganda, because they thought the French had their sights set on the headwaters of the Nile in those same great lakes. Control the flow of the Nile and you control Nile-dependent British Egypt, it was argued.

Feeling out the ground for the 'Great Powers' were their missionaries, the harbingers, as I believe they have been rightly described, of imperialism. The British had Robert Moffat studying the Ndebele language at his Kuruman Mission. He would soon become a constant, trusted visitor to the court of the Matabele chiefs, Msilikaze and his son Lobengula. Msilikaze is said to have worshipped Moffat as an individual but never came close to being converted to Christianity. Livingstone monitored the Matabele eastern flank from Bechuanaland, where he too failed to convert almost anybody, and would later move hopefully on to a position of influence on the Zambesi river north of Lobengula's fiefdom.

The missionaries, of course, spent a great deal of time with their Bibles. Ophir for them was gospel. It was just a matter of finding it. Merensky had set up his Berlin Mission on land controlled by the British-hating Boers in the mountains just south of the land of the Matabele; indeed, he overlooked the road, known as the Missionary Road, and the Limpopo river crossing everyone had to take into Matabeleland. The Portuguese, whose colonisation of the east spanned more than five centuries, were also probing the hinterland, which in the light of their long tenure they regarded as a legitimate sphere of influence. The British, noting that the Portuguese had made little progress from the east coast in all that time, saw no immediate threat from them in the race for Ophir. Not so from the Germans, and particularly the Boers, who were known to be working together.

British fears were well founded. Boer agents – tough, bush-wise hunters – had reported that there was gold to be found deep in the hinterland behind the potent and disciplined Matabele military screen. Moreover, the land here did indeed fit the definitions of both

Ophir and Shangri-La. Ancient abandoned mines with shafts too narrow for an adult European were found, and the overgrown piles of quartz beside them revealed that they had been worked for gold. These ancient workings were on the edges of a cool plateau offering verdant, well-watered arable and grazing land too high for the tsetse-fly and, most important, thinly populated by a quiescent Matabele slave-tribe, the Shona.

There was also, paradoxically, another lure. Neither the Matabele nor the Shona appeared to have any real knowledge of the value of their gold. Nor were there any legends or even myths of the ancient gold-miners.

Yet for almost a decade before the turn of the nineteenth century the balance of other political concerns in an increasingly volatile Europe confined these European powers to their existing spheres of influence. Confrontation in Africa could provoke the unmentionable but inevitable war in Europe between the aspirant Germans and the established British. For the time being, limited and probably expensive territorial gains in Africa were worth neither the risk nor the cost, even if there was, perhaps, a pot of gold at the end of it all.

This all changed when one Englishman, Cecil John Rhodes, decided he had become rich enough to implement his personal dream of a British Africa from the Cape to Cairo, and the German chancellor, Bismarck, turned 'Kolonialmensch'. But even the arrival of these two extraordinary egos would not of itself have opened up the road to Ophir had not a fateful meeting taken place in 1871 at the Soutspanberg Berlin Mission between Pastor Merensky and an itinerant German 'geologist', Carl Mauch.

This was the same year that Rhodes came to Africa to begin making what in its time would be the largest individual fortune the world had ever known. Mauch was also there to make his fortune from Africa's mineral wealth but until he met Merensky had had little luck. It is also patently obvious that both he and Merensky were furthering their national interests or, more simply, were willing agents of German imperialism.

Rhodes from the beginning was a political and financial voice to be reckoned with. Within a decade he would become a member of the Cape parliament and then its Prime Minister. At no time did he make any secret of his national interests, believing that if Great Britain did not occupy the hinterland by fair means or foul, the Germans would beat them to it.

Such dreams by a single, destitute, individual may seem extraordinary by today's standards but as early as 1872 when his fortune had yet to be made, Rhodes made a will in which he left his imagined estate to the British Secretary of State for the Colonies 'for the extension of the British Empire'. A second will in 1877 provided for 'a secret society, the true aim and object whereof shall be the extension of British rule throughout the world . . . and especially the occupation by British settlers of the entire Continent of Africa, the Holy Land, the valley of the Euphrates, the Islands of Cyprus and Candia, the whole of South America, the island of the Pacific not heretofore possessed by Great Britain, the whole of the Malay Archipelago, the seaboard of China and Japan, the ultimate recovery of the United States of America as an integral part of the British Empire, the consolidation of the whole empire, and finally the foundation of so great a power as to hereafter render wars impossible and promote the best interests of humanity.'

The only man even vaguely in his class of imperialist was Bismarck, who took Rhodes seriously and had his Afrika agents keep a careful eye on him.

Rhodes finally found his fortune in the rich diamond mines of the Transvaal at Kimberley. The German imperialist, Ernst von Weber, came there in 1873 and wrote an article urging the colonisation by Germany of the west coast north of the Cape Colony which had a 'superfluity of mineral treasures and could support a population 50 times as large as that of Great Britain'.

In 1874, Bismarck shook Great Britain off the fence and caused all Rhodes' worst dreams to come true when he declared South West Africa a protectorate of Germany. And it did not stop there. Almost the whole of Germany's colonial empire was laid out between 1884 and 1885 and Rhodes and the British became convinced that Germany's next move would be to join forces with the Boers, block the road to the north, then move on Ophir themselves. Rhodes was by then convinced that he knew where Ophir was and he wanted it to be 'Rhodesia' (literally) not some German mining colony.

But again we must step back a few years and try to overhear the conversation which took place at the Berlin Mission between Merensky and Mauch. By 1871 Mauch had been inside Matabele territory twice, ostensibly as a member of a hunting party mounted by the legendary elephant hunter, Henry Hartley. Also by this time the Boers had launched a series of diplomatic forays to the Matabele court at Bulawayo, culminating in a dubious mutual defence 'treaty' in 1847 between the Boer leader, Hendrick Potgeiter, and Matabele indunas which was subsequently ratified by Potgeiter's son, Piet, in 1852.

It is, I think, too much of a coincidence that the Potgeiter family were the political bosses of the Soutspanberg, which commanded the road leading to the best crossing point of the Limpopo river into Matabeleland, and that Pastor Merensky, citizen of the country most opposed to Britain, chose this site for his mission station.

In those early days the only whites Msilikaze would admit were a few favoured missionaries and hunters who rewarded him with part of their bag. The most famous of these were Thomas Baines, who was also a skilled artist, Frederick Courtenay Selous and Henry Hartley, all from Britain; the brothers Posselt from the Boer Republics; and the German, Carl Mauch, who had useful geological skills other than with a rifle, even though hunting was his great passion.

The years from 1865 to 1870 were the golden age of elephant hunting north of the Limpopo river; in fact elephants were all but wiped out on higher ground where an absence of the tsetse-fly allowed pursuit on horseback. Some hunters, like Selous, who also collected 'specimens' for the British Museum of Natural History, took after their prey on foot. Others like Hartley turned their attention to clandestine hunts for another lucrative natural resource – and here Carl Mauch came into his own.

Hartley had first found gold in quartz seams when he hunted in Matabele territory in 1865. Local informants also showed him what they described as old gold workings which had fallen into disuse a decade earlier when the 'Disturbers' (Msilikaze's original refugee Zulu *impi*) had overrun the country. Back in the Transvaal, Hartley approached the young geologist, Mauch, and invited him to join his hunting expedition planned for the winter of 1867, an invitation which Mauch accepted with alacrity even though he must have known that there were few elephants left and, if he was caught digging for gold, Lobengula might well have him put to death. Lobengula, in fact, had a favoured clifftop for just this purpose.

The group trekked deep into Shona country with little success. As they returned, however, Hartley wounded an elephant and in the course of pursuing it through the bush, he and Mauch stumbled upon several excavations which turned out to be ancient mine shafts. Mauch took out his hammer, examined several specimens and found them to contain gold. Along the Umsweswe and Sebakwe rivers more old diggings were found and Mauch abandoned hunting in favour of prospecting to establish the extent of this ancient eldorado. To keep these activities secret he put it about that, guided by honey birds, he was searching for wild honey to supplement the party's diet.

At the end of that summer on their way out of Matabeleland, Mauch came upon another promising reef in the southern Tati area and the party hurried home to plan an expedition to exploit these more accessible Tati lodes. Negotiations were opened with Lobengula who had that year succeeded his father, Msilikaze, and in December news of the gold 'broke' in the Transvaal *Argus*, soon to be followed by wildly exaggerated claims in the British press, one of which was entitled 'To Ophir Direct'. But Mauch kept to himself information, indeed an introduction, to an even more exotic secret.

We know that he visited his fellow-national, Pastor Merensky, at the Berlin Mission on his way through the Soutspanberg. It was either on this visit or on another trip a year later, Merensky told Mauch that the ancient gold mines were the work of a lost civilisation and, according to Merensky's native sources, they had left behind a monumental temple-city ruined and overgrown in the Shona jungle. Merensky also revealed that he had already passed on this story to an earlier adventurer, an American sailor, Adam

Renders, of whom nothing had been heard since. If Mauch could find Adam Renders, or any evidence of his passage, he might also find the lost city. Merensky knew his Bible. He wanted his fellow countryman to be the first to discover King Solomon and the Queen of Sheba's lost city of Ophir.

Rhodes, meanwhile, had been spending time at Oxford University getting a degree, and he read all of the newspaper accounts – especially 'To Ophir Direct' – with undisguised excitement. In Africa, however, there were more pressing affairs, not least the takeover bid which would make or break him. Rhodes had determined to buy out the entire Kimberley diamond field. Just one powerful entrepreneur, Barney Barnato, still stood in his way. By 1888 Rhodes had in effect 'cornered' the world's diamond market but there was still a fight over the terms of the trust deed for the new company, De Beers Consolidated Mines. Barnato had insisted on a company limited to diamond mining, but that was far too confining for Rhodes who had announced to friends that he wanted to use the De Beers company as his instrument for 'winning the north'. There was a final all-night meeting at the end of which an exhausted Barney Barnato conceded defeat with the comment: 'Some people have a fancy for one thing and some for another. You have a fancy for making an empire. Well I suppose I must give it to you.' As a result the mighty De Beers conglomerate has the right not only to mine diamonds and other minerals, but to conduct banking operations, build railways, annex and govern territory – and even raise an army. All this, as we shall see in a moment, can be traced back to the outcome of the conversation Carl Mauch had with Pastor Merensky.

In this interval the Boers had added to everyone's fears of an Afrikaner–German axis across middle Africa by first allowing the establishment of two 'freebooter' pocket republics, Stellaland and Goshen, and then annexing them into their South African republic. The British responded by declaring their 'protection' over the southern approaches to Matabeleland and installing a British commissioner there. When the Boer annexation took place under the eyes of this commissioner, 4,000 British troops marched north into what would in future be known as the Bechuanaland Protectorate and eliminated Goshen and Stellaland. For the moment the threat of further anti-British territorial gains which would block the road to Ophir was over.

That still left the Boers with unrestricted access to the north and the Boers were as ever restless, their young men agitating for the right to open up more land for farming. To the east all the political activity had also reignited Portuguese interest in the land of the Mashonas. Basing their case on century-old precedents and treaties they claimed to have with Shona and Manica chiefs they reinstated the Shona hinterland as their sphere of influence.

Frederick Courtenay Selous, the hunter-politician who will feature large in our story, sought to secure the Shona eldorado for himself by recognising the Portuguese claims and obtaining a gold-mining concession from them.

The British denied all such claims but they did acknowledge that a race between three European powers – Britain, Germany and Portugal, as well as the Boers – was under way and they began to call on their agents, missionaries like Moffat and Livingstone, hunter-explorers like Selous and businessmen like Rhodes, for information about this alleged Ophir. Was it worth the expense and perhaps the risk of war? Carl Mauch's description of the place which had been published years before in an obscure German journal were dusted off and re-examined. His conclusions of origin had been derided as amateur romanticism by antiquarians of the time (archaeology was still a science in its infancy) but leaving aside Mauch's exotic claim that he had actually discovered the Queen of Sheba's summer palace, what else had he revealed?

Merensky had warned Mauch that the journey would be both difficult and dangerous. He confessed that he had already tried to reach the 'ancient Ophir of Solomon' himself but had not pushed on to any ruins because of a notorious tribe called 'Makwapa' who robbed and murdered whites for their valuable possessions. Merensky later recorded: 'A guide of the Banyai tribe told us much about this mysterious spot (the temple-ruins), and thus we gathered that the Banyai revere these ancient buildings; that no living creature may there be put to death, no tree destroyed, since everything is considered sacred. He told us that a populous black tribe, acquainted with the use of firearms, had formerly dwelt there, but about fifty years before had gone northwards. We heard many details regarding the form and structure of these ancient piles, and the inscriptions they bore, but I cannot answer for their truth.'

Mauch, however, was tougher, younger and more intrepid. He also had established credentials with the Matabele as a hunter. Nonetheless, as his journal reveals, it would take him four months, from May until the end of August 1871, to reach 'the most valuable and important and hitherto most mysterious part of Africa . . . the old Monomotapa or Ophir'. Deep in Shona country he also found Adam Renders, of whom he was somewhat contemptuous because Renders had 'gone native', taking two wives, the daughters of a Shona chief. This might have offended Mauch's morality but it proved diplomatically useful because after much prevarication on the part of suspicious local people, Mauch was taken by Renders to 'quite large ruins which could never have been built by blacks'.

Mauch hung on in Mashonaland for nine months, his relations with the natives progressing from bad to worse until in the end he was only allowed to visit the ruins three times. His plight is reported in a note he sent to a hunter friend, George Phillips, in October. Mauch had not even dared to sign the note for fear of revealing where he was to the Matabele, but he identified himself to Phillips by reminding his friend of an incident they had had with lions. Mauch confirmed that he was living with a man named Renders, was in a bad way, having been robbed of everything except his papers and a gun, and needed help. He reminded Phillips not to bring any Matabele. Phillips went to his rescue and also met Renders.

Phillips' report confirms that Renders was an American and he had been living near the lost city for three years. It should be noted in passing that if there is to be credit for the 'discovery' of the ruins, which would become known as Great Zimbabwe, it should go to Adam Renders, especially as nothing is heard of him ever again. Renders was living with Mauch, Phillips stated, on a stone hill a few

From a drawing (probably by the talented Mrs Bent) in Theodore Bent's book, natives explore the massive passage between Great Zimbabwe's outer walls.

miles south-west of the lost city. It was a pretty place: a waterfall coming down from the ridges above which fell into a pan by their hut, to re-emerge as a gushing fountain several hundred feet below. The river had eroded a cave nearby and Mauch told Phillips that he and Renders regularly had to hide there with their Shona hosts to avoid Matabele raiding parties.

It is from George Phillips' account of this rescue mission that we get our first hint that Great Zimbabwe might be just one of many lost city complexes. When Mauch takes Phillips to see 'Ophir', Phillips comments on a zigzag pattern on the walls similar to a ruined wall he had seen while hunting in the western mountains. He had also heard of decorated walls in the south close to the Tati gold workings in Matabeleland.

Phillips re-provisioned Mauch, who was then able to make two more visits to Great Zimbabwe. Mauch wrote the first detailed descriptions and drew remarkably accurate plans and sketches. It was no easy task. Apart from the hostility of the locals the entire complex was overgrown with giant stinging plants. Massive ancient trees grew through some of the larger walls. Not a single building was in a state of repair or occupied. 'It was a very sombre environment', Mauch wrote. 'Masses of rubble, parts of walls, dense thickets and big trees.' But he hacked his way through them and was rewarded with a sight no European had seen before, a massive stone wall of immaculate construction with a decorated top. It left him in no doubt that he had finally discovered the 'rondavel' of the Queen of Sheba.

That was, of course, an enormous conclusion to jump to but it should be remembered that in those days the Bible was gospel, not a book of apocryphal stories. The consensus of opinion of the time, expert and romantic, was that Ophir was in Africa. It was perfectly reasonable, having already found the gold mines on which the existence of Ophir hinged, for Mauch to conclude that he had now found the temple Sheba is said by the Bible to have built at Ophir, especially as nothing of this magnitude had ever been found in 'darkest' Africa before. Even more so because the local people living in its shadow laid no claim to the ruin and told Mauch 'the walls were built at a time when the stones were still very soft, otherwise it

The first glimpse of the impressive Great Zimbabwe wall from a sketch by Mrs Bent.

would have been impossible for the whites who built the walls to form them into a square shape'. Mauch also interviewed an elderly African who described religious ceremonies, including sacrifice, which had been conducted in the ruins by his father.

Mauch now packed his meagre belongings and hurried south, compiling from his diaries two articles which would eventually be published in German in the *Geographischen Mittheilungen* in 1874.

Mauch wrote:

The ruins may be divided into two parts. The one upon a rocky granite eminence of 400 feet in height, the other upon a somewhat elevated terrace. The two are separated by a gentle valley, their distance apart being about 300 yards. The rocky bluff consists of an elongated mass of granite, rounded in form, upon which stands a second block, and upon this again fragments small, but still many tons in weight, with fissures, chasms and cavities.

The western side of the mountain is covered from top to bottom by the ruins. As they are for the most part fallen in and covered with rubbish, it is at present impossible to determine the purpose the buildings were intended to serve; the most probable is that it was a fortress in those times, and thus the many passages –

14

now, however, walled up – and the circular or zigzag plan of the walls would also indicate.

All the walls without exception, are built without mortar, of hewn granite, more or less about the size of our bricks. Best preserved of all is the outer wall of an erection of rounded forms, situated in the plain, and about 150 yards in diameter. It is at a distance of about 600 yards from the mountain, and was probably connected with it by means of great outworks, as appears to be indicated by the mounds of rubbish remaining.

Inside, everything excepting a tower nearly 30 feet in height, and in perfect preservation, is fallen to ruins, but this at least can be made out; that the narrow passageways are disposed in the form of a labyrinth.

The tower consists of similar blocks of hewn granite, and is cylindrical to a height of 10 feet, then upwards to the top conical in form. At the foot its diameter is 15 feet, at the top 8 feet.

The lost city's finest and most puzzling structure, a 10-m high, cut-stone, mortarless tower which is an almost perfect geometrical progression from base to tip.

It stands between the outer wall and another close to and parallel with it. This entrance has, up to the height of a man, four double layers of quite black stone, alternating with double tiers of granite. The outer walls show an attempt at ornamenting the granite – it represents a double line of zigzags between horizontal bands. The ornament is 20 feet from the ground, and is employed upon a third part of the south wall on each side of the tower and only on the inside.

Remembering Merensky's notes, Mauch then looked for 'inscriptions', finding none, a problem which has bothered origin theorists ever since. He did, however, unearth a soapstone beam protruding from a wall, a soapstone dish lying underneath a large walled-up boulder close to the Eastern Enclosure and, near the Elliptical Building, an iron object which 'was a complete mystery to me, but it proves most clearly that a civilised nation must once have lived here'. He sketched this object – it is an iron 'gong' of which several others would be found at Great Zimbabwe. Mauch's critics have, of course, derided this 'civilised nation' conclusion but others have shown that the gongs were most likely imported objects, perhaps trade goods. Others very like them have been found in various parts of Africa.

For Mauch, his most exciting find came on his last day when he revealed the collapsed wooden lintels of the doorways of the Elliptical Building, noting that the wood had not been eaten by insects, was reddish in colour and slightly scented. It was similar to the cedar wood of his pencil. Mauch instantly embroidered a whole theory of Solomon and Sheba around this wood, for which he has been much ridiculed; indeed, it can be said that it was what Mauch made of this wood that has resulted in all his theories about the ruins being scorned as romantic nonsense. Nonetheless, discoveries since have made many of Mauch's observations worth reviewing.

'It can be taken as fact that the wood which we obtained actually is cedar-wood and from this that it cannot come from anywhere else but the Lebanon,' Mauch affirmed. 'Furthermore only the Phoenicians could have brought it here; further Solomon used a lot of cedar-wood for the building of the temple and his palaces; further, including here the visit of the Queen of Sheba and, considering Zimbabwe or Zimbaoe, or Simbaoe written in Arabic (of Hebrew I understand nothing), one gets as a result that the great woman who built the *rondeau* could have been none other than the Queen of Sheba.'

Obviously these connections are very tenuous. As Mauch's critics have pointed out, for Solomon to have brought cedar-wood to Zimbabwe would have been Biblical coals to Newcastle. Mauch's theory also suffered another mauling when it was demonstrated that an indigenous Zimbabwe tree *spirostachys africana* has all the properties he describes.

Back in the 1880s, however, Mauch's reports set many imaginations alight, not least that of Cecil John Rhodes. What Rhodes wanted was proof positive that this was Ophir, material evidence which would transcend speculation. He began collecting every Zimbabwe artefact he could lay his hands on, starting with the items Mauch found.

The object which would delight his heart and, in my view, change the course of his life and arguably result in his early death, was at that moment travelling south through Matabeleland concealed in the baggage of a hunter, Willie Posselt, who had retraced Mauch's footsteps. In 1889, Posselt went looking not for ancient ruins but for 'King Solomon's mines' as described by Mauch, and he had the luck to hire a native guide who promised him stone images of a king and queen. These had to be of Solomon and Sheba, Posselt naturally concluded. The guide took him to a group of simple huts on a stone kopje where he was introduced to the chief. This chief, whose name was actually Mugabe (no relation to the present incumbent), ruled over the valley containing Mauch's ruins. Adam Renders is nowhere in evidence. Posselt was also told that the ruins had last been occupied by a tribe called the Barozvi who practised sacrificial rites, and that the area was still regarded as sacred by the local people.

Chief Mugabe was very reluctant to let Posselt enter the valley but the hunter was well armed and well endowed with trade goods. Posselt also had an armed Swahili bodyguard, Klass, who helped with the persuading. On this occasion, however, Posselt found nothing of interest in the valley ruins, certainly no statues of King Solomon and Sheba and he gave up and went back to hunting. On his way back, however, curiosity got the better of him and without seeking the chief's permission he climbed to the hilltop fortress that Mauch had labelled 'the Acropolis', a place which had been banned to Europeans heretofore.

The reason for that was immediately obvious. Posselt had trespassed on the most sacred site at Great Zimbabwe. In the centre of an enclosure around what most experts agree was an altar he found four soapstone birds carved on the tops of tall columns or stelae. These enigmatic birds, each exquisitely and individually shaped, decorated with chevron patterns, studding and attendant animals, faced east towards the rising sun. Posselt records:

> Each one, including its plinth, had been hewn out of a solid block of stone and measured 4 feet 6 inches in height; and each was set firmly into the ground. There was also a stone shaped like a millstone and about 18 inches in diameter, with a number of figures carved on the border.
>
> I selected the best specimen of the bird stones, the beaks of the remainder being damaged, and decided to dig it out. But while doing so, Andizibi [a relative of Chief Mugabe whose village was on the same hill] and his followers became very excited and rushed around with their guns and assegais. I fully expected them to attack us. However, I went on with my work but told Klass, who had loaded two rifles, to shoot the first man he saw aiming at either of us.

Posselt paid Andizibi with blankets 'and some other articles'. For this he got the one stone bird and the perforated stone. The bird on its pedestal was too heavy to carry, so he hacked it off! The other stone birds he hid, 'it being my intention to return at a future date and secure them from the natives'.

Word reached Cecil Rhodes of Posselt's successful treasure hunt and that he had brought back to South Africa 'some wonderful stones from a visit to King Solomon's Temple', and he arranged to buy one from Posselt, the first stone bird known to have been looted from the lost city. Rhodes was undoubtedly mesmerised by the bird; indeed, it became a kind of talisman for him. It is still in the bedroom of his house, Groote Schuur, in Cape Town – now the home of the State President – where last year I was allowed to handle it for the purpose of photography. Alta Kriel, the Curator of the Rhodes Collection, told me that Rhodes refused to have it kept anywhere else and it is rumoured that he preferred to be in its presence when making major decisions, of which the most major was, without question, the decision to acquire the country where the stone birds ruled and have its name changed to his own. This bird indubitably changed the course of African history and half a century later, my own.

Rhodes had two stone copies made for the gateposts of his house in England. The Norfolk pine staircase at Groote Schuur was refitted with newel-posts mounting carvings of the bird and ground-floor doors were fitted with protectors in the shape of the Zimbabwe birds. One cannot avoid the presence of the birds in that house even to this day. I worked in Rhodes' library on this book and there is no doubt that they have a strange, brooding presence. Rhodes took the real bird on fund-raising trips to Europe when he was seeking backers for an organisation called the British South Africa Company, in reality the cover name for his private army of occupation.

The British government was still refusing to have anything to do with an official colonisation of Ophir even though it appeared to be a genuine eldorado. But if Rhodes, who was now Prime Minister of South Africa, wanted to undertake this dubious work for them at his own expense that was a different matter.

Posselt records that Rhodes later told him: 'I take that stone bird you found in the Zimbabwe ruins; I place it on the table, and tell that where this bird came from there must be something else.' Within a year Rhodes and the bird had attracted sufficient funds and Queen Victoria signed a Royal Charter legitimising the British South Africa Company's invasion of Matabeleland and the occupation of Mashonaland.

Before he left England, Rhodes also took the Zimbabwe bird to the Royal Geographical Society and suggested that they support a 'proper scientific expedition' to explore the lost city led by an eminent Fellow of the Society, Mr J. Theodore Bent. Rhodes offered to contribute generously to this expedition; indeed, he provided most of the funding.

TWO

The Conquest of Ophir

Queen Victoria refused to grant a charter to Rhodes' British South Africa Company until he had obtained a signed 'concession' from Lobengula. She had no intention of being held responsible for licensing an invasion, especially one which could easily go disastrously wrong, even if it did add a golden prize to her empire. The Queen and her ministers must, of course, have realised that the Charter would allow Rhodes to invade and occupy Mashonaland. Perhaps she thought the condition of a concession would put a stop to the whole dubious business: Lobengula was no fool and would surely recognise the risks of letting Rhodes loose in his domains?

If that was the case then they both sorely underestimated Rhodes, who sat down to work on this problem with two of his closest friends, Leander Starr Jameson and Rutherfoord Harris. Both had practised as doctors in Kimberley which was now Rhodes' town. Jameson would become Rhodes' right-hand man (many have suggested that the relationship was more intimate than that) and Harris a specialist in Rhodes' dirty work. Jameson had a mercurial temperament and he enjoyed taking huge risks for Rhodes. Many paid off but when he tried to take over the Transvaal from the Boers, only Rhodes' intervention saved him from execution. Harris quite simply did whatever Rhodes told him. Jameson once described Rutherfoord Harris as 'as thick as they're made'. A more stable business associate of Rhodes from the Kimberley days, C.J. Rudd, was also involved in the plan.

Essentially they had to work out an offer that Lobengula could not refuse. Rudd had already been dispatched to Lobengula's court to see if he could buy a gold-prospecting concession from the

21

Matabele king. He joined at least three other concession hunters there. The Portuguese had also finally decided to do something about their lapsed concessions in the region and sent envoys to Chief Mutasa whose land adjoined Mashonaland to the east. Lobengula was in no hurry to give concessions to anyone and kept Rudd hanging around for weeks until Rudd concluded that only one course was open to him – what might tempt Lobengula were rifles.

The Matabele – a renegade offshoot of the Zulu – were famously disciplined under seasoned military tacticians. The aggressive young warriors were keen to rid their country of hungry white men and they begged their generals and Lobengula to provide them with the opportunity to 'wash their spears'. For most concession-hunters, including the British emissaries at Lobengula's court, the idea of a Matabele army armed with modern weaponry was enough to chill the blood and thus far they, the Germans, Portuguese and Boers, had baulked at the idea of giving Lobengula military ordnance even in return for Shona gold.

Rhodes, as was his wont, called for an expert analysis of the problem and upon receipt of an assessment by British-trained military advisers decided on perhaps his greatest gamble. Rhodes was told that without expert weapons instruction and target practice Lobengula's army would, quite literally, shoot itself in the foot. Issuing warriors trained in the use of the spear with modern rifles would reduce their efficiency rather than enhance it, at least in the early stages of any war. Armed with this intelligence Rhodes sent Rudd back to Lobengula with orders to offer the Matabele king 1,000 Martini-Henry breech-loading rifles, 100,000 rounds of cartridges, a gunboat on the Zambesi (or £500 in cash) and £100 a month. Rudd took £5,000 in gold coins in his saddlebag as a down payment. In those days it was a king's ransom and it was enough. This king, who by then was weary of badgering concession hunters and worried that the Boers might just ride in and take his kingdom, accepted. Better to give Rhodes a gold-mining concession than risk all that.

That left just one problem for Rhodes, albeit a major one. Trading guns to the natives was highly illegal under South African law, especially for a member, as Rhodes was, of the Cape parliament. The mere removal or conveyance of such articles across the Cape borders was similarly prohibited. Rhodes arranged for the rifles to be moved secretly, admitting in a letter to a member of Rudd's group: 'With great difficulty I have managed to get them through the Colony and Bechuanaland.'

These rifles are pivotal to our story. Without them Rhodes would not have got his concession and his charter. Without the presence of Rhodes and his money in Mashonaland none of the three scientific investigations, which would subject the Zimbabwe culture to minute scrutiny, would ever have happened. He and the Rhodes Trust subsidised all three.

Rutherfoord Harris, now a Cape Town merchant, applied for a licence from the resident magistrate to send a shipment of rifles to Kimberley. The licence was issued because no borders would be crossed. Once in the vast De Beers sidings – Rhodes' very private bailiwick – they vanished, just as an even larger illicit arms shipment would vanish a few years later when the same team tried to provide supportive ordnance for Jameson's abortive raid on the Transvaal.

Two clandestine teams were used to take packets of 500 rifles apiece across the border under permits issued by a Bechuanaland official. This smuggling did not quite go unnoticed but another official, Sir Gordon Sprigg, who made enquiries about the shipments was urged to look the other way, or more precisely not to look 'into matters which do not affect the Cape Colony'. The correspondence actually reached the Colonial Office in London but there they looked the other way too. A note in the file observes: 'Sir Gordon Sprigg evidently thinks that the rifles . . . were meant for Lobengula (*hinc illae lacrymae*) and I dare-say he isn't far wrong.' They were already well on their way to Lobengula. Jameson and Harris crossed into Bechuanaland ostensibly as hunters, picked up the cached rifles, and eventually arrived at the Matabele border post where they were met by one of Rudd's partners, J.R. Macquire, a British barrister and friend of Rhodes from Oxford who was there to see that the Lobengula concession was couched in the right legal terms.

In December 1888 Lobengula fixed his mark to a document, the key paragraph of which read:

Unto the said grantees their heirs, representatives and assigns jointly and severally the complete and exclusive charge over all metals and mineral situated and contained in my Kingdoms, Principalities and dominions together with full power to do all things that they may deem necessary to win and procure the same and to hold, collect and enjoy the profits and revenue if any derivable from the said metals and mineral subject to the aforesaid payment and Whereas I have been much molested of late by divers persons seeking and desiring to obtain grants and concessions of Land and Mining rights in my territories I do hereby authorize the said grantees, their representatives and assigns to take all necessary and lawful steps to exclude from my Kingdoms, Principalities and Dominions all persons seeking land metals, mineral or mining rights therein and I do hereby undertake to render them such needful assistance as may from time to time require for the exclusion of such persons and to grant no concessions of land or mining rights from and after this date without their consent and concurrence.

Rudd immediately took the road for Cape Town, leaving the lawyer, Macquire, at the court to defend the concession against the attacks Rudd was sure would come. And come they did but first there was the most extraordinary incident that could well have ended in the concession which paved the road to Ophir never seeing the light of day.

A pond called the Lemoen pan upon which all travellers relied for their water was found to be dry. A note fixed to a thorn tree told Rudd there was water 2 miles away but in searching for it he became hopelessly lost in the bush. Rudd dropped the concession, his money bag and a farewell letter to his wife down an ant bear hole, convinced he would not last the night. Wandering around in the dark, Rudd eventually heard the barking of dogs and found their Tswana owners camped nearby. They gave him water and, amazingly, he was quickly able to recover his possessions.

Thereafter, to make up lost time, he made a gruelling dash in a mule-drawn wagon: 'We drove on through the night in stretches of two hours with one and a half hour intervals.' Two days later he drove in to Kimberley and handed the concession to Rhodes, a record for the distance that would not be broken until the railhead was extended to Bulawayo. They travelled on to Cape Town and presented the document to High Commissioner Robinson who, as Rhodes commented, 'raised no difficulties as to the guns'. Rhodes, of course, interpreted this as a deed of occupation, which it is not. The powers to protect finds of 'metals and minerals' are somewhat ambiguous but it remains a mining concession, nothing more. The other concession-hunters immediately claimed the Rudd Concession was a fake and Portugal rejected it outright.

The Consul for Portugal in Cape Town, Eduardo A. de Carvalho, published a denial of Lobengula's claim to Shona territory:

Whereas a notice signed by order of LO BENGULA, king of the Matabeles, has lately been published in the Newspapers giving notice that the mining rights in Matabeleland, Mashonaland and adjoining territories have already been disposed of, and soliciting the assistance of all neighboring Chiefs and States in excluding all persons entering these territories hereafter, I EDUARDO A. DE CARVALHO, Consul for Portugal, having received instructions, make it known that His Most Faithful Majesty's Government does not recognise the pretended rights of LO BENGULA to Mashonaland and adjacent territories, over which the Crown of Portugal claims Sovereignty, and that therefore, all Concessions of Land or Mining Rights granted, or that may be granted, in future in the said territories of Mashonaland and adjacent are null and void, as the Government of Portugal does not, and will not, acknowledge any such concessions.

Lobengula, a clever and ruthless man in his own right, suddenly saw the full tidal wave of colonialism building on his borders. Press reports from Cape Town were read to him, no doubt with a little imparted tarnish from Rudd's competitors, which said that the King had sold his country and the grantees could if they wished bring an armed force into the country, depose him and put another chief in his place, 'to dig anywhere, in his kraals, gardens and towns'. Lobengula arranged to have the following notice published in the *Bechuanaland News*:

I hear it is published in the newspapers that I have granted a Concession of the minerals in all my country to CHARLES DUNNELL RUDD . . . As there is a great misunderstanding about this, all action in respect of said Concession is hereby suspended pending an investigation by me and my country.

Signed, Lobengula

British lawyers quickly advised Rhodes that this did not actually revoke the concession; indeed, while suspended, it confirmed that Lobengula had signed it.

Lobengula then asks a competing concession-seeker, E.A. Maund, to take two of his indunas to London to intercede with Queen Victoria, but he is too late. The lion at his gate is the inexorable Cecil John Rhodes. Lobengula's appeal to the Queen is that Rhodes is trying to 'eat' his country. True, but Rhodes has by then already consumed much more sophisticated adversaries – Barney Barnato for one – than this Matabele potentate.

The British fête the indunas, turn out the Guards, show them the Zoo, the Bank of England, Westminster Abbey and St Paul's. The indunas speak to each other on the new 'telephone', and are taken to the first big field-day military tattoo at Aldershot.

There is psychological double-dealing even at this level.

Macquire suggests to F.R. Thompson, the third member of Rudd's party, that when Lobengula heard from his emissaries that 'he was not strong enough for the white people, [he] will trek [north]. There is I think always a possibility of this and we should be prepared to buy all his rights from him if he shows the least sign of making a move.'

The British government, still wary of Rhodes' unbridled expansionism, hand the indunas, through Lord Knutsford, Secretary of State at the Colonial Office, the following bizarre reply to take home to their king:

> Lo Bengula is the ruler of his country, and the Queen does not interfere in the government of that country, but as Lo Bengula desires her advice, Her Majesty is ready to give it, and having therefore, consulted Her Principal Secretary of State holding the Seals of the Colonial Department, now replies as follows:
>
> In the first place, the Queen wishes Lo Bengula to understand distinctly that Englishmen who have gone out to Matabeleland to ask leave to dig for stones have not gone with the Queen's authority, and should not believe any statements made by them or any of them to that effect.
>
> The Queen advises Lo Bengula not to grant hastily concessions of land, or leave to dig, but to consider all applications very carefully.
>
> It is not wise to put too much power into the hands of men who come first, and to exclude other deserving men. A king gives a stranger an ox, not his whole herd of cattle, otherwise what would other strangers arriving have to eat?
>
> Umsheti and Babaan (the indunas) say that Lo Bengula asks that the Queen will send him someone from herself. To this request the King is advised that Her Majesty may be pleased to accede.

This is the most extraordinary reply. It suggests that Queen Victoria has realised that she has been deceived by Rhodes and senior British cabinet ministers and is now seeking to reverse these wrongs by sending a personal negotiator to sort it all out. Lobengula, delivered of this conciliatory message, points out that, 'I have not asked the Queen to send anyone to me.' This may have been a considerable mistake because nothing more is heard of royal intercession and within weeks Rhodes is granted his Charter.

Chartered companies had their prototypes in the seventeenth century with the Hudson Bay Company and the East India Company but by Rhodes' era of empire the charter system –

essentially the licensing of commercial colonialism – had been reduced to the British North Borneo Company, the Royal Niger Company, and the Imperial British East Africa Company. For the British government the advantage of these charter companies was that they fell short of full colonial responsibility, leaving the host country under no great obligation to intervene should the enterprise founder. Everyone knew that a war between the militant Matabele and Rhodes' Charter Company was a real possibility and they were right. In fact there would be two wars.

The British premier, Lord Salisbury, was at this time presiding over a British Empire at the apogee of its power but with all of Europe probing its weak spots. Salisbury was personally less than enthusiastic about more colonial expansion but he was certainly not prepared to compromise Britain's lead, least of all to the Portuguese.

But the factor which tipped the balance in favour of Rhodes was, paradoxically, David Livingstone, whom history has shown to have been as inexorable as Rhodes and almost as great a British imperialist. Livingstone's wife had died after he insisted she and other Church of Scotland missionaries join him on the malaria-infested Zambesi. When many of these missionaries died too, Livingstone opened a new string of missions in the healthier Shire highlands of Nyasaland. Livingstone was by now the great hero of African exploration and everyone's favourite missionary for his unswerving assault on the slave trade.

For the Portuguese, however, this little crop of Celtic religious institutions stood square in the way of their proposed trans-African linkage of Angola and Mozambique which would also secure them Ophir. Lord Salisbury at first attempted to stop the Portuguese by doing a deal on the disputed land, and the Portuguese initially agreed on condition that they got the Shire highlands. All of Scotland was up in arms when this deal leaked, with 11,000 ministers and elders of the Presbyterian Church of Scotland petitioning against it.

Lord Salisbury then decided that Britain might strengthen its own claims to the hinterland by making new treaties with tribal chiefs, superseding the ancient claims of the Portuguese. A young African expert from the Colonial Office, Harry Johnston, who was fluent in Portuguese, was chosen for this assignment, but Salisbury's Treasury baulked at the costs. Rhodes stepped in and offered to pay, actually sending Johnston a cheque for £2,000 – a huge sum in those days – along with the suggestion that he widen his sphere of operations with the money. Lord Salisbury, who knew little of Rhodes at this time, asked Lord Rothschild about him and was told that Rhodes was already 'good for a million or more'. Salisbury saw the chance to bring down a number of birds with one stone. He could clip the wings of the Portuguese, earn the righteous thanks of the Scots, stop Lobengula making life difficult for him with the Queen, and have Rhodes pay for it. Under a charter, Ophir would remain firmly within the British sphere of influence and with luck there was money to be made. If it all went wrong the upstart, Rhodes, would be blamed.

The charter received its royal assent at the end of September 1889, unbeknown, of course, to Lobengula. Rhodes moved immediately. He sent F.R. Thompson back to Lobengula to insist that the King – who still hadn't actually accepted the rifles – recognise the Rudd concession in front of witnesses and withdraw previous opposition. Remember, in Lobengula's mind, we are here still only talking a mining concession.

Reminiscent of the outcome of Rhodes' all-night session with Barney Barnato for control of De Beers, Lobengula found himself faced by a united phalanx of white men, the majority of whom had done deals with Rhodes. Lobengula studied them and observed: 'Tomoson has rubbed fat on your mouths. All you white men are liars, but Tomoson you have lied the least.' Lobengula gave the acknowledged concession into the safekeeping of the one man in this company whom he trusted, the missionary Robert Moffat, who immediately 'yielded to Dr Jameson's earnest importunity and gave it to him, to take away with him'.

Queen Victoria broke the news in some style to Lobengula that Rhodes was now her chosen man. A party of five officers and men of the Royal Horse Guards in full regalia pitched up in Bulawayo on 15 November carrying a letter which advised the King:

The wisest and safest course for him to adopt and one which will give least trouble to himself and his tribe, is to agree, not with one or two white men separately, but with one approved body of white men, who will consult Lobengula's wishes and arrange where white people are to dig . . . the Queen therefore approves of the concession made by Lo Bengula to some white men who were represented in his country by Messrs. Rudd, Macquire and Thompson.

Finally, the Queen, overriding Lobengula's dismissive response to her suggestion of a British representative at his court, nominated Moffat to the post. Moffat had received an advance copy of the letter which he had had time to digest before the guardsmen arrived. He and Jameson decided to doctor it. Rhodes' name was substituted for some 'white men', Jameson not Thompson was named as Rhodes' principal representative and the reference to the Queen's representative was simply left out. Moffat himself translated this laundered version to the King. Lobengula was not actually fooled. When the Guardsmen left he told them 'that the Queen's letter had been dictated by Rhodes and that she, the Queen, must not write any more letters like that one to him again'. Unfortunately he was so impressed with the Guards' glittering accoutrements he did not see through to their true colours. The officers commanding the unit had been secretly sizing up Lobengula's army and advised Jameson that 'the fighting strength of the Matabele had been underestimated, and that it cannot be reckoned at less than from 15,000 to 20,000 men' – most of whom were now spoiling for a fight.

Rhodes was not concerned. He sent the famous scout, Selous, behind the lines to make his own assessment and speeded up his plans for the occupation of Ophir. Selous also arranged some insurance for himself. In an article in the British *Fortnightly Review* Selous all but named the Mazoe valley in Mashonaland as Ophir, calling it 'the fairest and perhaps the richest country in all South Africa . . . an utterly deserted country roamed over at will by herds of eland and other antelope'. What he did not mention was that in September 1889 he had obtained a dubious Mazoe concession from two headmen of the Korekore tribe, the chief, Negomo, having refused him. The paper they signed said they had also never paid tribute, directly or indirectly, to the Portuguese. Let us also not forget that it was Selous who had previously recognised Mashonaland and its gold as a Portuguese sphere of influence.

When Selous returned to Cape Town in December he offered to sell his concession to Rhodes. The terms were never publicised but one version is that Rhodes gave Selous 100 square miles of Mashonaland under the protective umbrella of the charter and its police force and £2,000 in cash. Selous was thereafter Rhodes' man and led the Pioneer Column to Ophir, having persuaded Rhodes to follow a route which cleverly bypassed sensitive Matabele kraals.

Deliberate confrontation with the Matabele – 'to get it over and done with' – had been actively considered. In October 1889, E.A. Maund discussed with Jameson the difficulties of occupying Ophir, and concluded that they should employ a kommando of 500 Boers who would be given farms as compensation, 'and a police of 1,500 to protect the diggers'. Rhodes was obviously behind such a final solution as is revealed in a letter Maund had written to Rutherfoord Harris: 'I have spoken freely to Helm [another missionary confidant in Lobengula's court] and Carnegie, and they with Moffat are convinced that Rhodes is right in his decision that we will never be able to work peaceably alongside the natives, and the sooner the brush is over, the better. There is a general idea here that if this advance is not made in the coming winter, the Boer filibusters will make it then, and that will be an additional incubus.'

On 6 January 1890, Selous independently added his weight to these time constraints in a long letter to the *Cape Times*. 'Now or never is the time to act,' he said to his principals.

On 7 December, Frank Johnson and an American with experience of the Indian wars, Maurice Heany, signed an agreement with Rhodes to 'raise in South Africa an auxiliary European force of about 500 men for service under the British South Africa Company.' With this pocket army they undertook 'to carry by sudden assault all the principal strongholds of the Matabele nation and generally so as to break up the power of the Amandebele as to render their raids on surrounding tribes impossible, to effect the emancipation of all their slaves and further, to reduce the country to such a condition as to enable the prospecting, mining and commercial staff of the British South Africa Company to conduct their operations in Matabeleland in safety and peace.' Lobengula was either to be killed or, preferably, taken hostage. This licence to kill had a life of one year and it commanded a suitable reward for its two principals – £150,000 and 50,000 morgen of land. Rutherfoord Harris was the only witness to the agreement.

Thankfully it was never carried out but the circumstances of its cancellation are shrouded in mystery. Johnson later claimed Heany got drunk and talked to an official who in turn leaked it to the High Commissioner in Cape Town. Rhodes backed away from the plan, called Selous in Kimberley, and agreed the course of non-confrontation. Jameson went personally to Lobengula's court with a cover story. He told the King that under the terms of the Rudd Concession, a party of miners were coming to dig primarily in the old Tati field on the Missionaries Road. Jameson knew that this well-trodden field would not overly concern Lobengula and he added a codicil that if there was insufficient gold at Tati he wanted permission to move the column of miners to a more promising area.

Two months later, on 31 January, this transparent ruse worked. Lobengula said a mining caravan could move on to Mashonaland – he even offered labour to help clear the road – and Jameson sped south to make the arrangements. Rhodes had anticipated Jameson's successful diplomacy. On 10 January he presented the British High Commissioner with the details of the mining party, to be led by Selous: 'some 80 wagons, accompanied by 125 miners [white] and about 150 [black men] for clearing and making a road for wagons; these with the men for the wagons, would represent all together a body of between 400 and 500; besides these a certain number of mounted police to act as scouts.' The commander of the Bechuanaland Border Police would provide 200 of his own men and 250 British South Africa Company police would be committed to the protection of the column. The former would remain in Bechuanaland, the latter would stay with the column. After crossing into Matabeleland, the BSAC police would be under the command of its own officers. Military considerations were the responsibility of a close friend of Rhodes, Sir John Willoughby, Bt.

The British High Commissioner approved. At the meeting Rhodes had been careful to refer to his party as 'miners' which appears to have been naively accepted by some (Moffat) and derided by others. Sir John Kirk is recorded as saying: 'It is a matter of course that we have granted a charter with a view to driving the Matabeles out of the country across the Zambesi and settling the whole country with "volunteers" whose services were paid for by free land grants. Of course this is quite contrary to the provisions and spirit of the charter.'

Not to mention Lobengula's concession.

Everyone knew that Rhodes was assembling in Mafeking a pocket invasion army. Along with the recruits (who had been deliberately enrolled from influential families in the Cape in case the column needed rescuing) came equipment which left nothing in doubt: military-style uniforms, revolvers, rifles, Maxim, Gatling and Nordenfeldt machine-guns and a powerful steam-driven searchlight. The men were formed into three troops, two of mounted infantry, one of artillery. The accompanying police force had been doubled to 500 men and there were now 186 wagons.

The column crossed into Matabeleland in July and was immediately shadowed by an impi of between 200 and 300 men. Lobengula sent protesting notes to the commander of the military force, Lieutenant-Colonel Pennyfather, ordering him to turn back. Pennyfather replied that he was a servant of the Queen and only she could order him back but he allowed Lobengula's note to be taken on to Rhodes. This all used up valuable time as the column moved on. The plan had been to form a defensive ring of wagons (a laager) every night but the column was spread out over two miles and this proved impractical. Thereafter, the column was split in two and advanced in parallel, forming a square laager at night. The searchlight was turned on and swept the bush, and explosive charges were laid outside the square and exploded throughout the night.

In the Cape, Rhodes had become Prime Minister.

Why did Lobengula not attack, as the majority of his young warriors were urging? The answer is still anyone's guess. By now the King knew of the tenacity of Rhodes and his minions and probably realised that his options were cooperation or bloody confrontation, if not with Rhodes then, almost certainly, with the Boers. Lobengula was aware of Zulu history and the inevitability of having to face a massive British army should British subjects die. The Guards had given him a foretaste of that and his envoys to Queen Victoria, still men of influence, had seen it in action at Aldershot. He knew of the fate of his Zulu relative, Cetewayo, who had also sought alliance with the British to forestall Afrikaner encroachment on his domains. The British still found an excuse to invade Zululand and while routed in the famous Battle of Isandhlwana (1879), a huge British army was then sent to Zululand to crush the Zulu nation and depose Cetewayo. Restored to power he was again deposed by rivals and died a fugitive.

Uncannily, Lobengula's eventual fate would be a tragic echo of this.

But in my view the overlooked factor in Lobengula's story and one which bears on ours is his attitude to gold. Astute and sophisticated in many other ways the King seems genuinely not to have recognised that gold was driving this army of treasure hunters. He must, therefore, have found it very difficult to believe that they were prepared to risk dying for it. Lobengula apparently knew nothing of ancient Ophir and the lost gold mines of Mashonaland and appears to have had little or no interest in the ancient Zimbabwe culture created by the power of gold. Land, slaves, and particularly cattle he would go into battle for, but not gold. This mistake essentially cost him his kingdom.

It has also been variously suggested that Lobengula, like his ancestors, still had a nomadic streak and he had already made plans to move his kingdom north to the Zambesi. That may indeed have been the purpose of extensive raids made to the far north by his impis throughout the time he was dealing with Rhodes. Be that as it may, for this little band of 'Pioneers', soon to be lauded as archetypal Victorian heroes, it was still an enormous gamble to take on Lobengula's huge, tactically adept army; indeed, I am certain it was only the King's restraint which saved them. Rhodes may even have assessed this risk and 'factored in' the real chance of a devastating Matabele attack. Applicants for the 'Pioneer Column' were very deliberately chosen from the sons of the most influential Cape families who would swiftly have demanded revenge and retribution had their scions been massacred by the natives in the north. As with the Zulus, a British army would inevitably have followed such a massacre, just as one did with Cetewayo after Isandhlwana.

Lobengula saw this threat. By clever manoeuvring through the indunas leading his regiments the young warriors were held in check, although it was often a close call. When, for example, the Bechuanaland contingent tried to turn back, the force returned in a panic after running into 2,000 advancing Matabele.

On 1 August the Pioneers spotted the low-lying hills which marked the start of the Shona plateau and Selous rode ahead to see if he could find a suitable pass for the wagons: 'My feelings may be better imagined than described when I say that [having ridden up a promising-looking pass] I saw stretched before me, as far as the eye could see, a wide expanse of open grassy country, and knew that I was looking over the south-western portion of the high plateau of Mashonaland. . . . A weight of responsibility, that had at times become almost unbearable, fell from my shoulders and I breathed a sigh of relief.' They named it Providential Pass.

On 14 August the column debouched onto the plateau and a halt was called for rest and recreation. Selous told them that they were just a short ride from the Queen of Sheba's much vaunted palace, and King Solomon's mines were all around them. Virtually every commercial mining operation these prospectors would now set up would be based on the evidence of gold-bearing reefs from ancient workings. In fact over the next decade it would be recognised that there were all but *no* worthwhile reefs which had not, to a greater or lesser degree, been worked by the ancients.

Ophir was theirs.

They laid the foundations of Fort Victoria, which grew into a thriving little agricultural town by the time I stayed there half a century later. A game of rugby was played and Sir John Willoughby

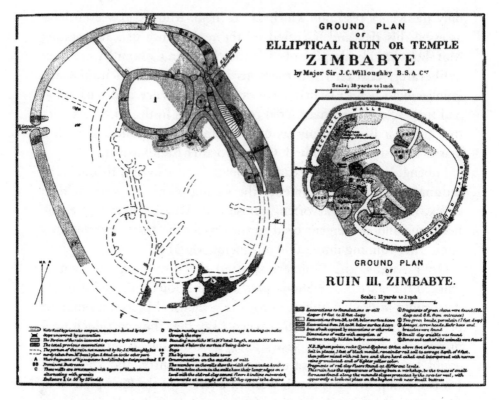

The first maps of Great Zimbabwe drawn rather well by the military commander of Rhodes' occupation force, Sir John Willoughby.

led a party to the ruins and spent the day searching for treasure. None was found, but Sir John was captured by the magic of the place and would return to spend a great deal of time here; indeed, he would be the second European to dig seriously among the ruins.

One man, *The Times* correspondent, left the others and made a careful and thoughtful tour, filing the only objective early description of the lost city. Hereafter, Great Zimbabwe would be seen either through the rose-tinted glasses of the Romantics or the clinical gaze of the archaeologists.

The Ruins themselves lie at the base of a striking and precipitous granite kopje, inhabited by one of the Mashona tribes under a chief called Moghabi.

The first feature to be noticed on approaching the kopje is the existence of an outer wall, about 4 ft high, running, apparently, right round the entire kopje; but owing to the tall grass and dense jungle-like undergrowth it was found impossible to trace this wall more than half a mile.

Next came indications of a second and inner wall, which it was also impossible to trace for any distance for the same reasons. Then amid a perfect labyrinth of remains of small circular buildings – a mighty maze, but not, apparently, without some plan – south-west of the kopje and 300 yd from its base, we find ourselves confronted with the startling and main feature of these remains – namely a high wall, of circular shape, from 30 ft to 35 ft high, forming a complete enclosure of an area 80 yd in diameter.

This wall, about 10 ft in thickness at the base, and tapering to about 7 ft or 8 ft at the top is built of small granite blocks, about twice the size of an ordinary brick, beautifully hewn and dressed, laid in perfect even courses, and put together without a single atom of mortar or cement.

The three main pattern styles used by the Zimbabwe culture. Experts say they must have been influenced by patterns on imported artefacts.

This strange enclosure is entered on its western side by what at first sight appears to be a mere gap in the wall, but which closer examination reveals to be what was once evidently a well-defined, narrow entrance, as shown clearly by the rounded-off courses.

Inside the building itself, which is most difficult to examine, owing to the dense undergrowth and presence of quantities of trees hundreds of years old, which conceal traces of, seemingly, a series of further circular or elliptical walls, and close to the entrance an outer wall, here 30 ft high, stands a conical shaped tower, or turret 35 ft in height and 18 ft in diameter at the base, built of the same granite blocks and consisting of solid masonry.

Lastly, the remaining feature of the building to be touched upon in this brief account is that on the south-east front of the wall, and 20 ft from its base, runs a double zigzag scroll one-third of the distance round, composed of the same-size granite blocks placed in diagonal positions.

On the kopje and hillside itself, too, there are numerous traces of remains of a similar character, circular buildings wedged in amongst boulders of rocks, walled terraces, at least nine in number; and, built on the very summit, an enormous mass of granite blocks, to be used apparently as a fort, and which owing to the complete absence of any disintegrating forces in this climate, is in an almost perfect state of preservation. The view obtained from the summit of the kopje commands a panorama probably unrivalled in South African scenery.

What may be the origin, history, and intention of these curious ruins and, in particular, of the large circular building with its cone-shaped turret, is, as far as the members of the present expedition are concerned, a perfect mystery.

The more scientific and learned element is mute in the presence of these prehistoric remains and stand in silent amazement at their magnitude and solidity. No one, so far, has been bold enough to come forward and suggest some solution of the problem they present, or offer some explanation of the sermons they most infallibly preach.

One thing is certain, however, that the area covered by the numerous walls and circular buildings points clearly to the existence at some time – perhaps 'before the ages' – of a large and semi-civilised population, at a time when slave labour was procurable to an unlimited extent.

From the natives themselves, as is invariably the case with all South African natives in similar circumstances, we can glean no information whatever respecting these ancient relics under whose shadows they dwell; nor do they appear to entertain any superstitious reverence for them.

They found them there, as did their forefathers, and there their interest in them and information about them begin and end.

Perhaps upon the advent of the expected white they will begin (and judging from our experience the process seems to have already begun) to recognize their value as a medium of obtaining blankets, limbo and beads from the grateful and enthusiastic visitor. Then, at any rate, they will be led to regard them, at least from a practical and business point of view, much as the Egyptian Arabs regard their Pyramids, the Swiss peasant his glaciers, or the English verger his cathedral. It is satisfying to learn that efficient steps have been taken to protect them from both the thoughtlessness and the Philistinism of any prospector or adventurer.

The Portuguese have suggested that these ruins form portions of the remains of the city and the palace of the Queen of Sheba, 'in the land of Ophir'. Again ancient Portuguese records refer repeatedly to people in this part of Africa, whom they found to be established long before their own arrival, and whom they represent to work for gold in the far interior. To these people they give the name of Morisco [Moors?].

With regard to the word itself – Zimbabye – its etymology and orthography, like most native names, it can be variously and equally correctly spelt Zinbawe, Zinboaoe, and Zinbabye. The Portuguese traveller Lacerda, in his journey through the Zambesi region in 1797, speaks of a tribe, Cazembe (near Lake Nyassa), who in answer to his enquiries regarding the course of a certain river, described it as running close by their Zinbawe, or royal residence. This fact, taken in conjunction with the existence of another Zimbabye in the Manica country, together with the ruins in this neighbourhood, would seem to fix the meaning of the word as palace or royal residence.

Be this, however, as it may, whether these ruins are to be attributed to either Moorish or Phoenician origin, or whether the circular building was a temple or a palace, and the conical tower the Queen of Sheba's tumulus, are questions which only the skilled antiquary and those versed in such matters should presume to decide.

In the meantime, many of us have been privileged to set eyes upon a spectacle which, with the exception of Mauch, as far as we know, no white man has ever hitherto been fortunate enough to behold.

This, by the standards of the time, was very balanced coverage – but it still left origin theorists with quite a narrow field of choice: Moors, Phoenicians or Solomon and Sheba.

Other 'considered' articles of the time were much more decided. Great Zimbabwe was: 'A fortified camp or station, established, it had hardly to be doubted, to control the enslaved population which worked the gold mines, and to protect the abler but scanty people which coerced and directed them and took away, like the Spaniards in Peru, all transportable fruit of their labour. Who they were may remain uncertain but there is no reason which makes it peremptory that they should have been indigenous.'

Of all the contenders for this title – and over the next few months the Hindus who conquered and held Java for generations, the Malays who conquered Madagascar, and the Arab people who founded the Sabaean kingdom were nominated – the outright favourite was the Phoenicians, given their history of long sea journeys in search of minerals.

For a truly Romantic view of the lost city, however, one only had to turn, then as now, to the 'tabloids':

Who were these soldier workmen of a vanished civilisation?

At whose bidding did they force their way into this barbarous place to dig for gold?

The country is dotted with the strange ancient relics of their work. The furnaces that they built to smelt the ore, the strong round keeps which they raised against the alarms of some besetting foe, the great stones on which they scored in indecipherable characters the record of their labours, perhaps the clue to their prize – these things remain and move the awe of the Matabele and his Mashona vassal.

Today, then, the Englishman is in the land of Ophir, opening afresh the treasure house of antiquity, equipped with resources of which the deft Phoenicians never dreamed.

It may be that he will come upon such relics among the abandoned workings as will throw a new light upon the story of his predecessors, and re-write a page of the world's history.

It may even be he will stumble into chambers of subterranean wealth such as Mr Haggard had imagined, secured with labyrinths like those of the Pyramids, with sliding stones, and all the appropriate witchcraft of an age when human life and human labour were of no account.

At least, before many years are out, we may expect to see the image of Queen Victoria stamped on the gold with which King Solomon overlaid his ivory throne and wreathed the cedar pillars of his temple.

For the far-sighted Rhodes, all this purple prose was of great help with fund-raising for the British South Africa Company. Moreover, he had already anticipated the huge public appetite for a more expert opinion on the true origins of the lost city. Mr and Mrs J. Theodore Bent were even now preparing to set sail from England armed with the credentials of the Royal Geographical Society and the British Association for the Advancement of Science.

THREE

Dreams of Avarice

In spite of all these intriguing leads, the thousands of mines scattered across the land of the Karanga have remained no more than mute evidence of an ancient eldorado. And for more than a century now not a single record, inscription, cryptogram, tablet or stela has ever been found at any of the grand *zimbabwes* to record the output of ancient mines or the people who worked them.

Perhaps one should say there is no 'Rosetta stone' here which has allowed a reading of the many inscribed columns, plinths, statues and a miscellany of stone objects found by Theodore Bent and others at Great Zimbabwe. Nor, as Bent much regretted, is there a trace of an oral tradition about gold.

When Bent asked these very questions of the natives in the area and on the actual site, it was as if gold had never been produced in Mashonaland. The Karanga, as we have heard, were completely ignorant of a gold industry ancient or modern and, as a result, made no attempt to gather the precious metals themselves. This is actually extraordinary and, so far as I know, unprecedented, for people still living among monumental works of this splendour. Yet the Karanga were also aware of the thousands of ancient gold workings dangerously littering the bush. How did they explain all this to themselves?

All the early explorers, dos Barros, Mauch and Bent, heard myths of ancient mining and building activities conducted by gods or, in one case, a white race. But these were no better supported than the tales told to dos Barros that god-like creatures had in ancient times been able to raise such monuments when the stones were still soft.

This ignorance of the value of gold and the tradition of ancient mining has been a problem for the Shona school. Their explanation

42

– that the Karanga did so well from cattle they had no need of gold and were quite happy to barter with foreigners for tools and trinkets which they did value – is in my opinion simplistic, a modern myth no more viable than the old ones. Were the Karanga deaf to the pleadings of early prospectors like Adam Renders who must have revealed the white man's hunger for gold, if only to his two Karanga wives?

If you believe the Shona school then it also has to be true that this complacency cost the Karanga their country. The gold in the dust beneath their feet would certainly have bought every man a Mauser and instruction in its use sufficient to free them of enslavement by the Matabele, the Boers, the Portuguese and even Rhodes. The great irony here is that it was Karanga gold, or the promise of it at 'Ophir', that bought Rhodes the breech-loading rifles and Maxims that he eventually used to suppress the Matabele and the Shona.

I prefer to believe that the Karanga were, at least originally, innocently ignorant of the international value of gold even if it does open the door to a currently politically unacceptable suggestion that ancient mining, certainly deep mining, was imported and directed by a foreign trading cartel using local, and not necessarily Bantu, labour. In the same way, perhaps, as these traders were ignorant of the economics and skills of cattle-raising.

The fact remains that it is pointless seeking information about ancient gold production from the Shona. It occurs, therefore, that the riddle might only be solved from the customer's end. More simply, thousands of tons of Shona gold went somewhere. Who at the time of Solomon, or before, had demonstrated a conspicuous consumption of gold? Solomon and Sheba both only ruled very small kingdoms in the North African hegemony.

My first lead came from an unexpected (and surely coincidental) source. Rhodes' bird, the stone statue he worshipped and used so successfully to raise money for the occupation of 'Ophir', thereafter Rhodesia, wears a pendant necklace. At least two of the other birds have them too. No explanation has ever been given for this singular piece of decoration. I have long doubted the prevailing notion that no cryptograms or meaningful inscriptions have ever been found at

Great Zimbabwe; I simply cannot conceive of a piece of art that is totally absent of meaning and there is a great deal of art in the various *zimbabwes*. I prefer the idea that we have simply not learned to read the cryptograms that are there, particularly the meaning of the extensive and varied decorative additions to the Zimbabwe birds.

So over the last three years I have spent what might be termed 'quality' time with Rhodes' bird at his house, Groote Schuur, in Cape Town, which is now the official residence of the State President. I had always assumed that his original bird, along with half a dozen others which had ended up in South African museums, had been returned to Zimbabwe in the 1980s. When I called the Curator of Groote Schuur, Alta Kriel, to make arrangements for the necklace to be professionally photographed, however, she told me this fascinating story – Rhodes' bird had not gone home. There *are* copies at Groote Schuur, but the black stone bird which sits on Rhodes' wardrobe in a corner of his bedroom is the original, thanks to the wife of former President Vorster. Apparently Mrs Vorster took an unusual interest in the house, which was not shared by other State Presidents; Nelson Mandela is said to have moved out of the old place, concerned at the damage his lively grandchildren might do. But Mrs Vorster recognised that they were treasures and when South Africa was minded to send the Zimbabwe birds home she had Rhodes' will re-examined by lawyers. As she had suspected, Rhodes had stipulated that his private collection should not be broken up or disseminated, so this seminal bird, although indubitably stolen for Rhodes by the hunter-prospector Willie Posselt, still sits in his bedroom, unknown to the general public, to this day. In African terms this is quite the equal of the saga of the Elgin Marbles.

But to return to the necklace that Rhodes' bird – and others collected by Theodore Bent at Great Zimbabwe – wears. . . .

In the course of my research into the 'ancient Moors' who for as long as records exist have dominated the trade between the Middle East and East Africa, I came across an intriguing name for the most ancient Egyptian word for gold, a name used several thousand years before the birth of Christ and a millennium before Solomon and Sheba.

That word is *nub*. *Nub* was produced from mines in the deserts of ancient Egypt but they were small in number and never prolific. Seemingly when the demand for gold exceeded the Egyptians' own supply, they took over the kingdom of Nubia – the 'kingdom of gold' – to the south. Egyptian imperialism, and the trade which came from it, was from then on almost always in a southerly direction.

The earliest Egyptian hieroglyph for *nub* is a symbol which the eminent Egyptologists, Rossellini and Lepsius, believe represents a bag or cloth with hanging ends through which alluvial gold was separated. There is a picture of this process on a building at Thebes. Auriferous sand was placed in a bag made of sheepskin with the woolly side inwards; water was then added and the bag vigorously shaken by two men. The earth particles were carried away while the heavier particles of gold stuck to the fleece. One such mythical golden fleece was, I assume, pursued by Jason and the Argonauts.

To get back down to earth – to earth with specks of gold in it in fact – alluvial gold is without doubt the first form in which Zimbabwe gold was traded to foreigners. As we shall see there are many accounts of Hottentot bushmen trading it with 'old Moors', having carried it to the coast in vultures' quills.

The Egyptians were well aware of the difference between alluvial and mined gold. The former was called *nub-en-mu*, 'gold of the river', while mined gold was called *nub-en-set*, 'gold of the mountain'. Mined gold obviously eventually came to dominate the market and in the course of the thousands of years we are considering, the hieroglyph for gold (the bag with strings) was replaced with another sign more representative of the use to which refined gold was being put – a necklace of pendant beads.

At least five Zimbabwe birds wear pendant necklaces that have never been explained. Moreover, the only other view on this change of hieroglyph from fleece to necklace, advanced by the Egyptologist Elliot Smith, actually strengthens our speculative Zimbabwe–Egyptian connection. Elliot Smith believes that the necklace hieroglyph was the determinative of Hathor, the hawk-headed goddess who had the responsibility for gold mines in Egypt and abroad!

Finally, there is even a possible element of dating in the fact that the Zimbabwe birds who stood guard over a countryside riddled with gold mines wear *nub* necklaces rather than golden fleece *nubs*. If there was a gold trade between the ancient Egyptians and the foundling Zimbabwe culture it would more likely have come into existence during the last millennium of the Egyptian dynasties, when trade via the Indian ocean was more advanced, rather than 3,000 years earlier. Be that as it may, I was no longer in any doubt that if I had to look for ancient markets for Zimbabwe gold, markets so old that the Karanga of the late twentieth century could no longer remember them, ancient Egypt had to be my prime choice. Once that had been established, the research proved easy.

To say that the Egyptians were obsessed with gold is to understate the case. They worshipped it from the beginning of their civilisation 4,000 years ago with a passion which never faded even when the empire became a Graeco-Roman colony. The earliest worked gold was from alluvial sources, but the Egyptians soon went on to mining proper with a transitional stage of 'open cast' extraction from surface outcrops which soon became trenches and then underground mines as the seams were traced down. Gold production in a desert is not a popular line of work and the more powerful countries dominated the trade because they were able to put slaves, convicts and prisoners of war to such hard labour.

Pictograms, inscriptions and stelae detailing the State hard at work producing gold litter Egypt's ancient sites. By the time of Menes (c. 3100 BC) a 'gold standard' ('one part of gold is equal to two and a half parts of silver measure') was already in existence. By c. 1320 BC the Egyptians were already working gold abroad, confirmed by an epistle from the sun-god, Ra, to Pharaoh Seti I: 'I have given thee the gold countries.' If, as seems to have been the case, Zimbabwe was at least potentially the most prolific gold country south of Egypt on the increasingly familiar Red Sea route, it has to be a strong possibility that Mashonaland was in the hawk-headed sun-god's gift.

Turin Museum even has a Rameside papyrus map, the famous *Carte de mines d'or*, which shows quarries, auriferous mountains, gold mines, and miners' houses. These have always been thought to describe Egyptian desert mines, but the site is not located and could just as easily be the Inyanga mountains where dozens of ancient mines and hundreds of residential *zimbabwes* have been found.

The same applies to the way gold was worked. Diodorus Siculus wrote a detailed account of these in the first century BC, a time when 'ancient Moor' traders were known to be working their way down Africa and would certainly have heard of the gold of the Shona hinterland. Theodore Bent believed he had found a connection between ancient Egyptian and ancient Karanga gold-working systems when he found mortars and crushing stones in lines near ancient workings. Similar mortars and crushing stones in lines near ancient workings were found in the recent excavations of the fifth- to sixth-century Egyptian mining town of Bir Umm Fawakhir in the Eastern Desert. Diodorus may also have given us an answer to another outstanding Zimbabwe enigma – why were the mining shafts so narrow?

> The gold-bearing earth which is the hardest, they first burn with a hot fire, and when they have crumbled it . . . they continue the working of it by hand . . . the entire operations are in charge of a skilled worker who distinguishes the stone and points it out to the labourers. The boys there who have not yet come to maturity, entering into the tunnels formed by the removal of the rock, laboriously gather up the rock . . . piece by piece and carry it out into the open to the place outside the entrance. Those who are about thirty years old take this quarried stone from them and with iron pestles pound a specified amount of it in stone mortars, until they have worked it down to the size of a vetch [fine grain].

These descriptions are from the last centuries of dynastic Egypt. But from the very beginning – *c.* 3000 BC, perhaps even earlier – there are records of gold becoming the reserved and spiritual currency of the pharoah.

From *c.* 2900 BC onwards, metals seem to have been monopolies of the court. The management of quarries and mines was entrusted to the highest court officials and sometimes the sons of the pharoahs. Often these responsibilities were handled by the priesthood; indeed, it seems most likely that the metallurgical sciences, and alchemy, first saw the light of day in the laboratories of the Egyptian priests. This priestly connection with gold from time immemorial will also have a bearing on this story.

The ancient religious record perhaps most concerned with the gold trade is, of course the Bible; in fact, gold is the first metal mentioned in the Hexateuch, which includes Genesis, the narrative of which was probably first cast into a written form in the tenth century BC. A number of other clues hover around the start of this last pre-Christian millennium, including the gold-rich voyages of the Phoenicians, the Solomon and Sheba legends, including that of Sheba building a temple in southern Africa, and the Pharoah Rameses' imperial leanings.

Six foreign sources of gold are listed but not located in the Bible: Havilah, Ophir, Sheba, Midian, Uphaz and Parvaim. Then in Genesis 2: 10–12 it is recorded that a river went out of Eden, 'and from there it was parted and became into four . . . the name of the first is Pison: that is it which compasseth the whole land of Havilah, where there is gold . . . and the gold of that land is good: there is berillium and the onyx stone.' Zimbabwe has several large rivers including the mighty Zambesi which most certainly encompasses 'the whole of the land' and so convinced one of our witnesses, the first Curator of Great Zimbabwe, Richard Nicklin Hall, that he called his camp Havilah. Rhodes' early prospectors soon discovered that Mashonaland is also extremely rich in precious stones.

By the time of Solomon gold was the metal of 'conspicuous consumption' by the rulers of North Africa. One of the most conspicuous was the 18th Dynasty queen, Hatshepsut, who launched the famous Egyptian expedition to 'Punt'. The whereabouts of Punt (which harbours a host of legends including that of a mystical African Christian King, Prester John) will be explored later but even a quick glance at Hatshepsut's expedition demonstrates how important gold (and foreign trade) was to the pharaohs.

Hatshepsut was a divine pharaoh having, as she put it about, been conceived by the hawk-headed god Amun-Ra. Her temple has paintings and inscriptions illustrating her birth and the extraordinary voyage she was so proud of. There is even the suggestion that the evocation of Ra, who was her celestial father, was a southern African who penetrated her mother's body 'with the flood of divine fragrance, and all the odours were those of the land of Punt'.

As the historian Felipe Fernandez-Armesto puts it, Hatshepsut needed 'crowning glories'. Uniquely among women, she had proclaimed herself sovereign of Egypt, ergo she became a living god, which was not normally open to living women. She needed to demonstrate godlike prowess. 'In antiquity,' Armesto points out, 'Riches – like pilgrims – gained imputed sanctity and power roughly according to the distance they travelled.' We know that Hatshepsut's fleet sailed down the Red Sea, and that they contacted an African tribe, and we are aware from the temple paintings that her traders went ashore to tropical conditions near the sea and traded for gold, incense, ivory, panthers (probably leopards or cheetahs), monkeys, turtles, giraffes, ebony and antimony – and of course, gold. All this exotic plunder they traded for Egyptian foodstuffs, and the natives were seemingly very content with the exchange.

The temple inscriptions admittedly gloat about Egyptian sagacity which allowed them to trade gold 'measured out with bull-shaped weights' for 'bread, beer, wine, meat and fruits'. Be that as it may, the spoils from this voyage gave Queen Hatshepsut 'crowning glories' sufficient for her lifetime and became one of the legends in the records of old Egypt in which gold plays a seminal part.

The most enduring of these legends is that of the Phoenix, and there is an inevitable association with the sculptured birds found at Great Zimbabwe. The Phoenix lived in Africa and was immortal; indeed, it had neither a beginning nor an end. Its colour was a beautiful green. Several Zimbabwe birds carved from green soapstone have been found; in fact, green soapstone was the favourite material for what are considered religious artefacts found at Great Zimbabwe. The Phoenix of legend resembled an eagle, as do the Zimbabwe birds, and had bright golden wings, a golden tail, and a solid crest of gold upon its head. When it grew weary of life it built a nest of sticks and the broken limbs of trees, a process which took a considerable time. Eventually the bird dropped a golden egg that instantly set the nest aflame and it and the nest were consumed. The golden egg transformed into a shell from which a white worm emerged and instantly sprang into the full-sized rejuvenated Phoenix.

Rameses II, arguably the greatest of all the pharaohs (dubbed 'the Great' by nineteenth-century Egyptologists), is often exemplified with a Phoenix by his right hand, although by Graeco-Roman times this had become an eagle. In fact, there are raptor-like birds on virtually every stela, bas-relief and decorative panel of ancient Egypt, and nowhere more numerous than in the vast array of stone monuments raised by Rameses the Great. His uniquely long rule of almost a hundred years is also (and perhaps significant to this story) the era in which Egypt became an imperial power in southern, 'black' Africa, imperialism motivated in no small part by the royal lust for gold.

Rameses the Great had some 200 wives and concubines and he acknowledged 96 sons and daughters. He outlived the first 13 of his heirs. His imperial ambitions were fostered in his youth when he accompanied his father (Seti I) on numerous campaigns in Libya and the gold-rich kingdom to the south, Nubia. As a builder in stone employing the mortar-less techniques also found at Great Zimbabwe, Rameses the Great engaged in an orgy of conspicuous consumption of his gold reserves, even though by the time of the Middle Kingdom (*c.* 1307–1196 BC) Egyptian mines were contributing less and less. Nubia, now part of the Egyptian empire, added to Rameses' coffers but neither of these sources could surely have provided the gold to pay for the construction of the following:

In Nubia (Nilotic Sudan), six temples, of which the two carved out of a cliff side at Abu Simbel, with their four colossal statues of the king, are the most magnificent.

On the west bank of the Nile at Luxor (Thebes), Rameses completed his father's funerary temple and then built one for himself, which is known as the Rameseum and is the best known of Rameses' accomplishments.

In the Wadi Tumilat, he built a border town Per-Atum (biblical Pithom) as a store city and customs post on the trade route from Nubia.

In Egypt he completed the great hypostyle hall at Karnak (Thebes) and continued the work on a large temple Seti I had been building at Abydos. He built a temple for himself at Abydos, his resident city, and endowed the town with four more major temples and a number of lesser shrines.

His most notable secular work is arguably the sinking of a deep well in the eastern desert on the route to the Nubian gold mines.

In truth there are few ancient Egyptian sites of any importance that originally did not at least exhibit the name of Rameses. He was determined that the world should recognise his prosperity, and apart from his own constructions he was not above inscribing his name on the monuments of his predecessors.

During his long reign, until the later part of the 20th Dynasty, Egypt and Rameses enjoyed suzerainty not only over Nubia but also Palestine, Syria and other adjacent territories of the Hittite Empire. Thereafter, under the weak kings that followed Rameses III, internal decay ended Egyptian power beyond its borders. Rameses II also must have known of Queen Hatshepsut's spectacular voyage down Africa in the dynasty which preceded his own. I have always found it very difficult to accept that a king of Rameses' expansionist inclinations, colonial ambitions and appetite for gold did not himself exploit this prime source of African gold. He was certainly the pharaoh who elevated the significance of gold in the Egyptian ideology of kingship. The pharoah's divine status as both 'Living Horus' (the falcon god) and son of Ra (the sun-god) was symbolised by his golden jewellery and regalia. In *Gold of the Pharaohs* by Hans Wolfgang Muller and Eberhard Thiem, published by the scholarly Cornell University Press, the authors (without apparently recognising it) offer another intriguing link to the stone birds at Great Zimbabwe. Reminding us that the Egyptian hieoroglyph for gold is a beaded necklace, Muller and Thiem observe that this is often augmented by 'a falcon or solar disk to signify "Golden Horus" or "Gold Sun".' A cursory examination of the Zimbabwe birds shows that several of them are carved with both necklaces and solar disks.

The New Kingdom, *c.* 1550–1070 BC, of which Rameses II's reign was the most glorious part, saw gold and precious stones becoming a royal monopoly. During the 18th and 29th Dynasties private citizens started to be rewarded with golden gifts by the pharaohs. Generals and officials received, as marks of special favour, golden swords, vessels, military decorations and chains of 'gold of honour'. The flow of gold to service this largesse must have been huge and it was still a flood a thousand and more years later in the Graeco-Roman period (*c.* 332 BC–AD 642). The Ptolemaic Dynasty was notorious for its displays of gold as an expression of the pharoah's wealth and divine status. Ptolemy II, Philadephus, was described as 'the Golden' and, according to Muller and Thiem, 'the mountain of gold that brightens all the lands'. They add: 'The visual climax of the *pompe* of Ptolemy II was a family portrait group in solid gold: golden statues of Ptolemy II and his deified parents, Ptolemy I Soter and Berenike I, stood in golden chariots set atop golden columns.' And this did not end with death; even more gold was required to see the pharaohs through to the afterlife.

The mummies and the funerary trappings of the pharaohs, as we know especially from the fabulous New Kingdom tomb of Tutankhamen, were festooned with gold jewellery, amulets, gold masks, gold coffins, gold accessories and gilded furniture. By Graeco-Roman times this use of gold as the flux of transition to a comfortable afterlife (as we know from the gilded mummies of the Bahariya Oasis) was no longer limited to the royal circle.

The desire to acquire gold, in a sense an addiction that could never be assuaged, spread out to encompass the whole of North Africa; indeed, it and other 'luxury' marine imports could be said to have created a unique society of marine traders, the Phoenicians, not just the best-known king and queen of ancient history. This trading nation occupied a strip of Mediterranean land covering a total area of about 4,000 square miles (less than the area of some English counties). Initially they were known as the Sea People but as their little nation grew into a world power the Sea People acquired territory on the Mediterranean and named it the Palm Land (Phoenicia).

The Phoenicians are pivotal to the early origin theories of the Zimbabwe culture because their deep-keeled ships allowed them to trade worldwide. Similarly, they seminally influenced their neighbour to the east, another little state called Netu (Palestine) ruled by a king called Solomon. Fabled for many things, in particular his wisdom, Solomon's driving passion was gold. His lover of legend, the Queen of Sheba (Yemen) had similar appetites and was an adept and highly successful import–exporter.

For Solomon to have had any involvement in the trade which resulted in the Zimbabwe culture – what H. Rider Haggard who rode with Rhodes into Mashonaland would immortalise in *King Solomon's Mines* – we need a rough idea of when Solomon and the Phoenicians were trading partners. Unfortunately, Solomon's era and the fabled Exodus of the Jews from Egypt are both the subject of running disputes as to when they occurred. Some say the Exodus was 1,200 years before the birth of Christ (which would lay it in the lap of the 19th Dynasty of Seti and Rameses I and II), others that it was 300 years later, others still that the whole story of David and Solomon was fiction made up in about AD 400. The two main schools of thought have Rameses II witnessing the departure of the Jews (*c.* 1290–1225 BC) or, 200 years earlier, Amenhotep II (*c.* 1490–1436) credited with the title 'Pharaoh of the Exodus'. There is even intriguing speculation that Queen Hatshepsut, whose fleet later brought back all the 'luxuries', including gold, from Punt, may as a princess have reared Moses.

There was definitely a time window between 1200 BC and 900 BC when the great empires of Assyria, Egypt and the Hittites did not dominate the Middle East and mini-kingdoms could have arisen. Be that as it may, there can be little doubt that over a thousand years before the birth of Christ a minor king called Solomon whose dreams went beyond the bounds of avarice ruled for some forty years a little Middle East country which is now Israel, and that he and a Phoenician king, Hiram of Tyre, made a much-publicised voyage down the Indian Ocean coast of Africa, returning with 43 metric tons of gold. Even accepting that biblical stories of great derring-do are apocryphal and boastful, this is an incredible hoard; indeed, even in the face of the compelling evidence that Solomon's dreams did go beyond avarice, it is still hard to countenance.

But why then quote the tonnage (in the measures of the time) so specifically? Admittedly speculating (with a little help from a mining friend), but if we allow the Shona gold collectors a ton a month, which is a huge amount if it is accepted that the first gold was alluvial, we are still talking almost four years of output. It is inconceivable how many eagles' quills would be needed to ship that amount! My mining friend then considered the primitive nature of the extraction processes in the ancient Zimbabwe fields, and opined that a few tons a year would be his preferred guesstimate. But then we would be talking about the production of decades, which is equally ridiculous. Unless, of course, there were more people collecting gold than has been acknowledged before.

Hiram's expedition certainly returned home and shared with Solomon an enormous hoard of gold. Had anything like it been seen before it would not have featured so large in the Bible. And if 43 tons is a dubious return from gold-rich Mashonaland it is even more questionable from the two other gold-producing countries, Ethiopia and Somalia, where Hiram's ships might have called. Then there is the problem of transporting gold in these quantities. This little band of Phoenicians and Jews could certainly not, on their own, have trekked up to Mashonaland and carried back 43 tons of gold through tsetse-fly and malaria-infested bush which, centuries later, almost brought Rhodes' expedition to its knees. Unless there had been some kind of gold market, collecting point or trading post with access to porters.

Was the easily defended acropolis hill community which preceded the grand *zimbabwes* a very early gold market or trading post? Did the Phoenicians, or possibly even earlier Moorish traders, set it up? An intriguing fact to support this idea will emerge shortly; Great

Zimbabwe in medieval times certainly had buildings from which foreigners sold imported goods.

The Phoenicians were after all the old world adepts at trading with primitive people. We know they went to markets in south-west England to buy Cornwall's tin, and some believe their unique ships took them as far afield as South America. As for porterage, Ezekiel 27:12 specifically mentions that the Phoenicians were slave-traders. In the earliest days of slave-trading, this human cargo was usually previously employed in the transportation of heavy goods, like ivory, to the coast.

That Solomon enjoyed close relations with the Phoenician King is confirmed frequently in the Old Testament, suggesting that in the beginning the two countries were operating almost as one. They had, initially, similar polytheistic religions and shared gods like Baal, Astoreth and Moloch, all of whom were worshipped amid sacred stones, pillars, towers and high places. Later, of course, the Hebrews came to worship just one god.

Apart from the joint expedition to Punt, the Bible is littered with references to the intimate early trading relationship which, given the size of his kingdom, brought Solomon disproportionately great riches, and a legend to match; II Chronicles 2:13 says that King Hiram's father was a Phoenician, his mother a daughter of the Jewish tribe of Dan. In the same book Hiram is reported as supplying Solomon with materials for his famous temple and ornaments to decorate it. I Kings 5 and Ezra 3:7 describe the Phoenician trade with Hebrews, the latter supplying wheat, honey wine and oil for various Phoenician luxuries like gold and the famous cedar trees (which Mauch thought he had found at Great Zimbabwe).

It is also recorded that Solomon married a Phoenician princess, that the daughter of the King of Tyre and High Priest of Astoreth married Ahab, King of Israel, and that Athaliah, daughter of Jezebel, a Phoenician princess, married Ahaziah, King of Judah, and so on.

I think we can accept with reasonable confidence that these two little nation states had strong blood ties and mutual trading interests, more than sufficient to support the biblical stories that they were partners in the expedition to Ophir that returned with tons and tons of gold. Moreover, this intimate Jewish partnership with the far-ranging Phoenicians will acquire considerable significance as this story reaches its climax. I am further convinced, even though he grew to be more and more enigmatic, that Theodore Bent regarded the Phoenicians and the Hebrews as one, specially in matters of trade and influence in south-central Africa. If that is the case, he was uncannily prescient.

Sadly, however, there is a seminal problem with all these Romantic theories that has in the past always stopped them dead in their tracks. A thousand or so years before the birth of Christ the expert opinion is that there were no resident natives in Zimbabwe. Or rather I should say, no 'Bantu' here. For the Zimbabwe culture to be an all-Bantu construct in line with the current 'definitive' origin theory, everything we have been talking about needs to have happened about 1,500 years later.

Contemporary Bantu are understandably implacable in their insistence that these unique stone works were raised by their ancestors, and them alone. But are they right? There are indications from almost every quarter that other influences were at work here, influences which increase in number the further back you go. Could this impasse, which has been holding the truth at bay for a century, be broken if, as I have suggested, the originators of the Zimbabwe gold trade and the authors of the Zimbabwe monuments are regarded, at least for the sake of argument, as different? It is surely obvious that the former must date from earlier times; indeed, the only question is how much earlier?

In his respected treatise *Africa: its People and their Cultural History* (New York, McGraw-Hill), Professor G.P. Murdock says that the Bantu only reached the north-east African coast from the interior between AD 575 and 879. This broad band is generally accepted. Others have pointed out that since the Bantu in southern Africa came down from the north as part of a general movement of expansion it is unlikely that they could have reached Mashonaland and further south in any large numbers before the sixth to the ninth centuries AD.

However, radio-carbon dating would soon make of all this guesswork a political time bomb that has been ticking ever since.

From well-conducted excavations on a site in the acropolis, the monument where the stone birds were found on the high kopje overlooking Great Zimbabwe, Messrs Robinson and Summers took charcoal from the hearths of early inhabitants, which gave them a carbon dating from the fourth century AD – several hundred years before expert opinion says there were Bantu here. Rare for archaeologists of that time who were newly armed with the miraculous tool of radio-carbon dating, Summers and Robinson did not suggest that this was the earliest period of occupation. In any case the dating method was only accurate to within plus or minus 150 years. Ergo, their Great Zimbabwe acropolis site could have been established by or before the start of the Christian millennium. It is also accepted nowadays that ancient communities can remain unchanged for hundreds or even thousands of years. The first Portuguese missionary to actually live with the Karanga 500 years ago, for example, left an account of a rural Shona society all but identical to the one I found there in 1947. So if there were people living on the Zimbabwe acropolis in what appeared to be settled communities, who were they? Packed into this question, however, there is so much political dynamite no one appears to have dared to answer it.

Dr Peter Garlake, whose book *Great Zimbabwe* (Thames & Hudson, London, 1973) remains the bible of the Shona school, goes no further than to propose that 'early iron age groups must once have lived or camped in the vicinity . . . infiltrating country previously occupied only by late Stone Age hunters . . . able to coexist in some areas without competition or conflict for many centuries'. Dr Garlake does not specify that by 'early iron age groups' he means Bantu, whereas his 'late Stone Age hunters' were people of a different race – itinerant bushmen (San People). Admittedly he does support, albeit unwittingly, that the San People once occupied the Zimbabwe countryside alone but he begs the question: for how long? If, however, we accept my proposal that people who collected and traded gold were the true originators of

57

the Zimbabwe culture then this is not a question that may be begged; indeed, it is the fundamental question.

Nowadays, archaeologists admit that they can rarely, if ever, pick up on and employ their skills other than to reasonably well-established ancient sites. There simply is no sufficient build-up of evidence from anything but settlements of some antiquity. Layers of traceable materials at the so-called lowest levels of the Zimbabwe acropolis site are therefore a good indication that there was an old settlement or the regular gathering of Stone Age people here.

Recent research has also indicated that pastoralists did not quickly take over from hunter-gatherers because theirs was the easier life. The opposite is true. When pastoralists first infiltrated the bush areas of hunter-gatherers, keeping their cattle alive and properly grazed was much the harder work. The reason that the pastoralists, like the Bantu, eventually won out is that cattle grazing drives out the hunter-gatherer and then expands exponentially as the cattle multiply. Eventually, as exemplified by today's Kalahari bushmen, the hunter-gatherers end up scratching a living from neo-desert land that won't support livestock or agriculture.

You can see the process still at work and seriously threatening wildlife in modern Tanzania. The local Bantu, the Masai, have lived as a cattle-dependent society for thousands of years and have only been stopped from covering the entire country with their livestock by wildlife protection laws. A Masai man genuinely believes that he has been put on earth to protect the world's cattle (which made for some very interesting defences against charges of cattle-theft in colonial times). Not surprisingly, full-time hunter-gatherers in Tanzania have become extinct.

The point is that this process takes a lot of time. Did it take the amount of time we require for San People to have met Solomon's priests and Phoenician gold traders, the 'ancient Moors' who are the shadows in the background of every ancient record of trade in southern Africa?

It is time to take a proper look at those 'late Stone Age hunters' cum gold traders, the mysterious San People, but that is no easy task because if Great Zimbabwe is the lost city of Africa, the San are most certainly the lost tribe. Their origins will be traced later. Here, for a moment, let us think that which has previously been unthinkable – that the San People were the *original* gold traders of south-central Africa and created the first settlement, albeit transitory, at Great Zimbabwe. Did they then, over a period of about a thousand years, slowly intermingle with the early Bantu immigrants until (as happened everywhere in south-central Africa) the exponential expansion of the cattle culture across gold-rich ground made them the dominant Karanga race that in medieval times would crown its achievements, like the Kings of Egypt and Israel, with spectacular monumental buildings?

Here again, however, that very awkward question of population numbers creeps into the equation. There certainly weren't any Bantu here a thousand years before Christ; were there viable populations of San? Consideration of the Sans' role in the early cultural development of southern Africa has been inhibited until fairly recently by the 'bushman' stereotype. Just as the Australian rediscovered their Aborigines about twenty-five years ago, the South Africans are now rediscovering the San, not least because the San, like the Aborigines, are demanding that large parts of their country – for some San *all* of the country! – be restored to them. The wave of interest in the San People that has swept through South Africa in the last few years is not, however, a significant movement in support of San territorial claims, but concern that the race should not become extinct before a claim of any kind can be filed and tested.

Already emerging are some quite extraordinary statistics based on hard evidence that these lost people of the far south were just the tip of an iceberg. There were San communities in Tanzania, Zambia, Zaire, Malawi, Mozambique, Angola, Namibia, Botswana, Zimbabwe, Lesotho, Swaziland and South Africa. And while these communities may have been small and transitory (although there is no strong proof either way of that) they were the *only* communities of modern humans. Moreover, it appears they were around for an immensely long time, a time that makes the territorial claims of 'modern' Bantu immigrants appear rather dubious.

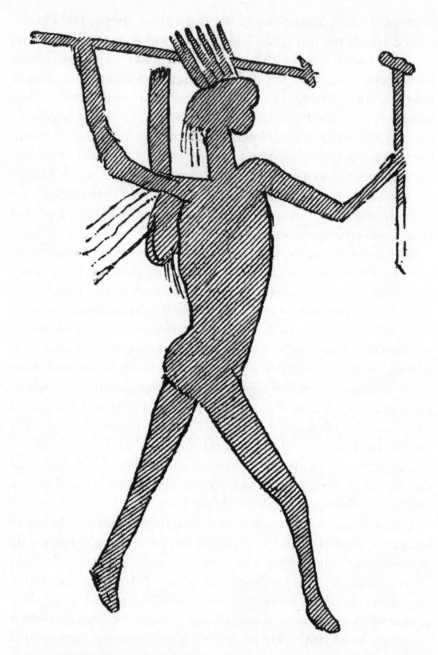

Were the San (Bushmen) the first native Africans to work and trade Zimbabwe gold? They left evidence of their presence in drawings across the length and breadth of south-central Africa.

Unlike the builders of the Great Zimbabwe monuments, the San People left a wealth of pictorial evidence of their presence in the form of glorious, highly creative and meaningful pictures and engravings, or, if you like, pictograms. The San painted extensively in the area of Great Zimbabwe and all the other grand monuments; indeed, their art is a cultural treasure to equal the monuments. In 1996 a survey was undertaken of all the rock art records in the countries above which produced a total of 14,118, of which South Africa contributed some 10,000. The latter was obviously the product of better record-keeping. The husband and wife academic team of Professor H.J. Deacon and Dr Jeanette Deacon in their book *Human Beginnings in South Africa* (David Philips, Cape Town) have judged that figure to be a gross underestimate of the actual number of sites:

We know from recent surveys that when these records are checked in the field, even for small areas, the numbers can be quadrupled at least and there are many areas in all the southern African countries that have never been surveyed at all. Peter Garlake believes that in Zimbabwe alone there are at least 30,000 sites, and there must be many more in South Africa.

Another observation from this erudite book should be added:

Although most of the rock painting and rock engravings were done by the San, not all South African rock art was the work of hunter-gatherers. There are many sites mostly in the north and east of the country, with paintings in a distinctive 'finger painting' or 'late white style', as well as engravings that depict subjects different from those in the San art.

The Deacons believe that these were done by Bantu (Khosa, Zulu, Venda, Shona, Sotho and Tswana agriculturists) and their ancestors, 'within the last 2,000 years'. That certainly takes us back to the time of Graeco-Roman Egypt when gold lust was at its height. It suggests again that the San and the Bantu overlapped and may have cohabited, not just coexisted. Sadly, even the learned Deacons are not able to say how far back into the pre-Christian millennium of the Phoenicians, Solomon and Sheba these creative 'ancestors' of the lost people of Africa learned to trade gold.

And that is where I had got to in Cape Town last year when a copy of the *Cape Argus* was dropped on my stoep. MAN'S EARLIEST IDEAS ARE WRITTEN ON OCHRE, was the headline of an article by the *Argus* science correspondent, John Yield.

What are ochres?

Yield had more important questions to answer, however, and his intro was a quote from Descartes: '*Cogito ergo sum*' (I think, therefore I am).

Yes, but what are ochres?

Implacably, Yield went on: 'It is the ability to think and to translate these complex thoughts into actions that distinguishes modern humans, like homo erectus, or from the hominids like Australopithecus, which came even earlier, and from other species in the animal kingdom.'

Was this the San again?

'One of the keys to complex, abstract thought is the use of symbols, including geometric shapes. An international team of researchers led by South African archaeologists have discovered abstract representations engraved on pieces of red ochre in the Middle Stone Age layers at Blombos Cave, near Stillbaai on the southern Cape coast.'

Yes it was!

The discovery was apparently about to be reported in the prestigious American journal, *Science*, and the scientists led by Professor Christopher Henshilwood of the South African Museum in Cape Town, and professor at Bergen University in Norway and the State University of New York, Stony Brook, had evidence that modern human behaviour emerged in Africa at least *35,000 years* before the start of the Upper Paleolithic era in Eurasia. The San had a history of coherent, creative social groupings far, far older than I had ever suspected, and infinitely older than Solomon and Sheba.

Ochre is chunks of hardened red-ochre-coloured clay and it is thought to have been used for things like hide-tanning and pigments, but no other ochre pieces or artefacts older than about 40,000 years have provided evidence for abstract or depictable images which would indicate modern human behaviour. Among archaeologists, modern human behaviour means the thoughts and actions underwritten by minds equivalent to those of Homo sapiens today. Such cognitive abilities have, until now, been confined to depictable images found at Eurasia's Upper Paleolithic sites and date back some 35,000 years.

Two pieces of engraved ochre have now been found in the Blombos Cave, another seven are potentially engraved and there are some 8,000 other pieces, many bearing signs of use from Middle Stone age layers. That they were worked by members of a settled community is confirmed by the discovery of a number of bowl-shaped hearths. On one piece of ochre, both the flat surfaces and one edge are modified by scraping and sanding. 'The edge has two ground facets and the larger of these bears a small cross-hatched engraved design,' says Henshilwood. The cross-hatching consists of two sets of six and eight lines partly intercepted by a long line. The engravings on the second slab consist of rows of cross-hatching, bounded top and bottom by parallel lines, and divided through the middle by a third parallel line which divides the lozenge shapes into triangles. 'The preparation by grinding of the engraved surface, situation of the engraving on this prepared face, engraving technique, and final design are similar for both pieces, indicating a deliberate sequence of choices,' Henshilwood concluded.

Both pieces were found within layers of bifacial flaked stone points which occur only below the so-called Howeison's Poort horizons, which date to between 65,000 and 70,000 years ago. This truly ancient date for thinking, decision-taking, artistic people who could only be the ancestors of the San has subsequently been confirmed by two different luminescence-based dating methods. The engraved slabs are therefore about 77,000 years old!

'The Blombos Cave engravings are intentional images,' Henshilwood insists, and then lays down an idea which could be pivotal to our story, bearing in mind that Great Zimbabwe, indeed most of the hundreds of *zimbabwes*, are covered with 'intentional images' of a creative nature, many of them engravings. 'The Blombos Cave motifs . . . may have been constructed with symbolic intent, the meaning of which is now unknown. These finds demonstrate that ochre use in the Middle Stone Age was not exclusively utilitarian and, arguably, the transmission and sharing of the meaning of the engravings relied on fully syntactical language.'

If this is true of motifs made at the dawn of human time in a cave in the tip of Africa, then it surely must be true of the motifs so generously engraved on thousands of shaped Zimbabwe stones on which cross-hatching also features large. Moreover, these stones of 'symbolic intent' are set in a natural art gallery of thousands of San, or their students', paintings and engravings. Suddenly, the disreputable thought becomes feasible that thousands of years ago – well before the time of Solomon and Sheba and even the earliest Egyptian dynasties – this Zimbabwe countryside was home to a considerable population of modern (in the archaeological sense) artistic people settled enough to find time to decorate their dwellings and deify certain sites.

And these were a people whom we know from the earliest Western encounters collected and traded gold.

FOUR

Ophir Revealed

Theodore and Agnes Bent spend their first two weeks cutting their way in to the temple through thick, stinging jungle. Everywhere walls had collapsed. Passages were overlain with human and animal detritus. No maintenance had observably taken place for centuries. Ancient trees grow through walls, including a well-established pair of *muchechete* trees flanking the conical tower which Carl Mauch had excitedly labelled 'cedars', and from which he extrapolated his theory of Sheba's temple and the ancient Ophir of Solomon.

The Bents make an early, disappointed, note of an absence of ancient tombs or grave sites but put a positive spin on it by suggesting that the 'ancient inhabitants who formed but a garrison in this country' might have taken their dead for ceremonial burial at sacred sites elsewhere. On the Bahrein islands in the Persian Gulf they have seen acres of mounds containing thousands of tombs and no vestige of a town. This custom, Theodore Bent says, still prevails among the Mohammedans of Persia. He also makes an early observation here which has been uncontested since:

> The circular ruins repeat themselves, always, if possible, occupying a slightly raised ground for about a mile along a low ridge acting, doubtless, as the double purpose of temples and fortresses for separate communities, the inhabitants dwelling in beehive huts of mud around.

Today's improved view of this is:

> A family homestead at the capital [Great Zimbabwe] consisted of several *daga* houses. Among the elite these dwellings were linked

65

Theodore Bent, who at the end of the nineteenth century led the Royal Geographical Society's ground-breaking expedition to Great Zimbabwe.

Mrs Bent, whose photography and drawings produced unique and unrepeatable images of the Zimbabwe ruins at their most derelict.

by low stone walls to form a homestead. Each homestead, in turn, was linked to other homesteads by similar walls. These shared walls provided privacy, surfaces for decoration, and protection against bad weather and wild animals.

Down the years everyone has been concerned by the obvious paradox here. Why live in mud huts if you know how to build exquisitely in stone, of which there is an abundance locally? Bent notes that all the native villages on the Zimbabwe hill are built, understandably, on the sunniest spots. Over the years – possibly thousands of years – many feet of human spoil had been laid down, making excavation with an unskilled labour force difficult and time-consuming. He seeks out a dig-site in the shade where the locals had not seen fit to build huts. Even though it is difficult to persuade his 'shivering Kaffirs' to work here his choice of the shaded side of the hill fortress immediately produces exciting results. ('Kaffir' was more a generic than a disparaging term in his day; 'Blacks' would have been more insulting.)

The kopje on which the fortress, or the acropolis, is built is a natural defensive position protected on one side by giant granite boulders and on the south by a 90 foot precipice. On the only accessible side is a massive wall, in places 13 feet thick and 30 feet high, decorated with small round towers and monoliths. The fortress is served by a flight of steps through a narrow slit in the granite boulders. Every angle is protected from attack, so much so that Bent speculates that the occupants were in constant dread of attack and lived like a garrison in the heart of enemy territory.

Just below the summit Bent comes upon an odd little plateau approached by narrow passages and steps and a curious passage through the wall covered with huge beams of granite to support the weight of stone above. Steps on one side are made of the 'strong cement' (powdered granite) he has found elsewhere and one wall is decorated with the ubiquitous chevron pattern. This platform is spectacularly adorned with huge monoliths and decorated pillars of soapstone, one of which is more than 11 feet tall.

Africans found living in these mud huts among the Zimbabwe ruins knew nothing of the builders of the stone cities and their gold industry.

The team clears the dense jungle below this platform and soon comes across an altar. Contemporary accounts seem to share Bent's view of the religious significance of the site. Behind the altar a labyrinthine confusion of stone structures is revealed which completely baffles everyone. They follow a narrow gully 4 feet wide descending between two boulders and protected, for no apparent reason, by six buttresses which narrow to a zigzag passage 10 inches wide. Thick walls shut off separate chambers. 'In all directions everything is tortuous; every inch of ground is protected with buttresses and traverses. As in the large circular building below, all the entrances are rounded off.'

Bent speculates that this is the oldest of the ruins – later work has proved him right – and that it was built at a time when defence was the main object. 'When they were able to do so with safety, they next constructed the circular temple below and as time went on they erected the more carelessly put-together buildings around.'

The hill fortress enclosure has been used as a pen for Chief Mugabe's cattle but once cleared Bent is rewarded with spectacular soapstone birds and pillars, fragments of soapstone bowls and 'phalli'. Nothing like them has been found elsewhere in southern Africa. These phalli, mostly of soapstone, have been inserted into the stones of the altar and scattered all around it. They are carved 'with an anatomical accuracy which unmistakably conveys their meaning'. This does not deter Mrs Bent from taking sufficiently explicit photographs for her husband to make the observation that circumcision was practised by this ancient race and he draws attention to Herodotus's description of the origin of this practice: 'Its origin both amongst the Ethiopians and Egyptians may be traced to the most remote antiquity [Herodotus 2.37.104].'

They unearth no less than thirty-eight miniature phalli, one highly decorated with what appears to be a winged sun, 'or perchance the winged Egyptian vulture'. Bent compares it, printing accurate illustrations, with a small marble column of Phoenician origin in the Louvre, which has a winged symbol on the shaft and is crowned with an ornamentation of four petalled flowers.

MM Perrot and Chipiez, experts on the Phoenicians, are again called in to confirm that this is 'A sort of trade mark by which we can recognise as Phoenician all such objects as bear it, whether they come from Etruria or Sardinia, from Africa or Syria . . . we may say it is signed.' Bent takes a closer look at his Great Zimbabwe altar artefact and finds it is also crowned with a rosette of seven petals. These rosettes or flower patterns are also seemingly very distinctive as they were commonly used by the Phoenicians to indicate the sun. Phoenician stelae at the British Museum carry the rosette, often in conjunction with the half moon. Moreover, Bent's team find rosettes carved on the decorated pillars. The eyes of the soapstone birds appear also to be carved in the form of rosettes.

It is back to Herodotus for the significance of all this: 'The Arabians of all the gods only worshipped Dionysus . . . that is to say they worshipped the two deities, which in the mind of the father of history, represented in themselves all that was known of the mysteries of creation, pointing to the very earliest period of the Arabian cult, prior to the more refined religious development of the Sabaeo-Himyaritic dynasty, when sun-worship, venerated for the great luminary which regenerated all animal and vegetable life, superseded the grosser forms of nature worship, to be itself somewhat superseded or rather incorporated in a worship of all the heavenly luminaries which developed as knowledge of astronomy was acquired [Herodotus 3–8].'

Theodore Bent is evidently inclining towards the idea of a Semitic process of religious evolution at Great Zimbabwe, helped no doubt by his cartographer, Swan's, belief that the altars and other astronomical pointers are inclined towards northern stars.

The several Semite tribes are, we believe, descended from Shem, Noah's eldest son. They include the Phoenicians, the various Aramaean tribes (including Hebrews) and a considerable portion of the population of Ethiopia. They began to leave Arabia as early as 2500 BC in successive waves of migrations that took them to Mesopotamia, the Mediterranean coast, and the Nile delta. In Mesopotamia the Semitic people were in contact with the Sumerian civilisation and eventually dominated it. In Phoenicia they developed the most sophisticated and adventurous of maritime trades and are regarded as the first great seafaring nation.

The Hebrews went through Sinai into the Nile delta, settling eventually with other Semitic inhabitants in Palestine, and became the leaders of a new nation and a very potent religion, Judaism. In fact the three great monotheistic religions, Christianity, Islam and Judaism, all of them militantly evangelical, were born within the Semite hegemony. It is the Jews, however, who have maintained an unbroken tradition of commercial acumen.

Competition between the complex monotheistic religions which evolved within the Semitic sphere, in particular between Christianity and Islam, increasingly led to conflicts – and refugees. The most extended and bloody of these ancient conflicts were the Crusades and at the time when they raged between Islam and Christianity, Great Zimbabwe was probably at its most affluent. So was a king, 'Prester John', in a mysterious Afro-Christian kingdom to the far north. Hence the hope of European kings and popes who launched the Crusades that a flank attack on Islam might be mounted if contact could be made with Prester John.

Might this answer the riddle of Great Zimbabwe's lost gold? Did it contribute to war-chests now lost in the depths of time via earlier ancient links with the only other traditional stone-city builders south of the Pyramids? Theodore Bent grew ever more convinced of a Great Zimbabwe history along these lines as his team unearthed a wealth of ancient artefacts. Such Romantic possibilities were actively contemplated.

In the middle of all this exciting activity, however, Bent, makes an odd discovery which he does not regard as particularly significant but which for me started a whole new line of enquiry. The largest of the soapstone pillars in the hill fortress measures 11 feet 6 inches. The base of the pillar was found in situ, acting as the centre to a group of monoliths. 'The rest had been broken off and appropriated by a Kaffir to decorate a wall,' says Bent. It is hard to understand, given his love of classical cross-referencing, that Bent fails to appreciate that throughout the golden age of the Greeks and the Romans, walls were decorated with coloured scraps of broken stone and tile. Mosaic proved, in fact, to be the most durable of the decorative arts of these times. It would seem that even when the Zimbabwe culture had began to decay the people here were still sufficiently concerned with the aesthetics of their monument (and of aesthetics per se) to want to decorate it. Could it be that the art of Great Zimbabwe is the key to many of the enigmas?

Bent does acknowledge that other pieces he is finding are beautifully decorated *objets d'art*. The tallest pillar has patterns round it, as on the wall below the altar, orientating it to the setting sun. The rosette pattern is present on many of these pillars.

He provides evidence of old-world religious veneration of large stones like these Great Zimbabwe columns. Dr Gustav Kremer of the Akademie der Wissenschaft, Vienna, has written a famous account of the ancient cults and of their worship of stones, as have El Masoudi, Marinus of Tyre and Herodotus. There is also this account from Euthymius Zygabemus: 'This stone was the head of Aphrodite, which the Ishmaelites formerly worshipped, and it is called Bakka Ismak . . . they have certain stone statues erected in the centre of their houses, round which they danced till they fell from giddiness; but when the Saracens were converted to Christianity they were obliged to anathematise this stone which formerly they worshipped.' Bent himself suggests that the famous Kaaba stone at Mecca resembles a black schistose block he has found at Great Zimbabwe. Taken together it all adds up to an exceedingly old worship at Great Zimbabwe apparently dating back to the most primitive ages of mankind.

His team of diggers have now worked down to considerable depths on the shady side of the hill temple and these excavations begin to turn up what for me, apart from the Zimbabwe birds, are the most interesting artefacts found at Great Zimbabwe: fragments of decorated and plain soapstone bowls. Soapstone is a soft, mostly emerald green, talc schist which can be easily carved and highly polished. Bent is artistically impressed with these bowls:

The work displayed in executing these bowls, the careful rounding of the edges, the exact execution of the circle, the fine pointed tool-marks, and the subjects they chose to depict, point to the race having been far advanced in artistic skill – a skill arrived at doubtless by commercial intercourse with the more civilised races of mankind.

Seven of these bowls were of exactly the same size – 19.2 inches in diameter. The most elaborate of the fragments is a bowl which has depicted round its outer edge a hunting scene; it is very well worked and bears in several points a remarkable similarity to objects of art produced by the Phoenicians. There is here, as we have in all Phoenician patterns, the straight procession of animals, to break the continuity of which a little man is introduced shooting a zebra with one hand and holding in the other an animal on a leash.

To fill up a vacant space, a bird is introduced flying, all of which points are characteristic of Phoenician work. Then the Phoenician workmen always had a great power of adaptability, taking their lessons in art from immediate surroundings, which is noticeable all over the world, whether in Greece, Egypt, Africa, or Italy.

There are three zebras, two hippopotami, and the sportsman in the centre is obviously a Hottentot. The fragments of a large bowl, which has a procession of bulls round it, is also Phoenician in character.

Fragments of soapstone bearing what the Royal Geographical Society's explorers believed resembled the earliest Arabian alphabet.

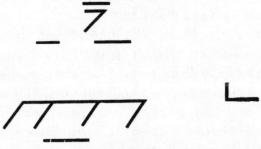

LETTERS FROM PROTO-ARABIAN ALPHABET

either side recall some system of tally, and the straightness of the lettering compares curiously with the proto-Arabian type of lettering used in the earlier Sabæan inscriptions, specimens of which I here give, and also with some curious rock carvings found by

LETTERS ON A ROCK IN BECHUANALAND, COPIED BY
MR. A. A. ANDERSON

These letters are thought to be part of the early Arabian alphabet.

This lovely artwork is, however, quickly set aside when the diggers unearth more fragments depicting, Bent believes, a religious procession, a hand holding a pot or censer containing an offering, and an arm of another figure with the portion of the back of the head with the hair drawn off it in folds. But it is a third fragment which, as Bent puts it, is the most tantalising of all. It is from a huge bowl – estimated at more than 2 feet across – and it appears to have writing round it. Mrs Bent carefully photographs this fragment and they compare it with letters from the proto-Arabian alphabet. There is certainly a striking similarity to letters which are found in the earliest Sabaean inscriptions. Bent asserts: 'It is an attempt at writing.' But it has never been translated and it is the only item resembling a cryptogram ever found at Great Zimbabwe.

The dig continues to be very rewarding. They retrieve an object similar to a drum, some 2 feet wide. Again of soapstone it is decorated on the sides and top with rings of knobs, four on the side and four on the top, with a hole in the middle. One theory is that it was a quern or grinding stone, but soapstone is too soft for such a purpose. It remains one of the most prized treasures found at the lost city and the most enigmatic; indeed, it has inspired an entire theory of Indian authorship for the ancient ruins of southern Africa. It remains at Groote Schuur in Cape Town where for some years, I am told, it was used as a doorstop.

Bent is particularly pleased with it because, though larger, it was all but identical to an artefact in the Fitzwilliam Museum at Cambridge. The Fitzwilliam stone is of white marble 6 inches in diameter with similarly disposed knobs in rows. This studded drum, attributed confidently to the Phoenicians, was found during excavations at Paphos, in Cyprus. Herodian (Book 5) also describes a sacred cone in the great Phoenician temple of the sun at Emesa, in Syria, which was adorned with knobs or protuberances.

Bent obviously believes he is accumulating strong evidence for his theory of a sun-worshipping Semite origin for the authors of the lost city – at the time I think I would have too – and is literally cock-a-hoop when he finds not one but eight of Herr Mauch's much-vaunted Zimbabwe birds. I cannot escape the feeling that this whole story hinges on a correct interpretation of the Zimbabwe birds and the enigmatic past from whence they flew. Are the ancestors of this flock the raptor-spirits, particularly eagles, to be found in some African cults? Or are they simple effigies of Egypt's feathered gods, like the hawk, Horus, protector of foreign miners? They were Rhodes' obsession as well, metaphors of a golden lost city he had yet to see. Through their influence on him they changed the course of history in this part of Africa; indeed, the shadows from their wings may be changing it still.

Apart from Carl Mauch, who is not a reliable witness, Theodore Bent was the first westerner with any archaeological expertise to examine these remarkable birds in situ. In all he found six large and two small ones. We already know that Posselt appropriated one for Rhodes who installed it in pride of place in his house in Cape Town. Bent also found a number of pedestals – stelae – still standing in the temple with their tops broken off which probably originally supported more birds. The tallest bird column stood 5 feet 4 inches high, the smallest 6 inches shorter. Each is essentially modelled on the same bird, but they are differently worked. The birds are exquisitely decorated and it is this decoration which makes them so fascinating for me.

One has wings tipped with the lost city's prevailing dentelle pattern. They all have the veiled rosette-eyes. There are a variety of patterns down the backs, some indicating feathers, others beaded knobs. Yet another has what looks like a necklace with a brooch in front. Two of the birds are distinctive and different to the others. They have fan-shaped tails and straight legs and they are perched on zones or cesti. Another, with nothing beneath its talons, has two circles carved below it and two on the wings. There are two raised ovoids thought to represent the sun, and chevron patterns.

The birds launch Bent on a frenzy of cross-referencing:

> I have little doubt in stating that they are closely akin to the Assyrian Astarte or Venus, and represent the female element in creation. Similar birds were sacred to Astarte amongst the Phoenicians and are often represented as being perched on their shrines.

Ancient Egypt, he reminds us, is littered with sacred bird sculptures:

> Horapollo tells that the vulture was emblematic of 'Urania, a year, a mother' while Aelian goes so far as to suppose that all vultures are female, to account for their character as emblems of maternity.
>
> The cesti and the circles point obviously to this, and these birds in connection with phallic worship are interesting as emblems, signifying incubation.

Lucian, who in his work 'De Syria Dea' describes a temple at Hierapolis, near the Euphrates, which as we have seen, has much in common with these temples at Zimbabwe . . . mentions a curious pediment, of no distinctive shape, called by the Assyrians 'the symbol', on the top of which is perched a bird.

Among Dr Schliemann's discoveries at Mycene, there are also images surmounted by birds.

All of this is very convincingly supported with drawings, photographs and invitations to his readership to see these comparable artefacts in northern museums:

A bird on a pedestal carved from 'rude stone fragments found in the Soudan [Sudan]' on display at the Ashmolean Museum.

Phoenician coins which have birds on pedestals as their focal object.

The curious zodiac of Denderah, where a bird is perched on a pillar and with the crown of Upper Egypt on its head 'which has recently been found on an archaeological dig in Egypt'.

'It is just possible', Bent avows, 'that the birds at Zimbabwe had some solstitial meaning, but as their exact position on the temple walls is lost, it is impossible to speak on this point with anything like certainty.' He adds: 'The very earliest Arabian tribes at the time of the Himyaritic supremacy, used the vulture as a totem.' The Zimbabwe birds do look quite like vultures. At this moment one senses that in Bent's mind the case for origin is all but proven.

Other interesting finds attesting to a cosmopolitan lifestyle at the lost city are mentioned almost as an afterthought:

In the vicinity of the temple we also came across some minor objects very near the surface, which did not do more than establish the worldwide commerce carried on at Great Zimbabwe at a much more recent date, and still by the Arabians – namely a few fragments of Celadon pottery from China, of Persian ware, an undoubted specimen of Arabian glass, and beads of doubtful provenance, though one of them may be considered as Egyptian of the Ptolemaic period.

One bowl is, however, so exquisitely decorated that he is obliged to concede that it is worthy of a good period of classic Greek ware.

> The pattern round it is evidently stamped on, being done with such absolute accuracy. It is geometric, as all the patterns on the pottery are. It is not hand-made pottery, for on the back of it are distinct signs of a wheel. Then there are some black fragments with an excellent glaze and bevel, also fragments of pottery lids, and a pottery stopper, pointing to the fact that the old inhabitants of Zimbabwe had reached an advanced state of proficiency in ceramic art. All that the pottery proves to us is that the ancient inhabitants of Zimbabwe had reached a high state of excellence in the manufacture of it, corresponding to a state of ceramic art known only to the rest of the world in classic time.

He is less impressed by a considerable quantity of iron weapons and implements, including a spearhead which had been gold-plated. 'I am inclined to set aside the iron implements as pertaining to a more recent occupation, though at the same time there is no actual reason for not assigning them a remoter antiquity.'

There is a reason for his interest wandering from these significant artefacts – he has found a gold foundry. Just below the temple under the fortress the dig reveals a smelting furnace flecked with gold, 'made of very hard cement of powdered granite'. The team is under no illusions about the importance of this discovery and, widening the excavation, they soon find evidence to confirm that it is indeed a metal-smelting furnace for the manufacture of gold from gold-bearing quartz. The furnace has a proper chimney, also of powdered-granite cement. Says Bent: 'Hard by, in a chasm between two boulders, lay all the rejected casings from which the gold-bearing quartz had been extracted by exposure to heat prior to the crushing, proving beyond a doubt that these ruins, although not immediately on a gold reef, formed the capital of a gold-producing people who had chosen this hill fortress with its granite boulders for their capital owing to its strategic advantages.'

Bent also found numerous clay crucibles, nearly all of them containing small specks of gold adhered to the glaze produced by the heat of smelting. In the same area he unearthed a number of water-worn stones also with gold stuck to them which he concluded were burnishers. Then there was a soapstone object with a hole in, which he decided was a hammer for beating gold into sheets.

Great Zimbabwe sits on the edge of an elevated plateau averaging 3,000 to 5,000 feet above sea level. The plateau, known as the Zimbabwe batholith, is largely Archaen granite some 3,000 million years old. The granite forms the bottom layer of the plateau, known as the Basement, and through this huge outcrops – kopjes – were raised up and later eroded.

Robert Swan is the best geologist in the party and describes the kopjes as 'suggesting the idea of huge bubbles on the surface of a molten mass'. In their explorations of Mashonaland prior to tackling the lost city, the team noted patches of stratified rock of quartzites and schists, crystalline limestone and magnesium. These belts of stratified rock are generally two or three miles wide and in them occur the gold-bearing quartz reefs. One such belt was found near Fort Victoria. Swan made a close examination of the quartzite rock they had found near the furnace, established that it contained only minute traces of gold, and decided it had probably been rejected as unworthy of processing. He took time off from cartography to visit the nearby quartz belt and to search for old workings and gold reefs but was again disappointed, finding a single poor reef and no evidence that this particular area had been mined. This was all somewhat puzzling because Mr and Mrs Bent were continuing to turn up fascinating artefacts associated with the crafting of gold.

Far and away the most exciting find after the furnace was the gold-crusted soapstone ingot mould. This mould has become almost a metaphor for all the mysteries of the lost city and was certainly the artefact which most intrigued me when I first heard of it; indeed, my first feature article for the Salisbury newspaper, *The Sunday Mail*, was about an ingot which had been found at the bottom of Falmouth harbour in Cornwall which matched the Zimbabwe mould.

So many different historical elements flow into its various features. It is cut from soapstone as opposed to any other rock, indicating strongly that it was made at Great Zimbabwe, which specialised in the carving of soapstone. The ingot shape is very indicative of ingots being a form of currency, or at least a standardised measure – but standardised to what system?

As soon as the Bents got the mould home they looked around for something to compare it with and in the School of Mines, Jermyn Street, London, they found a casting of the Cornish ingot (the original is tin). Bent's Zimbabwe mould is distinctively – or as he put it 'curiously' – shaped and the London ingot, he felt, 'corresponded almost exactly' to the Cornish casting. Looking at Mrs Bent's photographs I think it is fair to say that if this particular ingot wasn't actually cast in the Great Zimbabwe mould (and so far as I know nobody has ever checked that by so doing) the two are of the same system or, if you like, denomination. If the comparison is made with coinage, coins of a particular denomination – currency – all come out of moulds of a specific size.

If the Cornish ingot is a form of currency, or a measure in a standardised system, then it and the Zimbabwe mould are seemingly part of the same system. The shape – and let us not overlook the fact

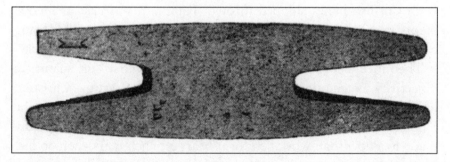

This ingot found in the Cornish harbour of Falmouth, and with a Phoenician 'hallmark', could have been cast from a mould cut from soapstone at Great Zimbabwe.

that it is a cross – is too distinctive to be otherwise. Today, gold is stored in bulk in the shape of bars of a specific weight and measure. There would be no point in casting crosses unless the measure in ancient times was a cross. The measure is the mould.

Zimbabwe – especially a fledgling Zimbabwe gold industry from the time of Solomon and Sheba – is a very long way from Cornwall. A link between the two, it has been often claimed, surely requires an impossible stretch of the imagination. Perhaps not. Very little serious work – certainly nothing definitive – has been done on the earliest possible beginnings of the Zimbabwe culture because, of course, in those distant days there was no culture. There was just gold.

We do know, however, from the existence of a very early Christian 'colony' in Ethiopia that the first Christian missionaries carried the gospel far and wide. There is another legend at least as long-lived as that of the Ethiopian Christian king, Prester John, which holds that Joseph of Arimathea, who was given Jesus' body for burial and provided the tomb where he was interred until his resurrection, accompanied the Apostle Philip on a preaching mission to Gaul and was sent on to Britain for the purpose of converting the island to Christianity. Joseph was a wealthy metal trader who is commonly held to have made regular buying trips to Roman Britain. Cornwall was in those days the country's chief mining district and was well known to the metal-traders for the quality of its tin. Falmouth was the port for this trade. There seems to have been a very ancient trade in precious metals between Arabia, Europe and Britain and the tin from Cornish mines shipped through Falmouth was cast as ingots, ingots shaped in moulds all but identical to the unique moulds being carved in soapstone by the Zimbabwe culture in the heart of Africa.

Theodore Bent, however, did not compromise his scientific objectivity by tempting his readers with legendary Cornish– Christian links; he steers well clear of it because he has something better: the Falmouth ingot is 'hallmarked'. 'This ingot of tin was undoubtedly made by Phoenician workmen for it bears a punch-mark thereon like those usually employed by workmen of that period,' Bent reports. 'Sir Henry James, in his pamphlet describing it, draws attention to the statement of Diodorus, that in ancient Britain ingots of tin were made of the shape of astragali [knuckle-bone crosses]. . . . Probably this shape of ingot was common in the ancient world, for Sir John Evans, K.C.B., has called my attention to an ingot mould somewhat similar in form, found in Dalmatia, and the Kaffirs far north of the Zambesi now make ingots of iron of a shape which might easily be supposed to have been derived from astragalus.'

In support of all this, Swan has finally located gold outcrops a few miles from Zimbabwe. New, smaller, ruined *zimbabwes* are also found, all of them close to ancient gold workings. At the bottom of some of the old workings Swan observes that the reefs continue to carry visible gold. On the edge of the escarpment Swan finds evidence that 'an enormous amount of alluvial [gold] has been worked'.

The team had begun to work on a theory that Great Zimbabwe was the capital of a gold-producing empire covering much of Mashonaland commanding a fiefdom of smaller gold-mining *zimbabwes*. Most intriguing were reports that they obtained from their workers, of a stone fort on the Sabi river which rivalled Great Zimbabwe. As the Sabi, with the Zambesi, were the most likely routes by which coastal traders could reach the Shona hinterland, Bent was particularly keen to inspect this Sabi fort.

The journey promised to be intrepid. There were no roads so the wagons could not be used to carry supplies or tents. Donkeys were employed, together with their drivers, and Bent hired an armed overseer, Mashah, who had been given a Martini-Henry rifle for saving the lives 'of a band of pioneers when on a wild prospecting trip'. Two days of chilly, drizzling rain resulted in four members of the party going down with fever and they were warned that their destination was presently the border of two competing raider-tribes, the Shangaans and the Ndebele. Undeterred, the indomitable Mrs Bent set out with them on horseback. They passed safely through a number of native villages, making notes of the arts and crafts, of a tribe who wove their hair into wicker baskets 'like miniature Eiffel towers' and the women who wore sandals on their feet. Ever cross-referencing, Bent observed that the chiefs carried long iron staffs and he mused, admittedly with no great conviction, about the Israelitish kings who 'ruled with rods of iron'. They were given a calabash of good beer 'which we drank with pleasure', Bent noting that the natives called it 'hava', as did the Arabians. They gave the chief a cup of tea 'which he detested'.

Four days later they entered the Sabi valley and the high plateau gave way to valleys and deep, rugged mountains. They stopped to inspect an insignificant set of ruins at a village called Luti perched upon a foothill of Mount Lutilo. The place was 'almost Alpine in character' but the fort, comprising three circles of stone poorly put together, was completely ruined. Bent notes that it did form a link 'in the great chain of forts stretching northwards' but they left it and moved on, arriving soon after dawn at extensive ruins called Matindela which Bent thought were probably those he was looking for although they were still some twenty miles from the Sabi river.

'The ruins certainly are fine,' Bent reports. 'But far inferior to those of Zimbabwe; they are perched on top of a bare granite rock about 150 feet high, a most admirable strategic position.'

The expedition spent three days here, coming to the conclusion that Matindela was more likely a temple than a fort because its north side was entirely vulnerable. The walls were half the size of Great Zimbabwe, entered via four square doors, and beautifully decorated.

'The great feature of interest here,' says Swan, 'is the arrangement of the patterns in the stone. To the south-east are herring-bone patterns, below a dentelle pattern running for six yards. Then the pattern stops altogether on the outside, but there are indications that it was continued on the inside instead. It starts again on the outside and runs on for 40 feet, finally going inside for another 13 feet. The wall has been battlemented, the outside portion being raised in front 2 or 3 feet higher than the back. The wall is 11 feet 6 inches at its thickest, and on the top of it we saw holes in which monoliths evidently once stood, as they did on the wall of the circular building at Great Zimbabwe.'

Outside this perimeter wall they found circular sub-walls regularly built of granite blocks, 6 to 15 feet across. The party assumed these were the foundations of stone huts. There were more than forty of them. Other foundation walls ran on down the hill.

In one sense their 'discovery' of the extent of this Matindela complex raised something of a conflict with earlier theories. This many ruins – Matindela's stone huts could easily have accommodated 1,000 people – made nonsense of the idea of an immigrant workforce. I suspect it must have been about this time that Theodore Bent started to think of words like 'authors' (which he would use in his final report) for the architects who created these structures rather than 'builders'.

Work at Matindela came to an abrupt halt however, when scouts reported the existence of yet another large ruined fort, twelve miles closer to the river, near a mountain called Chiburwe. This turned out to be a 40-foot circle with much better walls than Matindela, corresponding to the best of the building at Great Zimbabwe. They found a giant baobab tree which had grown up in the outer wall and knocked part of it down. Bent later checked this tree with Kew experts and was told that baobabs took hundreds of years to reach maturity. All over the plain below Chiburwe were more circular hut foundations.

It is now known that there are more than 200 substantial *zimbabwes* within the various tribal areas which the British South Africa Company named Rhodesia, and many more outside it. A great number of these have either abandoned gold-workings near them or gold-smelting facilities. Most of these monuments are not on any tourist itinerary; indeed, even today's tourist guides bemoan the general neglect of a heritage completely unique to this part of Africa and rivalled, as previously mentioned, only by the Pyramids in the far north.

Imagine what it must have felt like for Theodore Bent and his wife as they rode through splendid mountain country, successful not just in the discovery of yet another mountain fort but with a growing awareness that every day might reveal yet another 'undiscovered' stone city. Moreover, the fort near Chiburwe was pointing towards a river well capable of carrying to the coast the gold of this ancient empire.

An observation relevant to my own conclusions about the significance of Great Zimbabwe art is that all the Makalanga

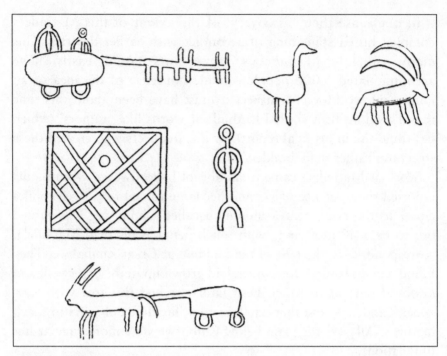

Informative Bantu 'cartoons' telling pictorially of whites arriving in wagons, drawn in the earlier Bushman style.

villages on the Sabi river – reached by Bent's party on the second afternoon after leaving Chiburwe – feature fine decorations, including drawings, one of which is a 'cartoon' of a trader driving a wagon with a span of six oxen. Bent realises that these are valid records but either does not really appreciate them or is not prepared to concede their proper relevance. He makes this rather patronising aside: 'I doubt not that those who follow after us will find attempts made to illustrate on their granaries a "Morunko" [white] lady [Mrs Bent] with long flowing hair trotting on that strange animal, the horse.'

These pictograms create new riddles rather than cast light on existing ones. Nothing as representational and specific has been found at any ancient *zimbabwe*. Nor has anyone yet interpreted – if an interpretation is even possible – the meaning of the marks on the stone columns at Great Zimbabwe, especially the ornately carved and marked columns topped by birds. Obviously they have information content, which is possibly arranged in message form. On one bird, for example, is a pair of horns identical to the horns of cattle featured in the bas reliefs of old Egypt. The several other animals and symbols, like the suns and the crocodile deity, are apparently positioned for status. This is surely not all decoration for decoration's sake.

Nothing like enough work has been devoted to the interpretation of the art of Great Zimbabwe. By comparison, the Egyptian monuments have been subject to rigorous study and as a result we know, for example, that the column of Horus, carved some 3,000 years before the birth of Christ, is a signpost. Horus, the hawk-god of royalty, is shown on a wall with a serpent, over other, mighty, stone walls. The serpent is a proven hieroglyph for King Serpent and the rest of the work tells us that the King lived in Horus' palace. Indeed, all the kings of ancient Egypt were considered to be the successors of Horus and were called Horus, followed by their own name.

The Great Zimbabwe stelae are in some cases more decorated than this ancient Egyptian cartouche and they all feature another animal below the bird.

If, hypothetically, you were to apply an Egyptian hieroglyphic translation to the Zimbabwe bird stela featuring a distinctive crocodile, it becomes a signpost. The bird denotes a royal palace of the god-king Crocodile. The crocodile is a common deity in central African cults.

So little is known of the message content of ancient Great Zimbabwe art, however, that we have no option but to assume that the 'cartoons' the Bents found in the Sabi valley villages were evolved among the rural Karanga long after the Great Zimbabwe culture had collapsed or, as some would have it, emigrated.

At this point the Bents make a peculiar diversion to the Portuguese port of Beira. This reconnaissance has added further fuel to the rumours that the team had interests other than in archaeology. More bluntly, were they spying for Rhodes, who was desperate for an outlet to the sea? Apart from an Arab house or two there are no stone buildings of any note there and even the earliest Portuguese explorers make no mention of Beira being connected with the Zimbabwe culture. It has, though, always been a strategic port for those occupying the hinterland. For Ian Smith's breakaway colony of Rhodesia, Portuguese colonial support for the supply of oil via the use of Beira port had been vital.

So far as I was aware the support of Portuguese colonialists could always be counted on. In fact, in the very early days, Rhodes' occupation of Karanga land had put the relationship under such heavy strain that pitched battles involving a considerable loss of Portuguese life had been fought a few months before Theodore Bent left the beaten track to explore Portuguese territory inland of the coast.

The real cause of this enmity was gold, not territory.

The Portuguese regarded all this land as theirs. What had begun as Vasco da Gama's search for Ophir and the discovery of those two dhows loaded down with gold of unknown origin, had ended with their occupation of Sofala port near Beira. They were the colonial presence and the hinterland was their sphere of influence. Theodore Bent would have been well aware of the importance of an east coast port to Rhodes, and he also took his mapmaker, Swan, along with him.

Beira sits on the estuary of the Pungwe river. A few miles south is the estuary of the Sabi river down which Bent believed ancient Shona gold was shipped. Midway between the two is Sofala.

Rhodes commonly used gentleman-spies; in fact, it was almost a condition of working for him. The most notable was Frederick Courtenay Selous, the hunter and animal-specimen collector who explored behind Matabele lines for Rhodes, then made the seamless transition to military scout and led Rhodes' Pioneer Column unerringly to Mashonaland. It was Selous, moreover, who suggested to Rhodes that time was of the essence if he wanted to control King Solomon's mines, because the Portuguese also had their eyes on this inland eldorado.

Was Theodore Bent enlisted in these intelligence operations? The Shona school is convinced he was, hence Rhodes' generous financing of the Bent expedition. Bent arrived in Mashonaland in 1891 when relations between Rhodes and the Portuguese had lapsed into an ugly stalemate. Six months previously a force of about 200 armed natives led by a noted Portuguese explorer, Colonel Paiva d'Andrade, had marched inland to occupy the kraal of the senior chief of the Manicas, Umtasa. Manicaland was situated directly inland from Sofala and the Portuguese claimed it had been their 'sphere of influence' for 300 years. In fact the Portuguese had never formalised a colonial claim on this part of Africa and had no formal treaties with Umtasa as, say, Rhodes had with Lobengula.

Selous, accompanied by A.R. Colquhoun, Rhodes' first Administrator in Mashonaland, had broken away from the Pioneer Column as it moved up-country and made a dash for the east to see Umtasa. Somehow these two returned with a 'treaty', granting Rhodes the mineral rights to Manicaland. The Portuguese moved in on Umtasa in response to this. Colquhoun immediately dispatched a patrol of well-armed white police and pioneers to 'protect' Umtasa, arriving just after the Portuguese flying column.

The British commander, Major Patrick Forbes, entered Umtasa's kraal with a few of his white mercenaries, took the Portuguese by surprise and 'arrested' them. Forbes then decided to try and take the land all the way to the coast. A small Portuguese fort at Macequece was overrun without much resistance and Forbes decided to push on and see if he could take Beira for Rhodes as well. A major political row had erupted in Portugal over the arrest of Colonel d'Andrade, however, and Rhodes, already in some trouble with Queen Victoria over the cavalier way he had obtained treaties from Lobengula, had Major Forbes recalled.

The Portuguese were not to be mollified. They launched what would be the first of many brutal East African colonial skirmishes with a hastily raised white force from the motherland who bravely battled their way back into Macequece fort via Beira, many dying of malaria. Rhodes' men had, meantime, taken up positions that blocked any further advance into the Shona hinterland and the gold fields. The much-depleted Portuguese militia attacked their position but were driven back by the fire of the seasoned shooters of the

British South Africa Company Police and the Pioneers, most of whom had been professional hunters. When the British – there were only fifty of them – advanced the next morning they found that the Portuguese had retreated and abandoned the fort.

When Theodore Bent arrived here a few months later the guns captured from the Portuguese were still on display in the British compound. Bent then reveals: 'Mr Swan had constructed a map of the route from observations and bearings taken at every possible opportunity by day and by night. And at the same time we had formed opinions on the country from our own point of view.' He adds, sounding as though he was party to the whole plot:

Umtali [the BSAC frontier post] is the natural land terminus of this route and the British South Africa Company hope to call it Manica and to make it the capital of that portion of Manicaland which they so dextrously, to use an Africander word, 'jumped' from the Portuguese.

There is a legend still told that the defenders of this fort of Massi Kessi were obliged to cast bullets out of gold nuggets when cheaper material came to an end. After this the inland country was practically abandoned to the savages. Old treaties existed but were not renewed; lethargy seemed to have taken entire possession of the few remaining Portuguese who were left here, a lethargy from which they were rudely awakened by the advent of the Chartered Company.

What better argument do we want for the reoccupation of this country by a more enterprising race than these forts abandoned and in ruins, and the treaties with savage chiefs long since neglected – consigned to national archives?

Here we see a secondary use being put to the research Rhodes had paid Dr Theal to do. It was not 'pure' research to feed Rhodes' interest in Ophir. He was checking on the validity of old Portuguese treaties! And we should also remember that Theodore Bent's brief from the Royal Geographical Society certainly did not extend to scouting rail routes for Rhodes or evaluating Portuguese treaties.

But if Bent was a spy or an agent for Rhodes it was all about to go very wrong. Queen Victoria was not pleased with any of this and she ordered her government to set aside all Rhodes' most recent 'treaties', although not the original one with Lobengula, and agreed a demarcation of territory with the Portuguese. It created Portuguese East Africa and left Rhodesia landlocked for all time.

Theodore Bent thereafter travels not to Great Zimbabwe, where there is still much work to be done, but to Fort Salisbury where he is welcomed and entertained by the administrators of the British South Africa Company who are now operating to all intents and purposes as the government of Mashonaland.

'The same motives, namely the thirst for gold,' Bent comments philosophically 'which created the hoary walls of Zimbabwe and the daub huts of Fort Salisbury, probably the oldest and the youngest buildings erected for the purpose by mankind, ever keen after that precious metal which has had so remarkable an influence on generation after generation of human atoms.'

But behind the philosophising lurk unpalatable home truths about Shona gold. So little of it is left, the whole occupation is turning into a costly farce. Bent attends a depressing first anniversary party:

A grand dinner was given to about eighty individuals at the hotel to celebrate the event: representatives of the military, civil, and business communities were bidden; gold prospectors, mining experts, men of established and questionable reputation – all were there, and the promoters underwent superhuman difficulties in catering for so many guests, and gave fabulous prices for a sufficiency of wine, spirits and victuals properly to celebrate the occasion.

It was ostensibly a social occasion to celebrate an ostensibly auspicious occasion; but one after-dinner speech became more intemperate than the other: the authorities were loudly abused for faults committed by them, real or imaginary; well-known names, when pronounced, were hooted and hissed; and the social gathering developed as the evening went on, into a wild demonstration of discontent.

Finally, Bent goes back to work. From contacts made at this party he learns that the prospectors are mostly not prospecting at all but simply looking for abandoned native workings and then burrowing down in the hope of finding the reef. In the process they have discovered dozens of *zimbabwes*. Almost the only recreation for a prospector is to loot ruins. The Bents mount a new expedition on horseback to the pretty Mazoe valley 25 miles from Fort Salisbury, where in the company of a gold prospector, Mr Fleming, they inspect a row of vertical mine shafts clogged with debris which Bent presumes are connected underground. He also concludes from the debris and large trees growing in the blocked shafts that they have not been worked for years.

On the hill slopes a mile and a half away they come upon a shaft which Fleming had cleared to a depth of 55 feet into which, with some difficulty, they are able to climb and there find ancient horizontal shafts connecting a maze of holes bored into the gold-bearing quartz. Shafts in the nearby Hartley hills go as deep as 80 feet. Bent concludes that these ancient workers had followed reefs with all the skill of European miners: 'All about here the ground is honeycombed with old shafts of a similar nature, indicated now by the same round depressions in straight lines along the reef where different shafts have been sunk; in fact the output of gold in centuries long gone by must have been enormous.'

Returning to Fort Salisbury, and talking to prospectors whenever he can, Bent concludes that these old workings extend up and down the country wherever there is gold-bearing quartz. Very often they are associated with *zimbabwes* – miles and miles of them up the Mazoe valley, all along the Nswezewe river, in the Tati district, Hartley and Fort Victoria areas: 'Everywhere in short where the pioneer prospectors have as yet penetrated, overwhelming proof of the extent of the ancient industry is brought to light.'

One of these hunter-prospectors, Mr E.A. Maund, attends the Royal Geographical Society to give a report on the Mswezwe district: 'On all sides there was testimony of the enormous amount of work that had been done by the ancients for the production of gold. Here, as on the Mazoe and at Umtali, tens of thousands of slaves must have been at work taking out the softer parts of the casings of the reefs and millions of tons have been overturned in their search for gold.' This reference to slaves stems from the discovery of long lines of 'crushing stones' placed at regular intervals around the workings. Bent observes that there are depictions on Egyptian monuments of gangs of slaves at work chained together in rows. The practice is also described by Diodorus.

The Mining Commissioner in the Mazoe district takes Bent's party to see the perfect model of an ancient *zimbabwe*-protected mining enclave. In a high valley they meet and dine on eland steaks with the white prospectors working the new 'Yellow Jacket' mine on the site of extensive ancient workings. Overlooking the site they climb a kopje to a ruin where the remaining walls are constructed with a 'wonderful regularity' to rival Great Zimbabwe. Enough remain standing to show that this gem of a fort had been almost 20 feet in diameter.

Already, however, creeping doubts are setting in that all this might be a literal 'flash in the pan' at least so far as large-scale modern mining is concerned. 'Strictures,' Bent reports, 'have been passed by experts that the gold reefs in the Mazoe valley "pinched out" and did other disagreeable things which they ought not to do.' With rare foresight he also goes beyond this and forecasts: 'The Mazoe valley is one of the pet places in Mashonaland: the views in every direction are exquisite, water is abundant everywhere, and verdure rich; and if the prospectors are disappointed in their search for gold, and find that the ancient have exhausted the place, they will have at any rate, valuable properties from an agricultural point of view.' Which ignores, of course, the fact that the Rudd concession was restricted to mineral exploitation.

Rhodesia did go on to build quite a healthy little gold industry but it was never eldorado. By the time I arrived in the Mazoe valley it was famous for its irrigated citrus and wonderful orange squash.

Theodore Bent did, however, decide that the prolific ancient gold workings in the Mazoe valley (to the extent that he was prepared to go along with such romantic descriptions) were probably the King Solomon's mines of ancient legend. Bent points out that this was also the opinion of the Portuguese writer, Couto: 'The richest mines are those of Massapa, where they show the Abyssinian mine from which the Queen of Sheba took the greater part of the gold which she went to offer to the temple of Solomon. It is Ophir, for the Kaffirs call it *Fur* and the Moors *Afur*. The veins of gold are so big . . . they expand with such force . . . they raise the roots of trees two feet.' These riches, says Couto, are traded at three Portuguese markets: 'Luanhe, thirty-five leagues from Tete south between two small rivers which join and are called Masouvo [Mazoe]; Bacoto, forty leagues from Tete [on the Zambesi river]; and Massapa, fifty leagues from Tete up the said river Masouvo.'

Bent calls this a 'quaint legend' but concedes that there is ample evidence of ancient alien influence to be found in the old shafts. At the new Jumbo mine in the Mazoe valley he is given fragments of delft pottery recovered when the shaft was cleared. Scraps of Nankin pottery are found in the same spoil. Bent is able to successfully barter for some large Venetian glass beads 'centuries old; the ancient trade goods given by traders to the subjects of the Monomotapa'.

And then he appears to promote a rumour of his own. I think I know Bent's mind well enough by now, his checks and balances, his prejudices and his strengths (both of which he possesses in potent measure) to make this judgement. He has never previously engaged in fiction – he is frankly too much of a Victorian for that and he knows a book comes next, a book he hopes will earn him scientific and intellectual credibility. So what is this story? 'It is rumoured amongst the inhabitants of the Mazoe and the Manica that long ago, in the days of their ancestors, white men worked gold and built themselves houses here.' Bent immediately tries to avoid this getting him lodged with the Romantics. 'The rumour most probably refers to the Portuguese, who at the three above-mentioned places had churches and forts, faint traces of which are still to be found in the district.'

But it doesn't really suggest that, and he knows it. If anyone ever worked gold hereabouts it was ancient Moors, not Portuguese. Bent is resurrecting the idea that there were Semites here once, people who would have looked white to the negroid natives; stone-city-raised Semites from Arabia who engaged 'thousands of slaves' in the mining of Mazoe gold.

In support of this he leaves us with an opinion of Corvo's from his journal *Provincias Ultramarinas*: 'The early Portuguese did nothing more than substitute themselves for the Moors, as they called them, in the ports that those occupied on the coasts; and their influence extended to the interior very little; unless indeed through some ephemeral alliance of no value whatever, and through missions without any practical or lasting results.'

I think we can safely conclude, even if he does not quite name them, that Theodore Bent has decided that the authors of the Zimbabwe culture were 'Moors' who came here first to buy alluvial gold and then founded a deep reef-mining and manufacturing gold industry.

FIVE

The Gold of Ophir

Ancient gold is the key to all the riddles of the lost city. Without a huge quantities of gold, the Zimbabwe culture and all its works – works much more monumental and extensive than Theodore Bent even dreamed of – could not have existed. But this single, incontrovertible fact immediately presented Bent with more riddles than it solved. He reasoned:

That the creation of a stone-bound Zimbabwe empire was a task beyond the skills and manpower of ancient Moorish trading caravans who may have been coming here since time immemorial.

That it was also beyond the competence of the Shona of Bent's time and, according to records going back 500 years, beyond the competence of their Karanga ancestors.

The Shona were entirely ignorant or, if you prefer, innocent, of the true value of gold. But some African hegemony must have been aware of it in the past or Great Zimbabwe and the other massive monuments would surely never have been built.

These golden riddles have remained thorns in the side of the Great Zimbabwe origin debate for more than a century and have never been satisfactorily resolved.

The more one looks at the paradoxes the more contradictory they become. For example, the deep mining of gold, as opposed to the simple collection of gold from river sand, are not skills just picked up. This applies even more to the delicate skills and apparatus required to smelt and work gold into plate, wire and jewellery.

It does not necessarily mean, however, that these gold adepts were white (Semite) aliens as the Romantic school founded by Carl Mauch would have us believe. They could have been coastal blacks of mixed origin (Swahilis), non-Bantu blacks (Hottentot and bushmen) and immigrant blacks from gold-producing countries (such as Nubians and Ethiopians).

Nevertheless, it is currently claimed, and has been for the last few decades, that the Karanga/Shona did spontaneously conceive, design, fund and build Great Zimbabwe and all the other monuments. It is easier to conclude, though (as indeed a lot of Bent's contemporaries did), that the Karanga were not the authors of the Zimbabwe culture. That suggests they were not the original gold miners either. There are even questions, as previously mentioned, as to whether enough Karanga were settled in this part of Africa when the Great Zimbabwe culture and the first stone structures were built.

As speculation is the only route open to us at this stage let me try and enhance Bent's suppositions of more than a century ago with some of the research that has been done since.

Having obtained the intelligence of itinerant Moorish explorer-traders that the Karanga hinterland is an eldorado, expeditions are mounted by, say, Egyptians, or Romans, Solomon's Phoenicians or Sheba's Sabaeans – or combinations of these. Biblical and other sources name all four groups and we know that their appetite for gold was enormous and insatiable.

The Hiram-Solomon expedition was away, according to the Bible, for three years so they must have made long stops somewhere. There are Carbon-14 traces of established settlements of indeterminate age on the hill overlooking the valley in which Great Zimbabwe is sited. They could date back to the pre-Christian millennium. Initially, these settlements could have been no more substantial than the grass mat structures of the San but if the assembly points turned into primitive trading posts or gold 'fairs', stone structures would sooner or later have proved better protection for the people, cattle for food (Hottentots kept both cattle and goats), the trade goods and the traded gold. Where suitable stone is available as with, say, Hadrian's

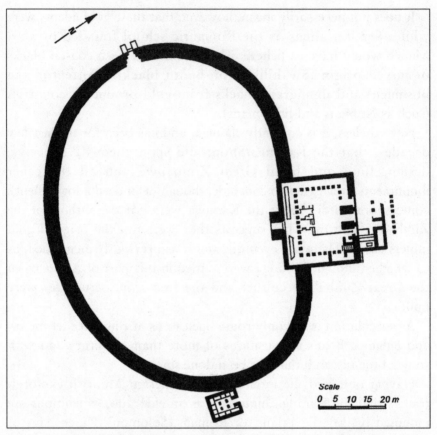

Ancient Awwam in Yemen, believed to be the temple of the Queen of Sheba, drawn to an identical scale to that of Great Zimbabwe (see opposite).

Wall, or Awwam in Yemen, where there is a stone ring that is virtually a mirror-image of Great Zimbabwe, stone structures almost always get built. British Iron Age round houses which are identical in structure and style to Karanga rondavels were there on many a site that would later become Roman forts and in time, Norman castles.

To begin with the aliens buy alluvial gold from the nomadic Stone Age bushmen and Hottentots now known as the San who are also well able to scramble down narrow shafts and work low adits when the outcrops are followed underground. Many die in the numerous accidents, leaving their bones to history.

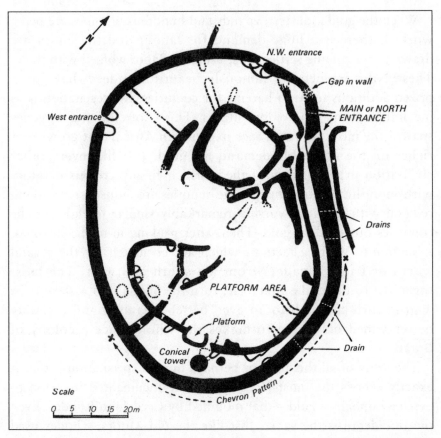

The 'temple' at Great Zimbabwe, drawn here to the same scale, is almost identical in shape and style to Awwam, Yemen (see opposite).

A new, more settled race – entirely dependent on their cattle – begins to infiltrate the rich Zimbabwe grasslands. At first they coexist with the San, picking up their skills as rock painters and engravers. Some integrate but by the middle of the first Christian millennium they are in sufficient numbers to push out into the neighbouring neo-deserts those of the San who have remained hunter-gatherers. Moorish traders find these new people even easier to trade with. Their cattle culture is not interested in gold and they happily swap the metal, meat and farm produce for the baubles, bangles, beads and iron tools the Arabian traders and their coastal cohorts, the Afro-Arabian Swahilis, ship up country.

When the gold industry expands and hundreds of mines are being worked, there is a huge demand for labour and the Bantu are drawn to the mining settlements, bringing Bantu women with them. These Nilot women are famously beautiful; indeed, have been prized additions to Arab harems for centuries. Miscegenation is as inevitable as the long empty nights. This exotic mixing of genes spawns the most advanced race in southern Africa, that grows ever richer on the insatiable demand for gold. Just like every other civilisation in the history of the world it finally crowns its glory with monolithic buildings, some temples, to house an evolving religion with icons of worship remarkably similar to those of the countries buying their gold. Then, after peaking in medieval times, it splits into warring factions which are no match for the several waves of Bantu invaders from the south and west. The most organised of these, the Matabele, turn the Shona into a slave tribe who in turn succumb to an even better-organised and certainly better-armed invader who makes the whole place a colony of Britain.

The irony of all this pure or perhaps impure speculation is that it exactly echoes the most recent and well-documented invasion to exploit Zimbabwe gold – that mounted by Cecil John Rhodes. Even the fine detail is the same. Just like the old Moors, Rhodes used explorer-traders (Selous and Posselt among others) to confirm the existence of gold in the unexplored hinterland. Carrying superior arms they brushed aside the indigenous opposition (as indisputably did the Bantu to the San), they built defensive forts like Fort Victoria, adjoining Great Zimbabwe, and Fort Salisbury. The forts were mud-walled at first but quickly fortified with stone.

These settlers lived initially in makeshift shelters but when they became a settled elite and money was coming in from the goldfields, they quit their tents and built protectively in the local stone. There was even a good deal of miscegenation with the beautiful native women (viz. Adam Renders) in those early days; in fact, the whites saw it as such a threat to their racial identity they established the infamous system of apartheid. Finally, they built monuments of local stone including temples.

Rhodes' expedition also lends obvious credibility to the idea that all this could have been achieved in ancient times by quite a small alien force. Rhodes did the job with about 500 armed men and a few hundred miners and then went on to dominate hundreds of thousands of Shona and Matabele for seven decades, a good many of whom came to be employed digging and processing gold and a wide range of precious metals.

But before we get carried away by the analogy, not one word of this, of course, would be acceptable to the present chief. President Robert Mugabe is so certain that the Zimbabwe culture is Bantu to the core he first named his political party after it, and later the country. Nor is it certain that he is wrong, even though the story is too complicated to be that polarised. In truth it would be preferable for him to be right if only because these fantastic buildings and the gold mines of Solomon and Sheba could then be promoted as the seventh wonder of the world that they truly are.

Sadly, however, the arguments advanced by the Shona school in favour of an all-Bantu Zimbabwe culture, are less convincing than the Romantic theories of alien authorship.

A dean of Harvard, Dr Mark Bessire, says in his book on Great Zimbabwe published in 1998, 'In return for gold, Great Zimbabwe received glass, beads, porcelain, and other luxury items that were relatively inexpensive in the countries where they were produced. Thus the ruling elite of Great Zimbabwe and the Swahili traders both gave up things they valued little. The ruler of Great Zimbabwe used the imported luxuries as signs of his status and power, and he gave some of them to members of the elite as rewards. Some imports may have been traded for cattle, which remained the people's measure of wealth.'

In my view, this is more than a little disingenuous. It describes a class of Swahili trader I have never met. Their contemporary brothers and sisters who run the *dukas* and much of the economy of East Africa are among the toughest street-traders you are ever likely to meet. To suggest that they ever 'gave up things they valued little' (things they would have risked their lives to carry hundreds of miles into the hinterland) is dubious.

101

Also, were the old Karanga chiefs, chiefs said to have built the largest stone city south of the Pyramids, incapable of working out that the more gold you traded, the more 'rewards' you could distribute and the greater your 'status'? Was this the first and only human society with a natural immunity to the lust for gold? It was never so in my time, it is certainly not so with the present-ruling Mugabe and, worse, it is patronising.

I am convinced that it was this intractable gold paradox which caused Theodore Bent to abandon any thoughts of a native origin for the ruins and to institute a search which might prove the presence of gold experts from outside the country. His resumed dig at Great Zimbabwe had begun to turn up physical evidence of a gold industry which was actually *wasteful* of the precious metal. Crucibles were found still liberally coated with a skin of gold. Other treasure hunters would puzzle over gold nuggets left lying in the dust of ruined floors. Large quantities of gold were found in native graves, but it was mostly in the form of wire and appears to have been valued no higher than the iron and copper wire also found on the bodies.

Mrs Bent noticed, and photographed, old Chief Mugabe wearing 'a string of large white Venetian beads of considerable antiquity'. Nor was this Karanga chief of Great Zimbabwe unaware of the value of decorated emblems of authority. He carried 'an iron sceptre, the badge of a chief, and a battle-axe lavishly decorated with brass wire'. Not a trace, however, of gold wire or plated gold *objet d'art*, even though Rhodes' treasure-seekers would reveal a wealth of both buried in the spoil beneath the hooves of Chief Mugabe's cattle, nor any recollection of a gold trade involving thousands of mines that had been going on for several centuries at least.

Thanks to Rhodes' investment in research we have excellent records going back more than 500 years, which show that Renders and Mauch were also simply following well-trodden footsteps. First ivory, then slaves and finally gold were the dreams of avarice which initiated and sustained European exploration of south central Africa, and long before that there were the ubiquitous Moors.

In 1487 John II of Portugal sent Pedro de Covilham and Alfonso de Payva to Cairo essentially as diplomatic spies with a particular commission to find out what the Moors knew of the sea routes to gold-rich Ophir. In those days, India, another known source of gold, was also a candidate for the lost kingdom, and Portuguese spies obtained copies of ancient Moorish sea-charts to the Indies. Senor de Covilham apparently obtained information which convinced him that Ophir was more likely to be found in south central Africa and he carried his search for the gold of Ophir as far south as Ethiopia.

He also carried a political commission from his King. Ethiopia was thought then to be the legendary lost Christian kingdom of the aforementioned Prester John, with whom European Christians since the start of the Crusades had been trying to find and link up with in the hope of outflanking the forces of Islam. This is not the place to pursue that trail, although Ethiopia and Great Zimbabwe have apparent links, not least ancient gold-workings. We will revisit the enigmatic John and his intriguing stone-bound kingdom in some detail later.

De Covilham was, so far as is known, the first European to seek to make a commercial-political treaty – a forerunner of Rudd's concession with Lobengula – for the gold of Ophir. Unfortunately we know nothing of the details because he died in the attempt. It seems likely, however, that he was able to get useful information out to his partner, Alfonso de Payva, because, within a decade, his fellow national, the mariner Vasco da Gama, also with a royal commission to find a sea route to Prester John, rounded 'the Fairest Cape' for the first time on record.

The next Portuguese marine expedition, by Alvarez de Cahal in 1505, secured the golden Grail when they navigated all the way up Africa's Indian Ocean coast to the old Arab port of Sofala (the closest to Great Zimbabwe) and found in its harbour two Arab dhows laden with gold. They took over the town, appointed a permanent Portuguese commander, Pedro de Nhaya, and garrisoned the old Arab fort in the name of the King of Portugal.

It is worth pausing here to consider some research which Theodore Bent presented in his report on Great Zimbabwe. Bent took the trouble to examine old Arab accounts from the start of Portuguese colonialism at Sofala in the hope of establishing who held power in the hinterland; it having become immediately apparent to the Portuguese that the Arabs only controlled the coastline.

The Portuguese mariner, Duarte Barbosa, reported to his King in 1514: 'The merchants bring to Sofala the gold which they sell to the Moors without weighing it, for coloured stuffs and beads of Cambay.'

An Arab traveller, Omar ibn l'Wardi', is on record as saying that the Arabs were being kept out of the interior by a fierce African tribe called the 'Zindj': 'Whose habitations extend from the extremity of the gulf to the low lands of gold, Sofala 't il Dhab . . . which adjoins the eastern borders of the Zindj . . . the most remarkable produce of this country is its quality of native gold, that is found in two or three meskalla, in spite of which the natives generally adorn their persons with ornaments of brass.' He also states that these natives have skill in working iron, and that ships came from India to fetch it.

Other exotic descriptions of these Zindj are provided by a writer who Bent calls the 'Herodotus of Arabia', El Masoudi. This Arab viewed the Zindj as naked Negroes dressed in panther skins who filed their teeth and were cannibals, fought with long lances and had ambuscades for game. They hunted elephants but never used for their own purposes the ivory and gold in which their country abounded.

Is this the genesis of the ignorance about gold?

Who the Zindj were is very unclear, even though El Masoudi's description fits well some of the warlike tribes of northern Kenya and Somalia among whom I have worked. They fight and hunt with long lances, ambush game, kill elephants and many of them file their teeth. So far as I know they do not eat people but I would not put it past a hungry Somali *shufta* a long way from home. Somalia also adjoins the Arabian peninsula and Ethiopia, thought by many to be the ancient gold-rich Land of Punt.

El Masoudi did claim that his Zindj descended from the north and Theodore Bent goes on to suggest that: 'The irruption of the wild Zindj tribes probably caused the destruction of the earlier civilisation.' Note his use of the phrase 'wild Zindj tribes', hinting at several incursions.

Almost everyone agrees that the culture that built the grand *zimbabwes* collapsed and had been derelict for hundreds of years before the Portuguese dared to pursue the gold of the hinterland. If it was violent Zindj incursions which caused the collapse (or a shortage of salt, as some have more prosaically suggested), what followed was the equivalent of the Dark Ages in Britain after the Romans. Several *zimbabwes* have produced evidence of burning, hastily abandoned damaged treasure, and bodies that had evidently met violent ends.

There are also the reports of the Matabele. By the time they crossed the Limpopo in quite modern times there was no evidence whatsoever of an extant Zimbabwe culture, least of all one administered by the Shona, hence the contempt in which the Matabele held the Shona. Burning and looting, they quickly reduced the Shona to a slave tribe who went into hiding whenever a Matabele raiding party hove in sight. Moreover, the Shona tribe that the Matabele subjugated in the 1800s appears to have been engaged in a social and agrarian lifestyle all but identical to the one reported in the 1600s by the first serious Portuguese missionary to the interior, the Jesuit, Father dos Santos. Dos Santos meets a high chief, Monomatapa – '*munhumatapa*'. It is the first reliable reference to any sort of African 'kingdom' in the region and today underpins the Shona school's case for a spontaneous Karanga history of the Zimbabwe culture.

The problems with this interpretation begin immediately, however, when one reads the good priest's detailed and affectionate descriptions of the lifestyle of the people among whom he has settled. Furthermore, dos Santos admits, '*munhumatapa*' is not the description of an empire, albeit past its best, but a generic term for 'high chief'. There are a number of *munhumatapas* around. Dos Santos' descriptions of rural Karanga life are in fact exactly the same as those Theodore Bent recorded at the turn of the last century: 'Feasts in honour of their ancestors, an infinity of fowls, curious pianos with bars of iron enclosed in a pumpkin, wine of millet, copper bracelets, little axes, spears, assegai-points, mattocks, arrows all made of iron and the beating of palms [hands] as a mode of courtesy.'

One can hardly blame Father dos Santos, who appears from his writings to have been a kindly man, well disposed to this rural community, for not believing that these were the people who conceived and built the lost city and carved the artefacts found in it. He discusses these mysteries – 'the many things which would otherwise have been obscure' – with a Monomatapa. These are the best 'oral traditions' ever recorded. He is told that in a previous age a high chief sent three of his sons each to govern a province. They refused to return their lands to the heir when the father died and the country became divided into four. Since then it had been subdivided again and again. The Monomatapa had nothing at all to say about the people who had built the grand *zimbabwes*.

The fact that Father dos Santos has related this story does indicate that an important local chief believed there had been better times. Subsequent researchers have built from it a history of the decay of the Zimbabwe culture produced by royal family feuds and territorial splits. My problem with it is that if the Monomatapa could remember these oral traditions and describe them to Father dos Santos, why not earlier ones of the building of the most impressive stone monuments in the whole of southern Africa? Surely these would have endured more than tales of family feuds? A great many civilisations have come and gone; indeed, cycles are the dynamic of civilisations, but it is almost impossible for them to vanish without trace if the descendants of the architects, builders, and artisans remain living on the site, which is what is being claimed for Great Zimbabwe.

The Portuguese did possess a description of Great Zimbabwe which the author, Jaoa de Barros, in his monograph of 1552, *De Asia*, claimed to have obtained from 'Moorish' traders. The fact that it is hearsay has always caused it to be questioned but it is intrinsically interesting in the sense that it came, allegedly, from Arabian sources:

There stands a fortress, square, admirably built, inside and out of hard stone. The blocks of which the walls consist are put together without mortar and are marvellously thick. The walls are twenty-five spans in thickness; their height is not so considerable compared with their breadth. Over the gate of the building is an inscription, which neither the Moorish traders who were there, nor others learned in inscriptions, could read. On the heights around the edifice stand others in like manner built of masonry without mortar; among them a tower of more than 12 braces [yards] in height. All these buildings are called *zimbahe*, as are all royal dwellings in Monomotapa.

There are no towers of this size other than at Great Zimbabwe. Sadly, however, nothing has been heard of that inscription, even though it remains the artefact everyone most wants to find. Theodore Bent came closest, with the cryptic etching he found on a large bowl and was later compared with the proto-Arabian alphabet. There is a reasonable correspondence but Bent admitted that the evidence was 'provokingly fragmentary' and nothing further has been adduced to the find.

Without exception, however, all the Portuguese and Arab accounts of the Indian ocean coast and its trade with the hinterland take for granted that the gold trade had been conducted by ancient Moors, with Swahili cohorts. As early as 1502, the Portuguese geographer Thomas Lopez, on a visit to Sofala province, reported being told 'there is a wonderfully rich mine to which, as they find in their books, King Solomon used to send every three years to draw an infinite quantity of gold.'

Father dos Santos says he was told of the remains of old walls and some ruins and that 'old Moors who have maintained a tradition of their ancestors claimed these to be in olden times the trading depots of the Queen of Saba [Sheba] from which were bought much gold'. Some Arabs actually called the region behind Sofala, Saba, and there is of course a major river through the region called the Sabi.

After two centuries of exploration and resident missionary activity, the Portuguese also come to the conclusion that the

Zimbabwe culture and its gold-rich empire pre-dated the Monomatapas and, indeed, might not be of central African origin at all.

On 17 April 1721, the Governor of Goa (East Africa was then administratively a part of the Portuguese–Indian Empire), Antonio Rodrigue da Costa, wrote to his King:

(1) There is a report that in the interior of these countries many affirm there is in the court of the Monomatapa a tower or edifice of worked masonry which appears evidently not to be the work of black natives of the country, but of some powerful and political nations such as the Greeks, Romans, Persians, Egyptians, or Hebrews; and they say that the tower or edifice is called by the natives Simbaboe and that in it is an inscription of unknown letters, and because there is much foundation for the belief that the land is Ophir, and that Solomon sent his fleets in company with the Phoenicians; and this opinion could be indubitably established if this inscription could be cleared up, and there is no one there who can read it. If it were in Greek, Persian or Hebrew, it would be necessary to command that an impression be made in wax or some other material which retains letters or figures, commanding that the original inscription be well cleaned.
(2) At the same time it would be suitable to examine whether in that land is a range of mountains called Ofura, what distance it is from the coast or seaport, and whether it contains mines of gold or silver.
(3) In the same way it would be as well to inquire into the most notable names of these parts, mountains, chiefdoms and rivers.
(4) To learn if the lands of Sofala are high or low, or marshy, or if they have any mountain ranges.

Thus, almost three centuries ago, the enigmas provoked by the lost city were posted for official investigation and the first list made of likely authors – Greeks, Romans, Egyptians or Hebrews.

Sadly, no Portuguese expedition complete with wax copying equipment for the cryptogram was ever mounted. The Portuguese never lost their interest in central Africa however – even though they were finally pipped at the post by Rhodes.

The Karanga attitude to the value of gold has been dealt with at some length because it appears to cast doubt on the seminal question of whether this ancient gold-based empire was Bantu at all. Others have proposed that the Zimbabwe culture was perhaps so aesthetically advanced it had no need to value objects for their (western) monetary worth, but for their beauty. Gold, an attractive metal but intrinsically no more attractive than copper, brass or silver if a monetary value is of no concern, was instead valued as an art material.

The best evidence in support of such a singular ideal is from a *zimbabwe*, Mapungubwe, just south of the Limpopo in what is now South Africa. In one of the first graves excavated was found a beautiful *objet d'art*, a gold rhino. In fact, as a piece of art craftsmanship the Mapungubwe rhino is unique. It is actually a fine example of wooden sculpture which has been plated with thin gold attached to the wood by tiny gold tacks. From the same grave came a beautifully executed gold bowl.

But as keeps happening with this story, one avenue of clarity usually leads to an even more enigmatic labyrinth. We cannot be sure that the inhabitants of these southern *zimbabwes* were an integral part of the Zimbabwe culture under the sway of Great Zimbabwe, nor can we be sure they were of the same race. I earlier questioned the idea that the first gold miners were not the Bantu Karanga.

Before the Bantu migrated here, southern Africa was roamed by Hottentots and bushmen and there is now little doubt that the Hottentots were the first southern Africans to recognise the attraction gold had for Europeans. They carried alluvial gold dust to the coast stored in vultures' quills.

Robert Ardrey, the American author whose passion for human origin-theory lured him into the writing of the immensely popular and influential *African Genesis* and *The Social Contract*, used to warn writers in this territory to 'publish – and duck', and there could be no better caution for what will be considered next.

Ardrey was a champion of Professor Raymond Dart, the father of African palaeontology who, in 1924, discovered the first man-ape (or ape-man) *Australopithicus africanus*, creatures who, after years of scientific debate to rival the one about the lost city, have been confirmed as 'human ancestors'. Professor Dart was very interested in the origins of the Zimbabwe culture and might also be called the father of the most intriguing of the alien-influence theories, namely that of the role of the little Hottentots and bushmen who were not Bantu. No certain evidence exists as to where the Hottentots themselves originated but with the bushmen, the desert-dwellers who took to wandering with the Hottentots, they were the first 'coloured' peoples to explore right down southern Africa.

When Europeans first reached the Cape there were villages of proto-San, calling themselves (phonetically) Khoi, living in villages behind the dunes where today we have our little house under Table Mountain. As I write I can see the long sandy beach where the Khoi (or Khoisan) used to hunt seals and gather shellfish, spending so much time at this work that the first Dutch settlers called them 'Strandlopers' – beachcombers. They were also known as 'Chinese Hottentots' because of their Mongoloid facial features. Professor Dart surmised that they could be descended from Asian stock which first reached the southern African offshore island of Madagascar, sailing before the monsoon in ocean-going outrigger canoes. They were most likely, according to Dart, Caucasoid-Mongoloid immigrants from Indonesia or from the Malay peninsula. They had domestic cattle and used wooden spears, slings and clubs and are represented today in the Hova people of Madagascar. It is a short sail from Madagascar to the east coast of Africa, directly east of Great Zimbabwe along latitude 20° south.

A second Indonesian invasion of Madagascar is thought to have occurred at the start of the Christian era, these migrants bringing with them a knowledge of terrace-irrigation for rice cultivation. One of the least-explored stone complexes in Zimbabwe is a mighty terrace-irrigation network in the eastern highlands. This was first investigated scientifically by a British archaeologist, Dr David Randall-MacIver. Randall-MacIver was certainly not a Romantic;

indeed, he founded the Shona school with his unequivocal report that the Zimbabwe culture was of comparatively recent origin – medieval – and of indigenous Karanga provenance. Nevertheless, Randall-MacIver felt obliged to describe the Inyanga irrigation terraces: 'The intelligent construction and mastery of gradients shown in the planning of these canals indicate a people with an agricultural knowledge far in advance of any of the Bantu tribes of Central and Southern Africa.'

There is even a written record in support of an Asian immigration to Madagascar in the journals of the Arabian writer, Idrisi (AD 1154) who reports that Indonesian traders (the al-Zabadj) visited Sofala for the iron ore which was mined in the mountains and was better than Indian iron.

But what has all this to do with the Mapungubwe gold rhino and a race of people who may have treasured gold more as an art material than currency for trade with aliens? After much careful archaeology Professor Dart concluded that San People were smelting iron and making tools at Mapungubwe long before the Bantu entered southern Africa. He and other experienced members of the digs at Mapungubwe and Bambandyanalo further concluded that the early population of these *zimbabwes* (which appeared to pre-date Great Zimbabwe) was of 'Boskop-Bush' (San) type and Hottentot in culture. We should also remember that the gold rhino came from an early-period grave. Dart's senior associate, Dr A. Galloway, examined many of the graves, and his conclusions were even more emphatic. In his opinion none of the skulls recovered from the early 'K2' level of the Mapungubwe excavation were specifically Negroid (Bantu). It should be added that Mapungubwe is arguably the richest cultural site next to Great Zimbabwe in south-central Africa. Its people produced fine pottery, traded with the outside world, and were, as mentioned, fine artists in gold.

Needless to say, in a country then evolving to Bantu rule these theories found little favour, even though they were endorsed by Professor Dart. The official South African archaeological record has, therefore, since 1970, promoted the conclusions of the less-well-known Dr G.P. Rightmire, who redefined Dart's proto-Hottentot skulls as 'Negroid'. Dr Galloway, however, was not to be moved; indeed, he found this pronouncement scientifically ridiculous: 'If the Mapungubwe skulls represent the antecedents of Setho-Shona [Bantu] people, then, to allow for this amazing biological change, the Negro must have entered South Africa and settled at Mapungubwe at least six thousand years ago – which is absurd.' And Galloway's judgement was upheld by arguably the most eminent anthropologist of the time, Sir Arthur Keith, and of course by Professor Dart.

These were all eminent men in their fields and it seems unwise, just because they were judged at the time to be politically incorrect, to reject their conclusions outright. We have, at least for the time being, to add to our list of potential authors of the *zimbabwe* culture a whole new race of people, observably skilled in the crafting of precious metals, who probably came to southern Africa via Madagascar. (The closest African gold-port to Madagascar in ancient times was, as it happens, Sofala.)

One of the remaining enigmas of Mapungubwe is that Stone Age hunting artefacts were found intermixed with 'Bantu' artefacts and human remains in the top two layers of Mapungubwe, 'reflecting the possible presence of hunter-foragers in the mixed farming community of Mapungubwe'. This is a politically correct way of saying that two racial types – San and Bantu – may have thrived side by side.

Mapungubwe is probably the one stone complex which has been consistently and scientifically studied for the last half-century. A comprehensive survey of all the work was published by the University of Pretoria as recently as 1998 but it is still riddled with intriguing enigmas. There were, for example, trade beads everywhere at Mapungubwe; in fact, the inhabitants appear eventually to have taken the glass trade beads, which they exchanged for gold, and melted them down to make bigger ones – labelled 'garden-rollers' by the archaeologists. Dr Gardner had decided that the beads emanated from Asia, which was interesting enough given Dart's theory of the origin of the Hottentots, but the other theory about the beads by the respected Professor van Riet Lowe, who now headed the work at Mapungubwe, was even more

The lost city of Great Zimbabwe on a clear day – more often it is cloaked in fine mists.

Towers of cut stone command the acropolis on a precipice above Great Zimbabwe. *(T.V. Bulpin)*

Not a trace of mortar in this, Great Zimbabwe's finest cut-stone wall. *(T.V. Bulpin)*

Western explorers a century ago found trees hundreds of years old growing through Great Zimbabwe's already ancient walls.

Sensuous curves – all Great Zimbabwe's walls and entrances have been designed aesthetically rather than practically. *(Mark Davison)*

Hardwood trees, centuries old, were found growing through the walls of Great Zimbabwe.

Finely worked stone beams from the *zimbabwes* remain a mystery but surely question the assertion that no 'inscriptions' have ever been found in the ruins.

Soapstone 'phalli' and a tiny mother-godess fertility figure.

The fabulous Zodiac Bowl found near Great Zimbabwe, with emblems of the 'northern' zodiac encircling an African crocodile icon. *(Mark Davison)*

Stone entrance to a 'slave-pit' tunnel found only in the early Inyanga *zimbabwes*.

A neat arrow-port in an early Inyanga *zimbabwe* considered to be a fort.

Dry stone terraces at Inyanga for which, experts suggest, more stone was moved than in the building of the Pyramids.

These structures in Yemen, once ruled by the Queen of Sheba, are virtually identical to those seen above.

Crowned Horus, the ancient Egyptian sun-god in the guise of a hawk, has echoes in the Zimbabwe birds.

A Zimbabwe bird displaying solar discs and a crocodile which, if it were Egyptian, could be read as a cartouche for the sun-god Horus protecting King Crocodile.

An Egyptian version on a like theme: a cartouche of the sun-god, Horus, protecting King Snake.

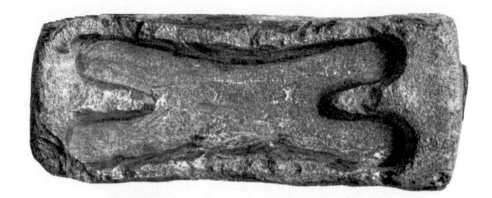

An enigmatic ingot mould in soapstone found at Great Zimbabwe. An ingot that might have been cast from it was found in the tin-mining harbour at Falmouth, Cornwall.

Several Zimbabwe birds sport beaded necklaces. In ancient Egypt the heiroglyph for gold – *nub* – metamorphosed into the sign for a necklace.

The Zimbabwe birds often feature solar discs and icons of animist gods, like the crocodile. All but one (Rhodes' bird at Groote Schuur) of the Zimbabwe birds have now returned home.

The Zimbabwe bird stolen for Cecil John Rhodes, which he believed to have mysterious powers, still guards his bedroom at his former house, Groote Schuur, in Cape Town. *(Mark Davison)*

Everywhere at Groote Schuur Cecil Rhodes commissioned Zimbabwe bird likenesses to grace his home. *(Mark Davison)*

Ancient cannon looted from the Dholo Dholo *zimbabwe* to which they were surely imported still guard the front door to Rhodes' old house in Cape Town. *(Mark Davison)*

Treasure hunters with gold from various *zimbabwes* at the end of the nineteenth century.

Messrs Neal and Johnson, Rhodes' licensed treasure hunters, commit archaeological vandalism with a 'dry-sorting machine'.

The Zimbabwe 'winged angels', looted secretly to British and American museums, are regarded by experts as the finest early carvings to come out of Africa.

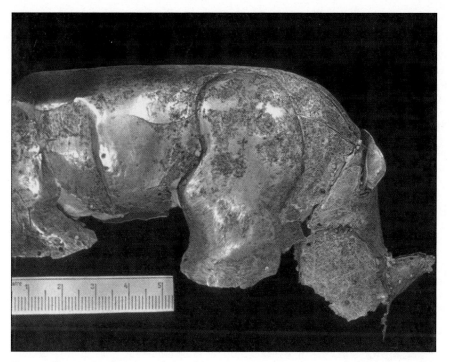

Extraordinary metal artistry from the ancient Mapungubwe *zimbabwe*; a wooden sculpture plated with gold attached by gold tacks.

Pottery figurines of obvious religious significance. But are they Bantu or the earlier shorter, sturdier San (Bushman) People?

AWWAM TEMPLE, MARIB	GREAT ZIMBABWE TEMPLE
Construction	
Dry stone—unroofed	Dry stone—unroofed
Plan	
Oval kidney shape	Oval kidney shape
Height of wall	
9,5 metres	9, 5 metres
Wall batter	
4,12 metres at base	4 to 5,9 metres at base
3,3 metres at summit	3,1 metres at summit
Orientation	
Main axis NW-SE.	*Main axis* NW-SE.
Short axis NE-SW.	*Short axis* NE-SW.
Wall decoration	
At summit only around $\frac{1}{4}$ of the better built portion of the wall.	At summit only around $\frac{1}{4}$ of the better built portion of the wall.
Religious use	
Mother Goddess cult embracing worship of sun, moon, stars and fertility gods symbolised in stone monoliths, phalli, etc.	Evidence of Mother Goddess cult, sun emblems, phallic objects and stone monoliths, bird stelae, etc.
(Glaser, E. *Reise Nach Marib*)	

The almost identical shapes, orientations, and dimensions of Great Zimbabwe and the Awwam Temple suggest the source from which the ancient Rhodesian builders drew their inspiration. The Awwam Temple at Marib *circa* 750 B.C. was the national shrine of the Sabaen Arabs for over 1 000 years, during a part of which period Southern Arabia controlled East Africa by ancient rights.

A comparison of the vital statistics of the Queen of Sheba's temple at Marib, Yemen, reveal it to be a near mirror image of Great Zimbabwe.

controversial. Van Riet Lowe nominated Egypt. This, like the Dart/Galloway Bush Boskop skulls was allowed diplomatically to fade into the background.

The 1998 Mapungubwe report reveals, however, that dedicated research has been completed on these particular beads by a team headed by Ms Sharma Saitowitz using colour spectography, chemistry and the analysis of the rare earth elements in the glass. Ms Saitowitz concluded: 'A particular type of glass used to make beads in Foustat [old Cairo] in Egypt is the same as the glass used to make the beads found on the southern African sites in the Limpopo river valley and elsewhere.'

It is time we rejoined Theodore Bent, who at the start of this chapter was making his way back to Great Zimbabwe, convinced that the gold trade was the key to the authorship of the lost city. 'Authors' had by now become his favoured term for the builders. This shift of focus resulted, I suspect, from the new information he had been collecting about the extent of ancient gold mining.

It was becoming clear that gold had been been dug and processed across a huge area of ancient Mashonaland, more than enough to satisfy even the appetites of gold-hungry hoarders like Solomon and Sheba. By the turn of the last century, 114,814 mining claims had been registered by white prospectors – more than half of them on the lines of ancient workings. These lines were often 50 to 200 yards long. The new Killarney and Surprise mines had been opened up on ancient lines 1,200 and 1,500 yards long. The depths of these lines of shafts averaged 30 to 50 feet; some exceeded 200 feet. There were also hundreds of adits extending deep into hillsides.

In 1899 Dr Hans Sauer, President of the Rhodesian Chamber of Mines, advertised: 'Our experience in this country now amounts to this, that, given a regular and extensive run of old workings on a block of claims, it is almost a certainty that a payable mine will be found on development of the ground.' Another mining expert of the time, Mr Walter Currie, confirmed. 'Experience has invariably proved that where old workings exist, they indicate more or less accurately the length of the payshoot below.'

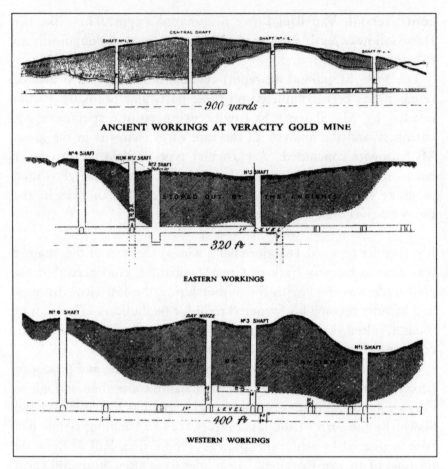

ANCIENT WORKINGS AT VERACITY GOLD MINE

EASTERN WORKINGS

WESTERN WORKINGS

Virtually the whole of the later Rhodesian gold-mining industry exploited deep mines established in ancient times.

Is it any wonder that when Theodore Bent then found at Great Zimbabwe a host of items dedicated to gold production which exactly fitted descriptions by the respected ancient archivist, Diodorus, Bent declared them proof of a long-lost alien influence?

An interest parallel to the ancient gold working of Mashonaland is to be found by studying the account of ancient gold workings at the Egyptian gold mines in Wadi Allaga, also given us by Diodorus.

There too the gold was extracted from the quartz by a process of crushing and washing, as we can see from the process depicted in the paintings on the Egyptian tombs. In any gold-producing quarter of Mashonaland, near old shafts and by the sides of streams, innumerable crushing stones are to be seen, used anciently for a like purpose, when slave labour was employed.

Diodorus tells us of the gangs of slaves employed. Of the long dark shaft into which they descended, of which a countless number are scattered still over Mashonaland; and after describing the process of washing and crushing he concludes: 'They put the gold into earthen crucibles well closed with clay, and leave it in a furnace for five successive days and nights, after which it is suffered to cool. The crucibles are then opened and nothing is found in them but the pure gold a little diminished in quality.'

Hence, it is obvious that the process employed by the ancient Egyptians for crushing, smelting and forming into ingots was exactly the same as that employed by the ancient inhabitants of Zimbabwe; which, in fact, when taken in conjunction with the vast amount of evidence of ancient cult, ancient construction, and ancient art, is, I think, conclusive that the gold field of Mashonaland formed one at least of the sources from which came the gold of Arabia, and that the forts and towns which ran up the whole length of the gold-producing country were made to protect their men engaged in the industry.

The cumulative evidence is greatly in favour of the gold diggers being of Arabian origin, before the Sabaeo-Himyaritic period in all probability, who did work for and were brought closely into contact with both Egypt and Phoenicia, penetrating to many countries unknown to the rest of the world.

The testimony of all travellers in Arabia is to the effect that little or no gold could have come from the Arabian peninsula itself; it is therefore almost certain that the country round Zimbabwe formed one at least of the spots from which the 'Thesaurus Arabum' came.

Case proven? Well, it is certainly very compelling. Suprisingly, however, Theodore Bent does not opt for Phoenician authorship as obviously as his detractors suggest or as Rhodes might have wished. We can see how he inclines towards a very ancient Egyptian origin long before Solomon and Sheba, but then accepts that this is in conflict with the Zimbabwe artefacts which appeared to support a Phoenician presence. In the end he sells Rhodes quite short by taking a step back from actually naming the authors, leaving us instead with something much more tantalising and mysterious.

The Zimbabwe culture, he says in his final (1892) report to the Royal Geographical Society, is the work of: 'A race coming from Arabia – a race which spread more extensively over the world than we have at present any conception of, a race closely akin to the Phoenician and the Egyptian, strongly commercial, and eventually developing into the more civilised races of the ancient world.'

Or more simply, he leaves the door wide open.

In summary, the extensive research conducted by this learned expedition on a site which would never be this pristine again, has really not eliminated anyone from the exotic list of authors with which we started. Well, perhaps the Romans. But we have also added a new contender – the 'Chinese Hottentots'.

SIX

Treasure Hunters

Confusion reigned supreme for more than a decade after Theodore Bent and the other experts of the Royal Geographical Society left the origin of the Zimbabwe culture up for grabs. Through this open door poured an army of treasure hunters. Close examination of Theodore Bent's cryptic conclusion shows, however, a number of intriguing clues of a revolutionary nature which I now believe he deliberately intended. Every word is carefully chosen: *'A race coming from Arabia – a race which spread more extensively over the world than we have at present any conception of, a race closely akin to the Phoenician and the Egyptian, strongly commercial, and eventually developing into the more civilised races of the ancient world.'*

The more astute of the treasure hunters, like Sir John Willoughby, read these clues and applied them to their digs.

Clue number one is the phrase – *'closely akin to the Phoenician and the Egyptian'*. Bent was an acknowledged Phoenician expert who, throughout his dig at Great Zimbabwe, had been identifying artefacts as Phoenician, one of which, the ingot mould, even appeared to bear a Phoenician hallmark. The use of 'akin' here actually eliminates the Phoenicians.

Clue number two is that these people (who are neither Phoenician nor Egyptian although 'akin' to them and originally came from the Arabian area) are *'strongly commercial'*. I am sure Bent chose this phrase particularly carefully. Who were the strongly commercial people of the Arabian area in ancient times yet not Phoenician or Egyptian?

Finally, the vaguest line of all which, in the sense that it narrows the field, contains the strongest clue of all – *'a race which spread*

117

more extensively over the world than we have at present any conception of . . .'. Phoenicians, Egyptians, and the lesser-known tribes of ancient Arabia do not fit that description at all.

I have read and re-read this enigmatic line in the hope of finding a word which would fit all the confusing movements Bent is describing: 'A race which spread more extensively over the world . . . eventually developing into the more civilised races of the ancient world'. The word is, of course, *diaspora*. Then another thought struck me, albeit one so far-reaching it dazed rather than enlightened. Was Bent describing, as vaguely as scientific rectitude would tolerate, *the* Diaspora, that great movement of a strongly commercial race which came out of Babylon in ancient times and went on to spread more extensively over the world than ever Bent could have guessed, becoming in time part of all the more civilised races of the world?

Was he describing the Jews? They certainly fit! In fact nothing else fits his description as well. Insofar as I am aware, Theodore Bent's conclusion has never been defined, or rather, broken down, in this way before. That is probably because Bent found nothing at Great Zimbabwe that could be directly linked to the Jews. He was personally contemptuous of the Romantic tales of the Jewish King Solomon and Sheba, commenting upon his arrival at the ruins: 'The name of King Solomon and the Queen of Sheba were on everybody's lips, and had become so distasteful to us that we never expect to hear them again without an involuntary shudder.'

I can also confirm that there are no significant traces of the Jews in the ancient records of exploration apart from some sailors on Hiram of Tyre's fleet. The earliest confirmed traders were Mohammedans, the earliest missionaries Catholic, and the local Africans sturdy pagan animists. Not a breath of Judaism anywhere here. Indeed, I suspect I would never have dared to introduce what might be Theodore Bent's secret theory – certainly secret thoughts – were it not for the fact that half a century after he dropped this hint, anthropological studies of a tribe now living directly south of Great Zimbabwe would reveal distinctly Jewish practices and traditions, one of these traditions being that the tribe was of mixed racial origin.

But we are not there yet. A galaxy of theories is about to rise in these southern African skies, each more cogent than the next, each one with its determined, sometimes fanatical, legion of supporters.

When Theodore Bent's *The Ruined Cities of Mashonaland* was published in 1892, and in spite of Theodore's repugnance for Solomon myths, it actually resurrected the legend of King Solomon's mines and the Queen of Sheba's love nest, perhaps because it was popular with the general public and soon became a best-seller.

Leaving the origin debate wide open made amateur archaeology, combined with treasure hunting, a favourite form of recreation in Rhodesia. Miners spread across the length and breadth of Mashonaland when Bent's book revealed that the ruins of the Zimbabwe culture all promised gold and were much more numerous than had been suspected. Digging in ruins was often more rewarding than mining.

The military staff officer of the Pioneer Column, Sir John Willoughby, who took his pioneers on that first works outing to Great Zimbabwe to introduce them to treasure hunting, led the pack. Willoughby was forever 'fossicking' in the ruins according to reports of the time. He became a close friend of Rhodes, often staying with him at his holiday cottage in the Cape, and seems to have enjoyed special rights to dig at Great Zimbabwe which Rhodes otherwise kept for himself. In 1892 Willoughby was granted 600,000 acres of land in Mashonaland.

A later Inspector of Rhodesian Monuments, Peter Garlake, would describe Willoughby as 'an insouciant British Army Officer who gutted three ruins in the valley and rummaged in the deposits just inside the north-east entrance to the Elliptical building'.

In truth, Willoughby obviously shared Rhodes' passion for Great Zimbabwe and while other treasure hunters would move on to smaller ruins producing better loot, Willoughby spent his time preparing the best maps of Great Zimbabwe. He is also the first to present evidence that Great Zimbabwe was much more important than the mining capital of a kingdom based on a gold industry: 'Though the gold belt, now known to extend for at least eighty miles, with a breadth varying from ten to fifteen miles, has its nearest point within five miles of Zimbabye, there are no traces of old workings anywhere throughout this whole area and its reefs up to their recent discovery were "virgin reefs".' This singularity has struck several expert visitors to the Great Zimbabwe district: 'Notwithstanding that gold-winning was the primary object of the ancients,' observes Richard Hall, 'and that there must have been a large population interested in gold-mining, the reefs in this district are absolutely virgin.' Hall names twenty-two such reefs opened up by Rhodes' miners which show no sign of having been worked earlier, adding '[Great Zimbabwe's] distance of between five and twelve miles from the nearest point of any gold reef . . . is the greatest yet known of any ruins, save those of road-protecting forts, from the quartz formation.'

Sir John Willoughby happily admitted that he was not an archaeologist and his searches had been conducted as 'thoroughly and rapidly as possible and without that caution which the expectation of an expert's report demands'. It also has to be said that treasure-hunting did not, in those days, attract the opprobrium it does today.

Assuming that he declared everything he found, which admittedly would make him unique in this company, his work did not enrich him, although a lot of his finds are very interesting. Like Bent, he dug up soapstone bowl fragments, pieces of china, porcelain beads, a soapstone game board, thirteenth-century painted glass (confirmed by the British Museum), a soapstone miniature bird, a three-pronged spear and an iron hammer 8 feet below the surface, portions of ancient crucibles showing gold and gold in flux, many phalli, and a copper-green enamelled, patterned bodkin. His finds add to the evidence of long-term alien influence at Great Zimbabwe and that this most splendid of *zimbabwes* had special religious significance.

But Rhodes, single-minded as ever, continued to promote Great Zimbabwe as gold-rich Ophir. 'You will find,' he wrote to a backer, 'that Zimbabwe is an old Phoenician residence and everything points to Sofala being the place from which Hiram fetched his gold.' Behind the bravura, however, Shona gold was proving very

120

disappointing and Rhodes was facing a financial disaster. Only the reefs around Great Zimbabwe had apparently not been worked. Could it be that the treasure house had been emptied thousands of years ago by Solomon, Hiram and their successors, leaving the place to decay into ruins? Had the golden bird flown, taking all its eggs with it?

The truth was that the British South Africa Company was financially on its last legs a year after the occupation, and the accounts laid before the shareholders at their first meeting in 1891 were frightening. With all but no income, 'general expenses' already exceeded £402,000, nearly half the total capital of the company.

Much the most poignant description of how desperate things were in the new Rhodesia is to be found in the last chapter of Theodore Bent's book as he attempts to leave the country. He had gone again to Beira, the port on the east coast to which the Rhodesians had been allowed access under the agreement recognising the coastal strip as Portuguese territory, and on the strength of which Rhodes had commissioned two of his most loyal cronies, Heany and Johnson, to open a road.

Bent reveals:

Ours is the only wheeled vehicle which has traversed [the road] in its entirety since the single pioneer coach went up to Umtali, after infinite difficulty and weeks of disaster, with such sorry tales of fever, fly and swamp, that no vehicles have since ventured to repeat the experiment.

Dozens of wagons lie rotting in the veldt . . . everywhere lie the bleached bones of the oxen which dragged them . . . fully £2,000 worth of wagons we calculated, ghostlike as after a battle. Then there are Scotch carts of more or less the same value, and a handsome Cape cart, which Mr Rhodes had to abandon on his way up to Mashonaland, containing in the box seat a bottle labelled 'Anti-fly mixture', a parody of the situation.

At a Portuguese settlement on the banks of the Pungwe river, Bent saw:

Two handsome coaches, made expressly in New Hampshire, in America . . . they are richly painted with arabesques and pictures on the panels; 'Pungwe route to Mashonaland' is written thereon in gold. The comfortable cushions inside are being moth-eaten and the approaching rains will complete the ruin of these handsome but ill-fated vehicles. Meanwhile, the Portuguese stand and laugh at the discomfiture of their British rivals in their thirst for gold.

What Rhodes desperately needed was some good news from King Solomon's mines but by now that too was in very short supply. 'The Directors are extremely anxious about gold news,' Macquire wrote to Rhodes in July 1891; 'any tangible news would have an excellent effect.'

What they got was the opposite and from a very eminent source. Lord Randolph Churchill had treated himself to a luxurious three-month safari in Mashonaland in 1891, subsidised by articles published in the *Daily Graphic*. Lord Randolph praised the settlers for their energy but poured doom and gloom on their prospects – 'It occurs to me that there must be upon this great continent some awful curse, some withering blight, and that to delude and to mock at the explorer, the gold-hunter, the merchant, the speculator, and even at ministers and monarchs, is its dark fortune and its desperate fate.' In private letters Lord Randolph's prognosis was even more specific and damning – 'The B.S.A. Co. funds have all been expended and no gold has been found.'

But if Rhodes was good at anything it was manipulating the assets of his various companies. The London board urged him to return home and 'smash Randolph with the public' and this he did, displaying Bent's new finds and continuing to stress that Great Zimbabwe was gold-rich Ophir. At the same time he 'stoked up enthusiasm' at board meetings of his rich companies in South Africa. These 'curious financial methods' often involved Rhodes 'wearing one hat, coming to the rescue of Rhodes in another of his hats'. Essentially, until his death of heart disease in March 1902, he kept his dream alive by ensuring that the financial wolves never quite got through Rhodesia's door, even though the exercise probably contributed to his death. In the last weeks he avoided going to his Cape Town club, for example, for fear that his condition would become generally known and depress share prices in his companies, particularly the rocky British South Africa Company.

On the ground in Mashonaland, Rhodes had taken control of gold affairs, reducing the 50 per cent company premium which had been restricting capital investment in gold mining, and licensing the treasure hunters to ensure the company got a percentage of these spoils. Great Zimbabwe was, however, excluded from any of the licences. Initially, an American, F.R. Burnham, who had fought bravely against the Matabele, was granted the rights to dig in the newly discovered Dholo Dholo ruins, fifty miles east of Bulawayo. Burnham lifted everyone's spirits when he recovered 641 oz of 'gold inlaid work and gold ornaments', some of which were given to Rhodes.

Two mining prospectors, W.G. Neal and G. Johnson, were at the same time desecrating native graves at a small unnamed ruin fifty miles to the south, stripping the bodies of gold necklaces, bangles and bracelets and other gold items 'strewn around', in all weighing 208 oz, which they sold for £3,000, a fortune at the time. Rhodes also later acquired this treasure and decided it was time he took control of these lucrative operations. The treasure-hunting company he licensed through the Charter Company was called Rhodesian Ancient Ruins Ltd, and it was operated by these same two lucky diggers, Neal and Johnson. Their licence was confined to the right to explore and work for treasure in several ruins in Matabeleland with a first option on other ruins. The British South Africa Company received 20 per cent of all their finds and Rhodes had a first right of purchase on everything. He is said to have accumulated over 200 oz of necklaces and beads. Other artefacts went to the BSAC's offices in London, but the bulk of these have just disappeared. One would have to be very naïve not to conclude that much more than this 'disappeared' in other ways and into other pockets in the course of a decade of open looting. As previously mentioned, however, Great Zimbabwe was fortunately not included in any of these activities, at Rhodes' 'express desire'.

Neal and Johnson dug through five Matabeleland ruins in the next six months, including a return trip to Dholo Dholo where they found their best cache of 700 oz of gold beads and wire bracelets. In the following year this industrious pair forked through some fifty other ruins but their luck, as with gold finds elsewhere in the country, had run out. They found a little bit of worked gold, or gold dust, everywhere they looked, but the average from each ruin was less than 10 oz.

If we consider that an estimate of 21,000,000 oz of ancient mined gold (worth in those days some £75,000,000) against a couple of thousand ounces still on or in the ground in 1895, this is surely incontrovertible evidence of a Zimbabwe culture engaged for centuries with alien gold traders. More simply, most of Zimbabwe's gold was exported from the country long before Rhodes or even the Matabele got there.

In 1900 the Rhodesian Ancient Ruins company was wound up and Neal gave all the information he had carefully compiled to a writer, Richard Nicklin Hall, who produced from it *The Ancient Ruins of Rhodesia*, a strange book which made Hall's name in the field of popular history. It also made Hall the new self-appointed expert on the authorship of Great Zimbabwe. Hall revealed to the general public for the first time that Great Zimbabwe was not a lone, lost city (albeit the most impressive one south of the Pyramids), but the likely capital of an empire encompassing hundreds of *zimbabwes* across the whole of south-central Africa, including at least half a dozen 'grand' *zimbabwes*.

Hall's book explores in some detail almost 200 *zimbabwes* from which we will consider just a few here, mainly for the extraordinary variety of artefacts which came to light in them. Other grand *zimbabwes* will be described by qualified archaeologists later on. Hall's favourite ruin was the acropolis which overlooked the temple, and his clear, succinct descriptions of these sites is a testimonial to the detail of his record-keeping:

The hill fortress is of labyrinthine character. The kopje on which it is erected is itself of great natural strength, being about 500 feet high, and having on the south side a precipice of smooth rock of 70 to 90 feet.

On the only accessible side there is a wall of massive thickness, being 13 feet high on the summit with a batter of 1 foot in 6 feet, and in height 30 feet in parts, with a flat causeway to the top, decorated on the outer edge by a succession of little round towers 3 feet in diameter, alternating with tall monoliths.

The approach to the fortress is protected at every turn with traverses and ambuscades. A flight of steps leads up from the bottom of the precipice and runs up an exceedingly narrow slit between the boulders. In front of the steps is a section of wall in dentelle pattern. At the summit of the hill are large boulders 50 feet high, with a little plateau approached by narrow passages and steps on either side.

The plateau was adorned with huge monoliths and decorated with pillars of soapstone, the patterns on which were chiefly of a geometric character, one being 11 feet 6 inches in height. The large semicircular area below this plateau contained an altar covered with cement. The labyrinthine character of these buildings baffles description.

Below in the valley he found some of the most spectacular monoliths, or stelae:

There are several large monoliths in the south-east wall of the elliptical Temple, some of which have fallen down. Evidence exists that they were equidistant. One of the largest standing was measured by Sir John Willoughby and found to be 14 feet 3 inches above the accumulated soil and 12 feet 3 inches above the top of the old cement floor. The foundation in which it once stood still remains in good condition.

The most impressive set of ruins after Great Zimbabwe is Khami in Matabeleland and again it is a city of substance covering an area of some two square miles. There are eleven distinct sets of ruins set across a long kopje in a spectacular landscape of kopjes and open valleys overlooking the Khami river. Two wide gullies lead into the remains guarded at several points by ruined forts which must have rendered the main ruins impregnable. The gullies have been paved with 'cement'. Neal found five pavements at one place, one on top of the other. Khami is extensively decorated, some herringbone patterns having been constructed of tooled blocks of a darker stone, diorite; elsewhere there are check patterns. Many of the walls are more than 100 feet in length, have stairways, and in one case a square door. Wild vines and fig trees were found in almost every ruin. Neal and Johnson used a small dry-crushing machine on a huge midden at Khami and from the washed spoils recovered over 40 oz of gold in beads, tacks, wire, small portions of gold bangles and pellets.

Head east from Khami in the direction of Great Zimbabwe on a line directly to Sofala Bay and you pass within a few miles of at least ten citadels, like that of Umnukwana overlooking the Bubi river. The ruins command the top of a 90-foot kopje and are regarded as the capital of a district containing some fifty minor and dependent ruins. Umnukwana itself covers an area of 300 by 60 feet with a massive main wall 300 feet long, 13 feet thick and 17 feet 6 inches high when Johnston and Neal surveyed it. There are a number of enclosures, one them 170 by 60 feet, served by rounded entrances.

Here the treasure hunters found a grave containing remains dressed with fine gold bangles, large beads weighing 2 dwt and a single bead of 1 oz 14 dwt, also smelted gold, a copper ingot, a pair of double iron 'bells', a boss or rosette of beaten gold with a presentation of the sun image, and a large soapstone bowl. Nearby is the Check ruins, regarded as the most beautiful of the *zimbabwes*, also on a kopje but invisible from the surrounding countryside. It gets its name from the fact that it is completely covered inside and out with decorations of the check or chessboard pattern. Neal reported that 'pannings of the soil from inclosures [sic] gave good returns of fine gold'.

North again brings one to the massive spread of the Thabas Imamba (or Momba) ruins, set on the highest point of the Imamba range. The walls enclose an area of over 200 feet by 80 feet. Thabas

Imamba has the most exotic history of any of the *zimbabwes*, for as oral records suggest, this was the capital of the Mombo clan, whose last king was 'skinned alive' here by invading Amaswazies.

West of here are four citadels, the Mundie ruins, of which the third is 160 feet in diameter with 14-foot-high walls. The space between the first and second structures had been cemented and from these enclosures 208 oz of pure gold ornaments were discovered. A grave contained human remains dressed with 72 oz of gold. In fact, Mundie was quite literally littered with gold, including 230 oz of gold in cakes. Neal observed: 'Gold was found scattered around the floors quite promiscuously in the two ruins. This was in all stages of manufacture. There were many gold-wire bangles pulled together out of shape as if torn or snatched by violent hands, and scattered beads and charred remains of unburied people evidencing a fight and a defeat of the ancient occupiers.'

And so it goes on, mile upon mile of ruins until the treasure hunters, tired of local names, start to name them after themselves. There is the Baden Powell ruin in the Sabi valley, the Selkirk, Gatling Hill, Mullen's, World View, Stone Door, and Yellow Jacket, until even these run out and Hall simply lists 'eighteen unnamed ruins in the Salisbury area', or 'Ancient Aqueduct Area and numerous unnamed ruins'. And this was the list after just a few years of white occupancy!

The most recent surveys, especially those from the air, would indicate that *zimbabwes* great and small could number 20,000. There are, as well, a few mythical lost cities, the most famous of which is the White City, alleged to contain stone figures, including a woman in a mourning position and a reclining man. Solomon and Sheba no doubt. They have vanished into legend. An American traveller, G. Farini, claimed in a book published in 1886 to have found a lost city in the Kalahari desert in the extreme north of the Cape Province. This was taken so seriously that several expeditions and aerial surveys were made in the 1950s and '60s but no city was ever found.

Apart from these ghosts virtually all the larger ruins gave up some gold. A number provided much more exotic treasure trove. There were old barrels of flintlock muskets, portions of a brass trumpet, two cannon which to this day command the front steps of Groote Schuur, a gold medallion embossed on one side with two birds fighting over a heart, silver twisted wire bangles, two huge lumps of lead weighing 60 lb, a large elephant tusk, bar silver, and what was described as 'a Jesuit priest's hoard', of which more later.

One or two very enigmatic curios also turned up. In a cave ten miles from Great Zimbabwe, Mr Edward Muller found a wooden platter or dish, 38 inches in circumference, showing a number of zodiacal and other astronomical signs – Gemini, Leo, Virgo, Libra, Scorpio, Sagittarius, Capricorn, Aquarius, a sun image, Orion and Taurus. The face of the bowl displays a crocodile, which was believed to indicate the northern circumpolar constellation. Rhodes acquired this gem and it is still in his bedroom at Groote Schuur, where it keeps company with the Posselt bird, also featuring a crocodile. The crocodile would indicate that this is Karanga work – but where did the local artist get his knowledge of northern zodiacal symbols other than from educated aliens?

Hall and Neal's *Ruined Cities of Mashonaland*, controversial as it has remained ever since, deeply impressed the one man it needed to impress, Cecil John Rhodes, so much so it earned Hall the appointment by the British South Africa Company of Curator of Great Zimbabwe. Hall's appointment was immediately condemned by British scientists, who wrote him off as a 'journalist'. In fact, he was well educated in England, qualified as a solicitor and, after coming to Rhodesia, was a local correspondent for several British journals, and editor of the *Matabeleland Times*, later the *Bulawayo Chronicle*, the first newspaper I ever worked for. In 1909 he travelled for five months down the Sabi and Lundi rivers collecting ethnological information. Hall eventually became a Fellow of several European and South African scientific societies and in addition to his books had numerous papers published in the journals of learned societies.

Hall's 'clearances' at Great Zimbabwe have been condemned as 'ruining Great Zimbabwe for archaeology'. What has been forgotten or ignored is that Hall's terms of reference from the BSAC required him to prioritise the 'preservation of the building' – or perhaps more accurately, the preservation of what had become Rhodes' private ancient ruin. Ignoring ever-louder howls of protest from foreign archaeologists he indulged in clearances which involved not just a wealth of trees, creepers and undergrowth, but fallen stones round the walls, the spoil from the Bent and Willoughby digs, and at least 3, 5 and in places up to 12 feet of what the archaeologists called 'stratified archaeological deposits'; that is, the layered history of the Zimbabwe culture, in particular the more recent stages of it.

Hall was utterly unrepentant. His job as he saw it was to preserve the *ancient* ruin, make it safe and improve access to it and if that involved removing the 'filth and decadence of the Kaffir occupation', so be it. This was bad enough but Hall did not stop there. Once he had cleaned and opened up the lost city he set about looking for evidence of what he called 'the ancients'. His predecessor, Bent, had already searched for and failed to find worthwhile grave sites. By the time Hall got to work, treasure hunters and white miners had located some 500 *zimbabwes* but they too found remarkably few graves. This was not for want of diligent desecration: everyone knew grave sites were the best places to find gold.

The total number of graves found by the time Hall went to press was just forty, one per ten *zimbabwes*, which everyone agreed was peculiar. Even Theodore Bent, who only ever knew of twenty-three *zimbabwes*, was mystified by this, suggesting that perhaps the alien authors of the Zimbabwe culture had removed their dead for burial at sacred sites in their homelands as was the practice in places like Bahrein.

Bent had gone on to suggest that 'the ancients were but a garrison in the country' but Richard Hall, now aware that he was in charge of the largest stone city south of the Pyramids, quickly rejected that view. The ancient gold mines, Hall pointed out, must have been worked by huge gangs of 'slaves', as was the custom in all the ancient countries of the world. A similarly large workforce would have been engaged in quarrying and transporting the millions of tons of rock for the buildings. A great deal of food would have had

129

to be planted, processed and transported by and for a large indigenous workforce. 'Such a vast slave population,' Hall decided, 'presupposes a vast population of the alien ancients to protect the town and the many and scattered gold mining districts.'

He was determined to find cemeteries, at least those of the 'Proconsuls or overlords . . . the chief stewards and taskmasters, or priests', which he expected would provide rich rewards of gold as 'the minimum amount of gold found with the remains of each ancient so far discovered has not been less than one and a half ounces.' He also anticipated no difficulties separating modern (Mombo–Monomatapa) burials from those of his ancients. On the basis of the few graves he had opened he asserted that the ancients were buried on their sides at full length whereas the moderns were interred haphazardly, often sitting upright. 'Ancients' were always buried under the original cemented floors or under the first or second floors above the original cemented floors. Medieval and modern people were buried near the surface and many feet above the ancients.

The presence of a considerable amount of solid gold ornaments decorated with old Zimbabwe patterns was an unfailing feature of an ancient burial, said Hall. Those of the Mombo–Monomatapa period had ornaments of iron and copper, sometimes banded with gold. The most recent burials only had copper, iron, brass and glass bead ornamentation. Hall further claimed that the pottery which he found invariably buried with the dead differed in design, glaze, ornamentation and material and that it deteriorated with each successive period until it became identical with the 'coarse articles' made by the natives of his day.

Graves that had been found and opened revealed, Hall remarked, evidence of a turbulent and violent history. At the Umnukwana ruin, seven 'undoubted ancients' were found who had not been buried. Surrounded by their weapons, they were lying under the soil just outside the entrance, evidently in the positions in which they had been slain. Broken bangles of solid gold and torn bangles of gold wire were found on the same site. Hall condemned what he called 'vandalism galore', which had caused considerable damage to the ruins as a result of a false belief among treasure hunters that the ancients buried their dead in the walls.

After five years of excavations, his own and those of Neal, Hall felt qualified to offer a detailed description of the ancient burial practices of the Zimbabwe culture:

On the death of an ancient a grave was sunk through the cemented floor, apparently under his own dwelling, and the grave was made apparently without any reference to the points of the compass. As all original floors have a layer of ashes underlying them, the ashes in the grave were removed and replaced by some sort of red earth in which the body was laid always on one side or the other.

His gold ornaments were buried on his person, and his cakes of gold still remained in the pouch on his waist, while, as in ancient Egyptian and present-day Kaffir burials, earthenware pots probably once containing grain, were placed beside him.

These pots of the ancients were of the finest clay, beautifully glazed, very thin, and engraved in the best style with the oldest Zimbabwe patterns.

His head either rested on a pillow of water-grooved stone as at Chum Ruins, or on a wooden pillow very similar to those seen in Egyptian museums and in ancient paintings of Egyptian tombs, resembling in shape and patterns the best of pillows used by the Kaffirs of today.

The wooden pillow was frequently covered with beaten gold fastened on by solid gold tacks weighing 3 dwt each, or were beautifully worked on both sides in gold wire with patterns of the oldest chevron decoration.

By his side if he were a great man, was laid his rod of office with the beaten gold head embossed with the Phallic sun image, and with solid gold ferrule six to eighteen inches long and weighing 1½ oz.

In these same Chum ruins, Neal found a 'giant'. One shin bone was over 2 feet in length. Hall speculated about the 'Tombs of the

Giants' created by the builders of the ancient stone monuments known as nauraghes on Sardinia which Theodore Bent had also compared with Zimbabwe stone structures.

Hall, it should be noted, quickly donned the mantle of antiquarian and was also in the process of formulating his own rules of archaeology for Great Zimbabwe. These have subsequently been much maligned, in my view unfairly. The 'science' of archaeology as we know it was still being invented when Hall worked at Great Zimbabwe and Hall implemented an early system of 'stratification' – layers of human activity – based on that suggested by Flinders Petrie in the same decade from his digs in Palestine. It may be that Hall interpreted his stratification to support his Romantic theories – most archaeologists do to a degree – but it also demonstrates that he was aware of and sought to practise scientific method. Hall was the first to spot 'a great waste of the precious metal [gold] which was so noticeable on every hand', and to extrapolate from this a material difference in the attitude to gold of modern Africans and the aliens he was now convinced had run the gold industry.

Gold in the form of broken bangles, tacks, and pellets were found on the original floors of the ruins 'as plentifully as nails can be picked up from the floors of a modern carpenter's shop'. Debris heaps of sweepings from the ruins produced gold pellets in profusion. At Khami, Neal, using his small dry-crushing machine on the debris heaps had produced an average of 16 oz of gold per month.

Based on the graves he had examined Hall insisted that the 'ancients' respected gold far more than the recent African kingdoms like Mombo and Monomatapa: 'With the exception of the Mombo chief buried in the rudely constructed stone circle at M'telegwa, very few of the Mombo skeletal remains had gold ornaments of any value, the gold generally being in bands at intervals on iron bangles, or gold beads at intervals on copper bangles. In these periods copper and glass beads appear to have been the favourite ornaments.'

Respect him or not (Hall was observably racially prejudiced), the fact remains that he had his hands on the lost city exclusively for more than two years – the longest full-time study ever – and he was both zealous and a good record-keeper. He saw things no one else would or could see. The vociferous condemnation of Hall by the archaeology lobby disguises the fact that even allowing for Hall's destructive housekeeping, modern archaeologists have provided few definite answers to key Zimbabwe riddles, not least what happened to the bodies of what must have been a large elite.

Perhaps Hall's greatest contribution to the debate is the extent to which his discoveries proved clear alien influence in the Zimbabwe culture even though such influence is still essentially denied by the Shona school. Hall alone made enough alien finds to make nonsense of that denial including, near to several furnaces, a lump of bronze 'slag', as well as melted-down tin for mixing with copper to produce bronze.

A complete ensemble of metal-working tools were found in hut ruins near the entrance to the conical tower including three gold crucibles, six pottery scorifiers, a pair of tongs, two shallow cross-shaped soapstone moulds, a drawplate for gold wire and, nearby, eight smooth river pebbles used to burnish gold sheets. Some 200 oz of gold beaten into metal sheets were found, as was gold wire and devices for drawing the wire. Hundreds of spinning whorls, mostly pottery but some of soapstone, were found in a single trench outside the Elliptical Building. Oral tradition suggests that cotton clothing was worn by the elite of the Zimbabwe culture, some threaded with fine gold wire.

Hall found Posselt's hidden soapstone birds and some new ones. A half-bird he unearthed fits the lower half of a broken bird in a museum in Berlin. And in the so-called Phillips ruin in the valley, Hall found the last whole Zimbabwe bird. Rider Haggard, who would use his experiences in Mashonaland as the basis for his novel *King Solomon's Mines*, coined his own theory about the religion the birds represented: they were 'sacred birds, figured, however, not as the Cypris, but as the vulture of her Sidonian representative, Astarte'.

Hall also accumulated huge piles of loose stelae, carved and plain, some perhaps door lintels. Many were still precariously decorating crumbling walls and as his job was to make the place safe he simply hauled them out and piled them out of harm's way.

Towards the end of his tenure, Hall called his camp at Great Zimbabwe 'Havilah' after the land from which, according to the Bible, Ophir's gold came. Here, in 1904, he compiled the second edition of his book which described his finds, his digs and his own, entirely Romantic view of the origins of the Zimbabwe culture. It is a slow, pedantic read but it was an immediate best-seller and is the only book on the Zimbabwe culture which has remained in print for a century. It enjoyed the support of several high academics, including Professor A.H. Keane, FRGS, late Vice-President of the Anthropological Institute of Great Britain and Ireland. Professor Keane summarised Hall's work in four scholarly articles, collectively entitled *The Gold of Ophir: Whence Brought and by Whom?* that included this condensed theory of the origin of the Zimbabwe culture:

Ophir was not the source, but the distributor of the gold and other costly merchandise brought from abroad to the courts of David and Solomon.

Ophir was the emporium on the south coast of Arabia which has been identified with the Mosha or Portus Nobilis of the Greek and Roman geographers.

Havilah [as named in the Bible] was the auriferous land whence came 'the gold of Ophir', and Havilah is here identified with the Rhodesias, the mineralised land between the lower Zambesi and the Limpopo – Mashona, Matabili, and Manica lands.

The ancient gold-workings of this region were first opened and the associated monuments erected by the South Arabian Himyarites, who were followed, not before the time of Solomon, by the Phoenicians, and these very much later by the Moslem Arabs and Christian Portuguese.

Tharshish [another Biblical reference] was the outlet for the precious metals and precious stones of Havilah, and stood probably on the site of the present Sofala.

The Himyaritic and Phoenician treasure-seekers reached Havilah through Madagascar, where they had settlements and maintained protracted commercial and social intercourse with the

Malagasy natives. With them were associated the Jews, by whom the fleets of Hiram and Solomon were partly manned.

The Queen of Sheba came by the land route and not over the seas, to the court of Solomon. Her kingdom was Yemen, the Arabia Felix of the Ancients, the capital of which was Maraiaba Bahramalakum. Her treasures were partly imported (the precious metals and precious stones) from Havilah and its port of Tharshish to Ophir, and partly (frankincense and myrrh) shipped at Ophir from the neighbouring district of Mount Sephar.

Sephar was confused by the Alexandrian authors of the Septuagint with Ophir, which was the chief emporium of the Sabaean empire.

In a word the 'gold of Ophir' came from Havilah [Rhodesia], and was worked and brought thence first by the Himyarites [Sabaeans and Minaeans], later by the Phoenicians, the chief ports engaged in the traffic being Ezion-geber in the Red Sea, Tharshish in Havilah, and mid-way between the two, Ophir in South Arabia.

This central position of Ophir explains how it became the intermediate emporium whither the fleets of Hiram and Solomon sailed every three years from Ezion-geber for the gold imported from Havilah and for the spices grown on the slopes of the neighbouring Mount Sephar, not far from the deep inlet of Moascha, round which are thickly strewn the ruins of Ophir.

These and the other Himyaritic ruins of Yemen show striking analogies with those of Rhodesia, while the numerous objects of Semitic worship and the fragments of the Himyaritic script found in Zimbabwe and elsewhere south of the Zambesi leave no reasonable doubt that the old gold workings and associated monuments of this region are to be ascribed to the ancient Sabaeans of South Arabia and their Phoenician successors.

Thus the eminent Professor Keane places Solomon and Sheba firmly back in the ring, this time with a clear Madagascar connection and a further hint of a Jewish involvement.

Need we go further? A Royal Geographical Society report, the Curator of Great Zimbabwe with more time on site than any other person, and a professor of the Royal Anthropological Society have now spoken almost with one voice. Is this not proof enough?

Again, the answer is an emphatic no.

The Rhodes Trust fired Richard Nicklin Hall, his work vilified by the British scientific establishment, after his patron's death. Waves of British university-trained archaeologists descended upon the ruins. They contemptuously discarded virtually everything about the authors of Great Zimbabwe that had been proposed thus far.

SEVEN

The Debunkers

If, as some Romantics have suggested, there is a Great Zimbabwe curse at work on those who desecrated the lost city in the first decade of the twentieth century, we find it hard at work. What's more, it is strikingly in chronological order. Carl Mauch is dead, having failed to get the scholastic position he felt his discoveries had earned him. He was forced to take a lowly job in a cement works and later 'fell' from the window of his lodgings.

Rhodes also met an early end and is buried in the Matopos hills in Matabeleland. Ambition finally spent, he insists on the simplest of epitaphs – 'Here lie the remains of Cecil John Rhodes'.

Lobengula is also dead. No granite tomb for him. He died, it is said, of hypothermia suffered while fleeing into the wilderness after his offers of truce were ignored. To this day the place of his death has never been established, although many have searched because he is known to have been carrying gold to trade for peace.

J. Theodore Bent is dying of a fever caught on another African expedition, still obsessively hunting the authors of the Zimbabwe culture.

Richard Nicklin Hall, once Curator of Great Zimbabwe, is out of work and embittered.

The row between the Romantic and Shona schools of origin theory rages on, not least over Rhodes' blatant use of Romantic images to fund his imperial ambitions and his financing of the Royal Geographical Society expedition. The Trustees of Rhodes' estate decide there is urgent need of damage control to protect their patron's name and they agree to fund a second scientific expedition under the supervision of the British Association for the Advancement of Science. Their brief is to lay the ghosts of authorship once and for all and they hand the responsibility to an energetic but unknown junior don from Worcester College, Oxford, David Randall-MacIver, aged thirty. He makes what amounts to a lightning tour of seven grand *zimbabwes* in five months and, in a book produced within the same year, rejects every theory we have heard so far.

His book, *Mediaeval Rhodesia*, rather than resolve matters, pours fuel on a fire that will blaze for the next decade. Randall-MacIver, largely through arrogance, polarises the two main schools of thought on the Zimbabwe culture for ever. Obviously well aware that he is about to stir the hornet's nest, Randall-MacIver admittedly starts in a conciliatory vein. He reminds his readers that he has nine years' experience in Egypt and the Orient and that 'nothing would have been more attractive to me than the prospect of extending my Oriental studies to South-East Africa'. But the boot is not long in coming: 'It has been necessary to abandon this dream, because it has proved to be incompatible with any respect for science and the logic of observed facts'.

To ensure there is no misunderstanding of where this boot is aimed, Randall-MacIver affirms that he is happy to have his 'wholly independent and original' report judged upon its own merits and that no reference has been made to 'various books which it is impossible to praise and would have been invidious to criticize'. That means all the books on the subject to date with the exception of Dr Theal's *Records of South Eastern Africa* which Rhodes paid for: 'Apart from the collection of documents embodied in that admirable work, there exists no bibliography with which the student need be troubled.'

If this is not insulting enough to people like Theodore Bent and Richard Nicklin Hall who have published hundreds of pages on the subject under similar scientific patronage to his own (the Rhodes Trust, the Royal Geographical Society and the British Association), Randall-MacIver extends it to all the amateur theorists as well: 'Before there was sufficient evidence on which to base any suggestions as to origin or date, popular opinion had confidently settled the question to its own satisfaction. It had decided that the

Rhodesian ruins must be of immense antiquity, and, following the mediaeval chroniclers with an uncritical credulity that would have been as admirable in their day as it is unworthy in our own, have pronounced Zimbabwe and all similar buildings to be the work of an ancient people from the East. . . . Journalists and popular writers professed, as might be expected, a knowledge of lost ancient history which the most learned Orientalists do not dream of claiming.' If arrogance were not enough he is then more than a little patronising: 'Still it was possible, of course, that these romanticists might prove to be correct; although only guessing, they might have blundered on the truth.'

As the title of his book indicated, David Randall-MacIver did not believe they had, but I will leave the profound and dismissive extent to which he felt so until we have heard his evidence. In the meantime he has at least supplied us with a label for all those who would disagree so vehemently with him. They were, henceforth, the Romantics. David Randall-MacIver actually used the phrase 'Romantics' when presenting his medieval theory to a public meeting in Bulawayo, which must have comprised Romantics to the man. It is a tough, pioneer town. David Randall-MacIver cannot possibly have suspected how close he came to being tarred and feathered.

Randall-MacIver's report also marks the moment when the lost city became a political pawn. It was felt by both camps, if covertly at first, that whomsoever could prove ancestors who were the authors of the lost city – White Semites v Black Bantu – had the moral right to rule Zimbabwe. When eventually it came to a bloody fight between these two camps 'Zimbabwe' would be on every black banner, ZAPU (Zimbabwe African People's Union) for the party which would eventually be led by Joshua Nkomo, and ZANU for the Zimbabwe African National Union led by Robert Mugabe.

Through these years I was the Controller of Rhodesia Television in Bulawayo. My daughter Lisa's maid, Annie Mutesa, was Joshua's niece. She and I, the police told us, were both on 'blacklists', she on ZANU's, me on both because of my position as a white television 'propagandist', albeit a rather pro-black one. Annie, who protected my children like a tigress, said it was probably better if ZANU took care of me because otherwise she might have to. Thankfully it never came to that; in fact, she was very upset when we left the country.

Mr Smith's parliament tried to diffuse the issue of the authorship of the lost city via a parliamentary order banning any suggestion that it was of indigenous African origin. I had earlier spent some time in the parliamentary press gallery with Robert Mugabe, he for the *African Daily News*, myself for the *Rhodesia Herald*, when the political row about the colour of the builders of Great Zimbabwe first began to rumble. At about that time, however, the *Daily News* was also banned. Robert, whom I had admired for his fiery commitment to his cause, went off to Mozambique to raise an army of freedom fighters. I, taking the hint from one of Mr Smith's ministers, went into voluntary exile in Britain and raised a family.

David Randall-MacIver gave the Zimbabwe nationalists their first secure political plank.

Richard Hall's writings had by then been comprehensively derided by a number of David Randall-MacIver's academic peers. Theodore Bent's work was also judged to be essentially Romantic. He was certainly guilty of quoting 'mediaeval chroniclers with uncritical credulity'. Randall-MacIver judged, in this climate of opinion, that he could afford, without unduly damaging his reputation at home, to displace Bent as well. I can understand his motivation. David Randall-MacIver was the first representative of the new school of British archaeology, founded by Sir William Flinders Petrie, to be given open access to the Zimbabwe ruins. The chance to be the first to reveal the true origins of what had to be perhaps the last essentially unexplored ancient culture on earth was a breathtaking opportunity and certainly not one to be missed. The temptation to produce an entirely new theory of its origins must have been irresistible.

By 1905 the railway line had been built to Beira along the route that Theodore Bent and others had scouted. David Randall-MacIver travelled up it to a huge fruit farm Rhodes had established in the rich Inyanga mountains. Four *zimbabwes* commanded the local peaks. Three of these were very roughly constructed – 'temporary refuges in times of great need. David Randall-MacIver went immediately to work and after a cursory examination labelled these 'forts' after noting that the southern building had 'loopholes' and entrances roofed with stone slabs. The fort, commanding the northeast of the estate, occupied a formidable defensive position on a sheer cliff above the Inyanga river. In his final thesis, one of his most dubious statements is: 'In the architecture [of the ruins], whether military or domestic, there is not a trace of Oriental or European style of any period whatsoever.' Yet here he is on Day One describing 'loopholes' which are, of course, a very common feature of forts everywhere, indeed the most common feature distinguishing a fort from a domestic building. Loopholes are, moreover, quite rare in the Zimbabwe ruins, so the existence of them in these Inyanga *zimbabwes* was of special significance, which Randall-MacIver would have to address, and correct, later.

Examples such as this, of emphatic labelling even when comments elsewhere contradict the labels, are common, especially when the labels are employed to support his thesis. The opposite is equally true. When unique features cannot be exactly fitted into his medieval timeframe or contradict his affirmation that there is no European architectural precedent, they are ignored or marginalised. An intriguing architectural feature of the grand walls of Great Zimbabwe is, for example, large well-made drains. Randall-MacIver does not address the enigma of so advanced a building technique and he does not choose to acknowledge that they are common to most grand monolithic buildings of Europe and Asia, for without them few of these monuments would still be standing. They are, however, very rare in the Zimbabwe ruins. Even more paradoxical is the comment he makes about the largest of the Inyanga forts: 'It much resembles that which Romans and ancient British marked out for their hill forts in our land.' How can this possibly square with 'There is not a trace of Oriental or European style of any period whatsoever'?

Fortunately we do not need to get bogged down with his inconsistencies at this stage because, faced with a truly extraordinary complex of stone works in these beautiful Inyanga mountains, Randall-MacIver's archaeological training and his sense of wonder reassert themselves. His youthful stamina allows him to make the first extended tour of a great number of stone walls, stepped as terraces, which had been reported in the region but because of their extent and inaccessibility had never been properly explored. Clambering up and over hundreds of walls only a few feet apart, David Randall-MacIver, led by a Major van Niekerk, after whom he named these terrace ruins, eventually achieved the summit of a stepped central peak 4,000 feet above sea level. All around him, for at least fifty miles, the plateaux and the hills were covered with walls. It was not, as he first thought, a formless labyrinth, but a walled ring of nine or ten hills, each constituting a separate unit complete with its own buildings and faced at the bottom from its neighbour by a boundary wall.

David Randall-MacIver was, quite understandably, awe-struck: 'There is scarcely a stone, out of all the unimaginable millions in a tract more than eight miles long and six wide [subsequent exploration would show it to be vastly larger], that has not been handled by a builder.'

Follow-up work by Rhodesian archaeologists would show that this massive complex was a conurbation covering a much larger area than Great Zimbabwe, embodying one of the largest ancient canal irrigation systems on earth. It is still all but unknown to the outside world and in spite of its tourist potential is neglected and, in places, vanishing.

To give him his due, David Randall-MacIver did see the true wonder of the complex, indeed lowered his academic guard enough to record in his monograph, albeit 'as told to me by a visitor': 'There has been as much labour expended here as on the building of the Pyramids, or even more.'

The labyrinth of walls lead uphill to even more intriguing, finely executed 'pit-dwellings'. Randall-MacIver finds both quartz and iron arrow heads in these buildings, sherds of patterned clay pots and a number of what he decides are 'altars'. Most of the hill complexes boasting a pit-dwelling also featured the remains of some six circular walls which he judged to be the wall foundations of once-thatched rondavels. Not a single building in this vast network of residences is in any state of repair, or occupied.

He inspects all this with great care. A typical pit is stone-paved and serviced by an awkward, stone-roofed passage, awkward that is for a full grown male adult of today. The one he measured was just 1.2 metre high and less than ½ metre wide – 'just wide enough for a man to creep though, crouching all the way'.

As previously mentioned the whole of southern Africa prior to the Bantu migration across the Zambesi was thinly populated by what are called 'Boskop-types', the Bushmen and Hottentots, some of whom still hang on in the Kalahari desert fringes. These tough little people would have been quite comfortable with these low, narrow passages; indeed, for hunters who originally used bows and stone-headed arrows, they would have been just about the right height.

David Randall-MacIver proudly records his finds – 'Armlets of heavy bronze, pot sherds, iron arrow heads, and Stone Age implements' – but nowhere does he suggest that these strange households might have been occupied by two races, an elite in the huts above, their subjects below. Was this oversight deliberate, because he knows that the best-loved theory of the Romantics was that the Zimbabwe culture was an elite race who enslaved the locals, working them in the narrow-shafted mines and as builders' labourers? The Romantics refer to these cellars as 'slave pits'.

Randall-MacIver then goes on to find timbers apparently used to bar the passages. These could only be inserted or removed from the outside, however! His own explanation of these enigmatic, portcullised, dungeons verges on the whimsical: 'The pit is distinguished from any of the other areas . . . by the special care and attention bestowed upon the [subterranean] stonework [it has been hardened]. This fact should be enough to prove that it was intended for the owners themselves.' This is surely dubious, as he has previously observed that no provision for light is made in the main pit-room although there is sometimes a light-well into the roofed access corridor.

Did the elite of this obviously affluent mountain kingdom really choose to dwell, or perhaps take refuge, in unlit dungeons after scrambling down passages built deliberately too low for people of their size? It is as ridiculous as the myth that ostriches, confronted by danger, bury their heads in the sand. Surely a more plausible explanation for these strengthened holts is as strongrooms for valuable goods in transit: ivory, slaves, or gold, especially as the Inyanga conurbations appear to span the trade route from the hinterland to the coast.

In the pit-dwellings David Randall-MacIver finds more Stone Age implements alongside Iron Age tools. 'We are confronted,' he records, 'with the curious, but by no means anomalous spectacle of a people who were perfectly familiar with metals and possessing admirably made tools but yet retaining the use of stone implements for the same purpose. It is quite evident that they belong to the same period and [the stone implements] are not more ancient.'

It may not be entirely anomalous but it is entirely possible, and surely more likely, that the different tools were made and used by two groups of people at different stages of social evolution. There is absolutely no viable reason for the advanced people who built this masterly irrigation system to use old-fashioned and less effective tools and weapons, any more than a hunter today would set aside a modern rifle in favour of a blunderbuss.

If Randall-MacIver found Iron Age and Stone Age tools in the same domestic strata I suggest his scientific integrity should have required him to propose a multicultural community for the Inyanga conurbations. And as 'primitive' races are almost invariably subservient to 'advanced' races (especially if they have been invaded and conquered) he should further have suggested that a master and servant, possibly a master and slave, relationship prevailed here. He does not. Archaeologists were not in his day allowed to have opinions on anything as intangible as relationships.

David Randall-MacIver undertakes a carefully stratified excavation of one of the better pit-forts, then makes a quite extraordinary announcement about the evolution of the Inyanga communities. The stratification indicates, he decides, that the most secure, well-built forts are *earlier* than later structures where less attention has been paid to defence. The Inyanga culture, he concludes, grew ever more secure and eventually abandoned its fortress mentality. Loose-knit hut complexes progressively replaced the hilltop pit-forts, firstly without corridors and eventually without cellars.

This seems the wrong progression for a naturally evolving indigenous race. Ancient Britons, for example, first lived in a variety of 'rude' dwellings or, if you prefer, 'loose-knit hut complexes' then, under threat of invasion, enclosed them in high, defensive palisades. In time, successful invaders integrated with the locals and this increasingly indigenous elite built castles with a portcullis and loopholes. The bulk of the peasants – the workforce – still lived rough under the castle walls.

Here in Africa, with no tradition of building in stone, Randall-MacIver would have us believe that medieval Karanga suddenly and spontaneously built castles, regressed to unprotected stone villages and ended up with uninhabited ruins. A model of that scenario which springs to mind is the Roman presence in Britain. Up went the defensive forts and citadels and down they came when the Romans left, leaving the locals to a centuries-long Dark Age. Randall-MacIver cannot afford, of course, to recognise that lesson of history in this context, however, because that is how the Romantics say it happened. So it remains a paradox.

Another paradox he is obliged to sidestep is generated by a question of his own: 'What purpose did the pit itself serve? The only answer that seems to fit the circumstances is that the pit was a refuge whenever the defenders were hard-pressed in siege. The fighting men, of course, would not go there – it would have been a veritable death-trap – but, like some of the modern kaffirs, they thought at once to keep their women in safety. Here in the fort they would be out of reach of flying missiles, and the narrow corridor could be defended by the last man.' This is almost laughable. Is he seriously suggesting that under attack from savage marauders you would force your women to crawl down a narrow passage into an unlit room, then lock them in with a latch that only the marauders can open? If you fail you have literally boxed in your women for delivery to the enemy; indeed, it is exactly the rationale he has advanced for the fighting men not to so trap themselves.

Nonetheless, he labels all this 'of African origin, and evidently akin to the race from which the present inhabitants sprang, for their dwellings show the same fundamental ideas of construction, and many of their implements and articles of daily use are identical with those among the modern inhabitants of the country'. Where he summons all this from is puzzling. Modern Zimbabwe dwellings bear no resemblance, say, to Great Zimbabwe's conical tower. It is in every sense unique.

Thankfully, David Randall-MacIver's sense of wonder now takes over. He trudges up hill upon hill, climbing walls in places just a couple of feet apart: 'Every hill that can be seen from the farthest point here is ringed with walls. Southwards . . . forts and pit-dwellings extend over the whole of the Inyanga for a considerable distance, and the forts at least are found down the road to Rusapi, and in the other direction almost as far as Penhalonga.' He decides that the whole complex was inhabited by a people who must have lived in perpetual apprehension of attack, 'and therefore protected themselves behind one of the vastest series of entrenchment lines to be found anywhere in the world'. Attack from whom?

The fortifications begin to peter out as he goes south. At Umtali no fortifications of any kind are found: 'So there seems to be a regular progression. The northern region nearest the Zambesi is fortified with the most extraordinary minuteness. A little further south, at Inyanga, the rigour of the defensive scheme is a little relaxed; then, at Umtali, the need for fortification seems to have been no longer felt. So it looks as if the enemy against whom these people were defending themselves was in the north, not in the east and south, and the distribution of their buildings suggest the probability that they themselves first settled in the north.'

Here, in fact, he is sharing ground with Romantics, a number of whom have proposed that the Zimbabwe culture evolved from a diffusion of old gold and stone cultures originating in the far north-east. He is, of course, breaking his own rules here because he has found nothing to physically confirm any such northerners. Randall-MacIver has obviously read the eminent Mr Theal's reports – it is the only book he allows as an acceptable reference to the history of these parts – so he also knows that 'old Moors' have reportedly been coming this way for at least a thousand years. Nevertheless, he affirms: 'No single object which can be recognized as foreign, of any period, whether early or late, has been found in the Inyanga ruins; and a chip of glazed stoneware traded there in the Middle Ages is the only foreign object that has been found at Umtali.' *Ergo* – no old Moors were here either.

Elsewhere, in another confusing reference, he acknowledges that the Shona hinterland is 'inexorably interwoven' with the foreign Arab settlements on the coast but warns 'that there is no historical warrant for ascribing any high antiquity to any of these east coast colonies'. This is not true. Among others there are 'historical warrants' to the fifth-century Pharaoh Sahu Ra (*c.* 3000 BC) and Menuhotep III (*c.* 2500 BC) sending ships to the Land of Punt which the consensus opinion locates either in Ethiopia or Somalia. The Turin museum has an Egyptian papyrus map thought to date from 1600 BC showing a gold-mining district in Nubia. Neku II (*c.* 611 BC) is recorded as sending an expedition under the command of Phoenicians to circumnavigate Africa: Herodotus reports that it was successful and we assume it was because in 470 BC Xerxes ordered it repeated. Randall-MacIver knows of these warrants but sets them aside as inadmissible evidence: 'Unaided documentary evidence does not permit us to suppose that there was any oriental traffic even with Sofala, the gate of the old gold bearing regions of the interior.'

He would not, for example, have given any credence to the famous thirteenth-century journals of exploration by Marco Polo, which offer detailed descriptions of how the Arabs navigated the very difficult currents off Madagascar. To be believed, Randall-MacIver insists evidence has to be dug up and confirmed by physical comparison to some authenticated artefact: 'The spade of some fortunate explorer may in the future, bring to light traces of settlements on the east coast just before and after the Mohammedan era, but we have no right to assume their existence until they are found.' He takes his own spade to the terraces and agrees that they are quite extraordinary. Streams had been tapped and directed into conduit ditches by small dams, allowing the water to be carried along the side of the hills. There are many such conduits and they often run for several miles. 'The gradients are admirably calculated, with a skill which is not always equalled by modern engineers with their elaborate instruments.' Randall-MacIver then casually breaks his own house rule banning speculation based solely on comparative evidence by comparing it with a system he has seen in Algeria. Later researchers have observed that the Inyanga layout is all but identical to terraces in the Yemen built by Sabeans.

So did all this 'skill which is not always equalled by modern engineers with their elaborate instruments' somehow spring unaided and spontaneously from the Shona earth? David Randall-MacIver continues to insist it did. If it did, what was it all for? Vastly more food could have been grown on the terraces than was needed to supply the local community. Cecil Rhodes probably supplied the answer to these questions with the thousands of tons of fruit his farms exported from Inyanga. Properly managed, the region can supply the nation with all the deciduous crops it needs. Certainly it did so in my day. Randall-MacIver is not supposed to offer opinions of this nature but faced with these magnificent decayed edifaces he cannot help it. He endorses the opinion of his respected guide: 'There has been as much labour expended here as on the buildings of the Pyramids, or even more.'

Randall-MacIver's first important revelation therefore (although he never lists it as such) is that at the dawn of the Zimbabwe culture a large number of people were engaged in labour so hard that we normally reserve it for criminals. Another large force was employed in the equally tough work of gold mining, which also involved the movement of millions of tons of rock.

All these people would have needed food – lots of food – and there can surely be little doubt that much of that food came from the Inyanga breadbasket, which raises the awkward conundrum of what impelled the people to do such alien work? What was their motivation and what were the imperatives here? No one has ever really dared address this seminal enigma of the Zimbabwe culture. It has too many racial overtones.

The Shona people are cheerful, enthusiastic, obliging, hard-working and exceptionally artistic. They do live, however, in a part of the world where it is very hot for a good part of the year and you do not, without very potent imperatives, choose to shift slabs of granite for a living. Nor is it necessary. Crops grow easily and prolifically here. Even under post-UDI sanctions Rhodesia was self-sufficient in food. There is frankly little point in building stone houses either. The clay from which the people build their rondavels is readily available all over the country and a thatched roof provides a perfectly adequate dwelling which is cool in summer and warm in winter. The clay – called *daga* – can be puddled to a very fine finish and, mixed with cattle dung, forms a hard floor which can be polished.

So what impelled the ancient people of the Zimbabwe culture to break with both ethnic tradition and reason and start transporting and assembling the heaviest of stone for structures of which they had no need? A lot of Rhodesian whites of my peer group and much of the Romantic school assumed it was done under duress, hence the Inyanga *slave* pits. David Randall-MacIver refuses to accept, however, that the people of Inyanga were slaves and he avoids the issue of imperatives. I suspect we may never know the answer to this riddle. Surely so dramatic a shift of work and cultural behaviour is pretty powerful evidence of a country and a population dominated by a powerful elite. This elite has proven skills as water engineers, stone craftsmen, builders and deep gold miners and it runs an administration which is able somehow to oblige the population to engage in unnaturally hard and seemingly pointless labour. These skills are not naturally the attributes of cattle-dependent semi-nomads.

Randall-MacIver found no evidence of an enriched working class. In fact he reported just the opposite: 'many of the implements and articles of daily use are identical with those found amongst the modern inhabitants of the country'; that is, of a poor rural peasantry. The peasants could have worked for food and favours as Dean Bessire has suggested, but again it is hard to see a large population of serfs shifting masses of rock across the centuries for no better reward than their daily bread and the occasional handout. Revolution is a more likely outcome.

If rewards are removed, it seems you are left with two other possibilities. Firstly, that there was a cultural imperative – the population built temples to their gods – and secondly, that the workforce was under duress, if not as slaves then as serfs; people eking out a subsistence existence from the land who were required to pay tribute to the lords of the manors, some of which could have been in the form of labour. This is the preferred Shona school solution to the labour riddle and one which could also go some way to explaining the fortified estates at Inyanga.

The Romantics have a not dissimilar explanation for the Inyanga castles. They say this is where the skilled alien elite first settled after crossing the Zambesi. They propose, with a good number of documentary references to back them, that Mount Darwin, a few miles closer to the Zambesi to the north of Inyanga, was known formerly as Mount Fura, a suggested corruption of Ophir. The only part of this that Randall-MacIver would have agreed with is that the Inyanga settlements are older than Great Zimbabwe and that their northern defensive orientation suggests that these first settlers saw the threat as coming from the north. Perhaps because there was more of their militant kind where they came from?

David Randall-MacIver leaves Inyanga for the bigger *zimbabwes* in the south, pausing briefly to inspect a collection of objects that has been found near the new capital of the eastern region, Umtali. This remarkable hoard comprises copper wire bangles, solid copper bangles, pieces of copper and iron wire, pottery figurines of animals, fragments of earthenware pottery and fragments of foreign stoneware with a sea-green glaze. At the very least it is a milestone to the passage of skilled metal workers, artists, traders and possibly, priests.

On an adjoining hill, where he is told there were many boulders 'on which naturalistic emblems and rude markings had been scratched', more figurines come to light, all of soapstone. The figurines are intriguing for a number of reasons. They are effigies of short-legged people with large heads, which would suggest an origin more associated with the bushmen than the Bantu. They are of soapstone, the chosen material for the Great Zimbabwe birds and the incised stelae, a material seemingly used only at the lost city. They are mostly female and it has therefore been suggested that they are icons of mother-goddesses. (The Romantics see an obvious association with the mother-goddess of ancient Egypt, Hathor, who in the guise of a hawk had special responsibility for the welfare of foreign miners.) They have especially intrigued contemporary Romantics because the larger figurines appear to be wearing space helmets.

Admitting that the figurines are unique and the site is an 'altar', Randall-MacIver nonetheless decides: 'The style of the work is, of course, quite Africa.' This is about the time when I started to lose patience with him. No soapstone figures have been found anywhere in Africa other than at Great Zimbabwe, so where is this all-African precedent drawn from? He completely ignores the report of the boulders 'on which naturalistic emblems and rude markings had been scratched', closing the subject as follows in his monograph: 'Neither here [Great Zimbabwe] nor anywhere else has anything of the nature of an inscription been found.'

The Umtali emblems and markings must have meant something to the people who made them and, given the nature of the other artefacts from the site, it is likely that the marks were of religious significance. Randall-MacIver even acknowledges this when he judges the site to have been 'an altar'.

It is my opinion that the figurines were among the most intriguing artefacts Randall-MacIver would see. Most experts since have agreed with his judgement that this was an altar of sorts; a number suggest that the figurines are pagan Madonnas or fertility charms. The most intriguing question they raise is whether the site was a 'mission' outpost of the Great Zimbabwe sect, or the other way around, a shrine on the road to Great Zimbabwe built by a cult that came *down* the trade route from the north. Was Randall-MacIver the first British archaeologist to examine a rural shrine of the ancient Zimbabwe diaspora? If so, he did not recognise it as such. The Umtali figures were given to the Rhodes Estate who sent them to the British Museum.

Randall-MacIver's first excavation proper is conducted at the Dholo Dholo ruin, one of the grand *zimbabwes* which forms part of the great southern complex. It is a peculiar place to start because these ruins were a favourite of the treasure hunters. Randall-MacIver appears unaware that the clay floors here have actually been washed for gold and other artefacts. He decides that Dholo Dholo is another fortified town. He notes the superior quality of the fine, small, stonework comprising the walls, and the complex decorations on these walls – chessboard, cord, herringbone and particularly beautiful inlaid patterns using serpentine rock.

As the first true archaeologist here he is particularly interested in the floors, which he describes as interlocking platforms of strengthened cement apparently made of powdered gravel rather than clay. He drives a number of trenches through these floors and through an adjoining area which he labels a midden (rubbish heap). He is convinced that the daga platforms once supported huts very similar to those on the platform-roofs of the Inyanga pit-forts. In the midden dig he finds items which excite him most: two large fragments of Nanking china. At last he can date the Zimbabwe culture to the satisfaction of his scientific peers.

He also finds bangles of solid copper, smelted copper, coiled copper wire studded with beads, fragments of tin, the bowl of an iron spoon, fused glass, ivory and glazed beads both plain and coloured. The most enigmatic of these discoveries are Stone Age implements alongside a pair of iron handcuffs, an ornamental silver pin surmounted by a cross, a bangle of twisted gold and enamelled copper wire, fragments of bell-metal (an amalgam of tin and copper) and beads of ivory and shell. In other words, scraps of goods that could have been carried in the pockets of half the trading races of the world, not to mention bushmen (shell beads) and proto-Karanga (ivory beads).

David Randall-MacIver makes a cursory, dismissive examination of this treasure trove and finally concedes an alien presence here. The gold wire coiled in alternate strands with enamelled bronze is 'perhaps the most beautiful thing discovered on the site . . . and it is difficult to suppose that the natives were conversant with the art of enamelling so that this is probably an article of oriental importation'. The glazed porcelain beads are identified as 'Cambray beads'. They are listed in ancient chronicles as popular trade goods and were made at Negapatum in India. But it remains all just medieval trade stuffs. The good item – meat for the archaeologist – is the broken china, because it meets his crucial formula of archaeological probity: 'There is only one means by which the antiquity of the Rhodesian remains may be gauged. This is by comparing them with those of other countries for which the dating is already independently established. The Nanking china is of a style known to be not earlier than the sixteenth century.'

But what is so significant about this? Accounts by contemporary explorers of his time such as the artist Thomas Baines, and Frederick Courtenay Selous, have long since suggested that the exquisite southern *zimbabwes* were major trading entrepots ruled by Rodzvi chiefs (the ill-fated Mombos) until about a century before the arrival of the first white explorers. There is also acceptable documentary evidence of this. Early photographs of Great Zimbabwe which Randall-MacIver must have seen show mature trees with lifespans of hundreds of years growing – indeed overgrowing – the conical tower.

There is even a debate about whether Dholo Dholo, Khami and Nanatali were part of the Great Zimbabwe empire. Subsequent aerial surveys have revealed some 15,000 primitive stone-walled *zimbabwes* running down South Africa as far as Kwazulu-Natal and it has been suggested that these owe their genesis to the spread of craftsmen cultures from the Sotho lands of the south-west among which gold-rich Mapungubwe may be numbered.

I sometimes wonder whether the fuss Randall-MacIver made of those sixteenth-century scraps of china – a storm surely in a broken tea cup – is not to do with the fact that his next dig, the big dig at Great Zimbabwe, is a failure. He finds gold and copper wire, bronze bangles, and glazed copper – but nothing new. These finds, he admits, are not 'of the quality of some which, it is rumoured, have rewarded the search of certain gold-seekers in past days'. What he really means is that treasure hunters beat him to it and he is right.

Randall-MacIver returns to his university and within the year his explosive theory, pivoting on the Nanking shards, is in print. It is summarised in five short paragraphs which sets the debate alight for the next century and will oblige the Rhodes Trustees to have it all re-checked two decades in the future:

> Seven sites have been investigated, and from not one of them has any object been obtained by myself or by others before me which could be shown to be more ancient than the fourteenth or fifteenth century AD.
>
> Not a single inscription has been found in the country.
>
> The imported articles, of which the date is well known in the country of their origin, are contemporary with the Rhodesian buildings in which they are found, and that these buildings are mediaeval or post mediaeval.
>
> That the character of the dwellings contained within the stone ruins and forming an integral part of them is unmistakably African.
>
> That the arts and manufactures exemplified by objects found within these dwellings are typically African, except when the objects are imports of well-known mediaeval or post mediaeval date.

No room for doubt here, so can we now let our enquiry rest? Many did. The Shona school essentially bolted the door and threw away the key.

Thirty years down the road, however, a test is being invented – the Carbon-14 dating method – which will revolutionise archaeology and show David Randall-MacIver's guesses to have been at least a thousand years out.

Also emerging at this time were tales of intrigue and skulduggery, confirming that Randall-MacIver really had missed the boat. The following story is particularly relevant because the ancient artefact it features was authenticated by Randall-MacIver's scientific supervisor, Professor Flinders Petrie.

I came across this story by extraordinary chance. A good friend of ours learned that I had been working in Rhodes' library at Groote

Schuur on original documents of the Shona occupation. She told me that John Rudd, the grandson of the Rudd whose name is now attached to the concession which opened the door to Ophir, ran a farm two hours from Cape Town and let rooms in the old farmhouse. We drove up the following weekend to an idyllic old Cape Dutch mansion set in the golden emptiness of the Great Karoo, the vast neo-desert that fills much of the northern Cape Province. Behind the mansion itself is a tower labelled 'Think Tank'. It was once the house's water tower, today it is John Rudd's library and it is where I was shown, and hastily read, Hans Sauer's *Ex Africa*.

But first, let me remind you of Randall-MacIver's rules of evidence: 'There is only one means by which the antiquity of the Rhodesian remains can be gauged. This is by comparing them with those for which the dating is already independently established.' I assume Sir William Flinders Petrie taught him this.

John Rudd had drawn my attention to a chapter in Sauer's book headed 'The New Conquistadors'. It was the graphic inside story of what had gone on behind the scenes in Rhodesia's frontier days.

Dr Hans Sauer's family was famous in South Africa at the start of the twentieth century and Sauer Street in Johannesburg is still one of its main thoroughfares. J.W. Sauer was Secretary for Native Affairs in Rhodes' Cape administration and his brother Hans was a doctor trained by Sir Joseph Lister at the Edinburgh Medical School. He became a close confidant of Rhodes and eventually a land agent for him.

Hans caught the gold fever of the time and was one of the first to spot the incredibly rich potential of the reefs on what became known as 'the Rand' around Johannesburg. With John Rudd's grandfather, Sauer bought up the land over these reefs and thus secured for Rhodes an even more massive fortune. Sauer got 15 per cent of the return from the diggings and was soon a very rich man in his own right. When Rhodes went in search of what was thought to be an eldorado of similar potential – Ophir – Hans Sauer trekked through Matabele country to see what he could find.

He was among the first of the treasure hunters to visit the Dholo Dholo ruin and his party immediately made extraordinary finds.

These included two cannon, one Portuguese and the other a British naval gun. The pieces now guard the front door to Groote Schuur and I was able to repay something of my debt to the curator there by informing her of how and by whom they were found.

Hans Sauer's companion, Bradley, was examining Dholo Dholo's daga platforms. Sauer wrote: '. . . when he stooped down and picked up an alluvial gold nugget weighing about an ounce. Searching further we all began to find small alluvial gold nuggets. We got our boys to flush the surface with buckets of water, and after washing away the dust and debris we collected about a hundred pounds worth of gold in two hours. The bulk of it was alluvial, but there were a few bits of ancient gold chains. I sent Rhodes most of the gold we had collected in the fort.'

Sauer was understandably secretive about his gold finds but it is what comes next that casts a revealing light on the true nature of the treasure-hunting of the time and how much gold and prized artefacts were removed clandestinely. Or more to the point, how little was left for archaeologists like Randall-MacIver to discover.

Returning to Bulawayo, now a frontier town of gold prospectors, Sauer was approached by two Americans – 'brothers-in-law, of the Western-cowboy type. One of the pair who would not take no for an answer, ultimately proposed to me that if I would tell him where we found the gold, he and his friend would go and explore the locality and would hand over to us one half of any gold or treasure they found.' Cutting this salutary story short, all Sauer ever saw from the deal was a copper axe, but:

The next time I saw Rhodes he told me the following story. When in London the two Americans called upon him at his hotel rather late in the evening. They entered carrying a heavy brown leather bag between them. For some reason or other they seemed anxious not to be recognised by people outside the hotel.

They had the appearance of conspirators with their overcoat collars turned up and their sombreros drawn over their faces. Having extracted a promise from Rhodes that he would not claim what they were about to show him they opened the bag which contained nearly £1,000 worth of alluvial gold, ornaments, beads, chains, bracelets and rings. All this treasure they had found in the ruins of the Insiza district, the bulk coming from the Dholo Dholo temple. They did not, however, tell Rhodes that one half of the treasure belonged to me!

It was from this same *zimbabwe* that Rhodes' licensed treasure hunters, Neal and Johnson, would later take another 700 oz of raw gold, plus gold beads, bangles and other items. As a very rough guide, the Dholo Dholo story indicates that only a fraction of the artefacts removed from the Rhodesian *zimbabwes* was declared or subsequently saw the light of day. Much of the worked gold was almost certainly melted down for ease of shipment and to disguise its origin.

From these same floors Hans Sauer retrieved 'an earthenware bead of a certain colour and shape which I recognised as Egyptian, having seen many similar ones in the museum in Cairo'. This so intrigued him he took it to London:

I showed it to Flinders Petrie, at that time attached to University College [of London] in Gower Street, who at once declared that the bead was of the XII Egyptian dynasty. On my showing signs of disbelief, he took me into a room where I saw a large number of slanting desks, with numerous strings of Egyptian beads stretched over every one of them.

The Professor then asked me to look at the end of the hole which pierced the bead, and examining this carefully, I noticed a small chip. I pointed this out to him, and he asked me to compare the beads on one of the desks which he designated. I found that all the beads on this desk had the chip at the edge of the hole and all resembled mine in size, colour and shape.

Professor Petrie then told me that the chip on my bead was present only in the beads of the XII Egyptian dynasty. The bead had probably been brought into Rhodesia thousands of years ago by Egyptian traders.

Let us assume for the moment that Hans Sauer is not inventing all this. The methodology fits all the archaeological criteria for a proper dating. Flinders Petrie is the top man in his field. His basis of comparison is a university collection of dated artefacts with a distinctive feature. Petrie's dating is not a throwaway remark. He had taken time to examine Sauer's bead and he takes Sauer to his comparative collection and obliges him to witness a singularity in this style of bead – a distinctive chip – that allows a positive identification.

What of Dr Sauer's motivation? He was an educated man from an important political family. As a medical practitioner his veracity and personal reputation were particularly important to him. He was a rich, well-known collector of African artefacts who never attempted to hide what he found on his trips to several *zimbabwes*; in fact, the 'Conquistadors' chapter in his book is devoted to describing such finds. His book enjoyed a wide international readership.

It is frankly inconceivable that Dr Sauer would have invented so detailed a story. He had absolutely nothing to gain and much to lose, not least his and Flinders Petrie's reputations; indeed, Petrie could have sued if the story was false. There are no rational grounds for disbelieving him. Reason demands, therefore, our acceptance of the fact that an identifiable artefact infinitely older than David Randall-MacIver's Nanking porcelain was found at this most affluent of *zimbabwes*. This would make it the oldest identifiable alien article ever found at any *zimbabwe*. There are also those beads from Mapungubwe which now enjoy a modern classification as the work of ancient Egyptians. If Sauer's bead was indeed Pharaoan Egyptian this story may have come full circle. We could be back in the time of Solomon and Sheba. At very least we are back to a time when the trade goods of the caravans of the old Moors included beads made well before the birth of Christ.

David Randall-MacIver would not, of course, have subscribed to this, although I must confess to wondering whether he would have changed his mind had he known the story and Professor Flinders Petrie's role in it. I am assuming he did not know because he would surely not have chosen to excavate at Dholo Dholo – indeed, base a dating of the Zimbabwe culture from artefacts found there – if he had known how extensively the treasure hunters had done the place over, Dr Sauer's party in particular. All in all, Randall-MacIver's monograph gives the impression of being a rushed job based, as he admits, on sites largely stripped of the materials he really needed. For the Shona school to regard it as their main plank of evidence in support of a stand-alone Karanga origin is, in my opinion, unsafe.

Randall-MacIver's work essentially adds nothing new to our enquiry because, while he affirms emphatically that the lost city is 'typically African', he says nothing about the origins of these Africans and their ancestral heritage. With hindsight I would even question that 'typically African' label. Virtually every corner of Africa has been explored since Randall-MacIver's time and nothing resembling my lost city (that is not probably part of the Zimbabwe culture) has been found. Great Zimbabwe is not typical of anything. It is unique.

But David Randall-MacIver did at least leave us with one new place to look. His work in Inyanga is, I think, the best and certainly the most revelatory. He observes, you will recall, that the Inyanga forts became less defensive in structure the further south of the Zambesi you go: 'It looks as if the enemy against whom these people were defending themselves was in the north, not in the east or south, and the distribution of their buildings suggests the probability that they themselves first settled in the north, and later extended their range. . . . It was therefore, a Negro or Negroid race of Africans, coming I do not know from what quarter, but possibly north of the Zambesi, who made these buildings.'

I have no problem with that; in fact it puts us right back on track.

EIGHT

Ophir Spinning

Far from resolving the origin debate as the Rhodes Trustees had hoped, David Randall-MacIver's dramatic conclusions provoked a decade of acrimonious debate. Battle lines were drawn, many of which are still in place today. Admittedly, Randall-MacIver had rubbed salt into long-open wounds by promoting his theory of a medieval lost city with almost evangelical arrogance.

'Many no doubt will bewail that a romance has been destroyed,' he lectured an audience in Bulawayo. 'But surely it is a prosaic mind that sees no romance in the partial opening of a new chapter in the history of vanished cultures. A corner is lifted on that veil which has shrouded the forgotten but not irrecoverable past of the African Negro. Were I a Rhodesian I should feel that in studying the contemporary natives in order to unravel the story of the ruins, I had a task as romantic as any student could desire. I should feel that in studying the ruins in order thereby to gain a knowledge of the modern races, I had an interest that the politicians should support and that the scholar must envy.'

This, in a country which had just bloodily suppressed the local Negroes, was either outrageously naïve or outrageously provocative. I suspect the latter.

Public meetings were called by Richard Nicklin Hall and his supporters to condemn David Randall-MacIver as an upstart whippersnapper, and a number of European academics supported this view simply on the limited time Randall-MacIver had spent on his excavations. At the same time Hall began a massive tome of rebuttal entitled *Prehistoric Rhodesia*.

Most damningly, Hall was also able to call into question Randall-MacIver's scientific process, showing it to be self-serving and

160

careless in key areas. Hall claimed straight away, quoting his excellent field records, that Randall-MacIver's most important archaeological stratifications of a trench, for which he claimed an unbroken progression from the present to the most ancient past, was not a pristine site. Hall (as Garlake confirmed with a new dig in 1958) had already removed several feet of deposits from the top of it. Hall in fact enjoyed the support of almost the entire South African historical establishment and a number of senior European academics. At least three other learned treatises all proposing a different authorship for the Zimbabwe culture to Randall-MacIver's were in preparation at this time.

What is most intriguing, however, is that the smoke and fire of this dispute seems to have disguised the fact that none of David Randall-MacIver's findings, or the conclusions of Richard Hall, added anything very revealing to the real origin debate. By that I mean the earliest beginnings of a stone-building phenomenon that has no precedent anywhere in south-central Africa was (and frankly, is still) a mystery to contemporary south-central Africans.

The Romantic and the Shona schools of thought had got stuck trying to date the grand *zimbabwes* – the jewels of what was, by the time they were all up, a highly developed Zimbabwe culture funded by a sophisticated gold industry. Hall had settled for his Phoenicians in league with King Solomon, although he had not a shred of hard evidence to support this idea of a large Semite occupation. Randall-MacIver believed the oldest remains in the country 'appear to be those of the northern district between Inyanga and the Zambesi' and on the strength of another piece of stoneware found near Umtali, affirms that the 'site may be considered to belong to the fifteenth century'.

Great Zimbabwe, he insists, is later (early sixteenth century) and the *earliest possible date* (his emphasis) is two centuries before this. His evidence is that Sofala, on the east coast, was at this time a flourishing port inhabited by a colony of Arabs who traded with the interior for gold: 'As Zimbabwe, being the great distribution centre, must have owed its very existence to the trade with the coast first opened up by the Arabs of Magadoxo, the *earliest possible date* for *any* settlement there [Zimbabwe] is the eleventh century AD.'

This method of dating the genesis of the very first stone structures is dubious. Arab settlements on the coast – even the earliest ones like that of Magadoxo – would only have become 'settlements' once trade with the hinterland had become reliable and sustainable. It takes hundreds, sometimes thousands, of years for settlements to grow into stone cities devoted to trade. So an eleventh-century Magadoxo or a 'flourishing' port at Sofala in the fifteenth century actually dates the *start* of the trade that created and sustained them to a much earlier period.

We are anyway not primarily concerned with the Arabs, Negroes and Swahilis who serviced the Zimbabwe/Magadoxo/Sofala trade between the eleventh and fifteenth centuries. I am now looking for the traders or tribes (or both) who first found gold and other valuable trade goods in the Shona hinterland and who built the very first stone enclosures for their cattle, or as protection for their camps and caravans. These are the original founders of the Zimbabwe culture. Romantic guesses about a Phoenician occupation certainly do not take us back as far as we need to go and Randall-MacIver's ruminations based on imported ceramics from a time when Great Zimbabwe was already a mighty monument are of even less help.

Even though they did not realise it (or admit to it), Hall and Randall-MacIver actually had a belief in common which should have caused them to recognise that the gold trade and the building of the grand *zimbabwes* had different evolutionary histories. They both believed the best buildings were built after invasions, albeit different invasions. In other words the construction of many of the best buildings had not been as a result of 'natural gradual evolution' but the other way around.

This could not have been the way it was with the gold trade. Nobody really disputes that it started before the arrival of the Bantu, with bushmen trading alluvial gold. It then went through major technological change from this alluvial gold-collecting industry based on barter, to deep-reef mining in long runs of deep shafts. There was also an associated gold-processing industry manufacturing gold bars and cast ingots, jewellery and art objects like the Mapungubwe rhino.

But neither Randall-MacIver nor Hall believed that the Zimbabwe culture's better buildings were the product of a similar slow evolution of style and craftsmanship. Hall visualised an invasion by Phoenicians who enslaved the natives to put up the grand *zimbabwes*. The society then became decadent and the quality of building declined. Randall-MacIver believed in an invasion across the Zambesi by Bantu from the north-east. Their best buildings – strong hill forts with fortified cellars – were the first to go up, 'protected behind one of the vastest series of entrenchment lines to be found anywhere in the world'. Later Inyanga buildings were inferior as the culture grew more secure.

Essentially, whether you believe either of them or not, Hall and Randall-MacIver are both saying that invaders *imported* the necessary skills. That for me is perhaps the most important thing the pair of them have to say; indeed, Hall may well have identified the genesis of the gold trade, Randall-MacIver the stone-builders. I am probably the first to suggest that both Richard Nicklin Hall and David Randall-MacIver, in this sense, did sterling work. All that has been remembered of their relationship, though, is the row, and it just went on and on. Even so it would be another twenty years before the Rhodes Trustees recognised that Randall-MacIver had not put the ghosts of the lost city to rest and that they needed to try again.

In 1929 they appointed Gertrude Caton-Thompson, another Oxbridge archaeologist who had also learned her trade under Flinders Petrie. Again a member of the British Association for the Advancement of Science, she dug more thoroughly than any of her predecessors, on nine ruin sites. I have no wish to denigrate Ms Caton-Thompson's work by giving it short shrift here; indeed, I am advised that it was an exemplary piece of early twentieth-century archaeology. But sadly she has little of a revelatory nature to add to our tale as she and David Randall-MacIver were to be contradicted in a decade or so on the crucial issue of dates by the new techniques of Carbon-14 dating.

Caton-Thompson dug an interesting trench under the conical tower, proving it was solid. This enigmatic tower evidently attracted her and she allowed a comparison with a minaret at Zanzibar, thought to be ancient, which also had a double chevron pattern built into its walls. Otherwise she largely supported Randall-MacIver's datings and his theories of how the people who did the work at Great Zimbabwe were housed. Like him she also avoided speculation on enigmas such as the stone birds. Indeed, she avoided speculation on any of the enigmas, which, as a result, left the issue of authorship somewhat more of a puzzle than it had been before.

Her final report included this apparently definitive comment on the key issue of authorship of the Zimbabwe culture and its buildings: 'If by indigenous we mean an origin born of the country on which they stand, then the ruins are in my opinion, indigenous in the full sense of the term.' The Shona school claimed this with glee, reading it as proof positive that the Zimbabwe culture was entirely of their making.

Take a close look at her phraseology, however, and you find that it might not mean that. Is Gertrude Caton-Thompson in fact covertly questioning an 'indigenous' Bantu origin? Personally I am convinced that she chose to be ambivalent. 'Born of the country on which they stand', is an odd phrase by any definition, but is obviously carefully chosen. Caton-Thompson was well aware of the history of the region and of the long-term influence of aliens like 'ancient Moors' who by medieval times could have been permanently resident, not to say integrated. Born of the country on which they stand, in fact.

Moreover, Caton-Thompson uses this peculiar phrase to answer the key question she has been sent in to resolve when she could very easily have made a simple, unequivocal answer such as: these monuments are the spontaneous, unassisted work of the Karanga cattle-herders who lived here. I think there is significance in her avoiding this plain answer if only because I can see no other rationale for her conditional answer. Was she really trying to suggest: we have no idea of the composition or the antecedents of the elite who created the Zimbabwe culture but whoever they were, they, not invading aliens, built these extraordinary buildings. Given that the rest of her report so closely reflected David Randall-MacIver's, was she in fact carefully choosing her own words to echo his evasive answer to this point: 'As to which particular tribe of Negroes erected the buildings I make no suggestion'? In the light of all this ambivalence I find it very surprising that Gertrude Caton-Thompson and her meticulous, encyclopaedic report, at least so far as academic opinion was concerned, closed the case.

Hereafter, the monuments were known as the 'Zimbabwe ruins', which is how they were referred to throughout my time in Rhodesia. Rather than an exotic antique connecting at least two cultures and linking Great Zimbabwe to ancient golden ages, it was henceforth simply the neglected evidence of a decayed black kingdom. And it is hard to convey how quickly public interest worldwide fell away in the wake of the Caton-Thompson report.

The concrete arc of the Mazoe Dam which the colonialists built over a river I now know to be the conduit for a vast treasure in gold was then at least as big a tourist attraction as these native ruins and certainly better publicised. No school party from Churchill High School, where I was a founder pupil, ever bussed down to Fort Victoria to see the largest stone temple-city south of the Valley of the Kings. So far as I know, no black school parties went there either. This is the real tragedy of the lost city. Not a day has passed since I have been involved with this project without some intelligent person admitting that they have never heard of the place. Perhaps one in a thousand, and this includes people with some knowledge of Africa, have even an inkling that Great Zimbabwe is the largest stone monument south of the Pyramids or that there are several thousand *zimbabwes*. An extraordinary international cultural attraction that Zimbabwe can patently ill-afford to lose has vanished almost as effectively as Atlantis.

But how do you lose the Incas or the Aztecs? Time has shown, I believe, that these early archaeologists, blinkered by scientific disciplines which have been relaxed a great deal since their time, failed to recognise that there are two seminal issues to be addressed here, not just the dates of the grand *zimbabwes*. To define the Zimbabwe culture we also need to know: (1) The origins and make-up of the original Bantu settlers; and (2) The elements that evolved into the Zimbabwe culture. These questions address the most intransigent of the riddles: how and from where did the natives acquire the know-how, the design skills, the decorative patterns, the architectural mathematics, measuring and levelling instruments and the business acumen to pay for the movement of tens of millions of tonnes of well-shaped tiles of granite? Moreover, if any one of these was alien in origin then the prevailing theory of authorship has to be rewritten and Great Zimbabwe and the Zimbabwe culture has to be accorded a very much more exotic history than it has been credited with for the last half-century.

On the information we have at the moment there is actually no justification for rejecting the idea that these were King Solomon's mines, and even the most sceptical of the archaeologists has never questioned that Great Zimbabwe was a temple of sorts. They have also largely sidestepped the question: a temple to whom? That said, I am not intending to lose our way in the Romantic mists of Carl Mauch's erotic theories. The pioneer archaeologists, especially Ms Caton-Thompson, have at least given us an idea of where to look for the founders of the Zimbabwe culture.

Mauch's idea that the actual Queen of Sheba built a temple at Great Zimbabwe can, I think, now safely be set aside. If Sheba's biblical trip to Africa is, however, apocryphal like so many other Bible stories, it is not yet safe to dismiss the possibility that the first itinerant traders here could have worshipped Sabaean gods and, when the gold trade was at its most lucrative, directed the building of a temple. They at least would have known how. The pivotal question now is not whether there was alien influence, but how much and how early did it come into play. Admittedly this has to be speculation, but there is no way forward (or more importantly, backward) if you deny, as the Shona school largely continues to do, the impact of material alien influence. The dramatic waning of interest by the international scientific community (and the tourist trade) which has caused Great Zimbabwe to remain all but 'lost' for the last century is in my opinion a direct result of this door being wrongly closed.

After Gertrude Caton-Thompson appeared to swing it shut, the lost city could only attract the attentions of poorly funded local enthusiasts either directly or peripherally connected to a body called the Rhodesian Historical Monuments Commission. Its brief was about the preservation and – where damage was hazardous – also the restoration of the *zimbabwes*. Few of these zealous enthusiasts were academically trained; indeed, one of the most active, K.S. Robinson, who would become Inspector of Monuments the year I arrived, was self-taught. Largely unsung and perhaps with the exception of some of the 'restoration', they all did an excellent job. Dr Roger Summers, who after training in the archaeology school of the University of London was Secretary, later Chairman, of the Historical Monuments Commission from 1950 to 1967 and from his post at the National Museum, Bulawayo, gave energetic leadership to this disparate crew. And in the end their work was distinctive and unique because of a sensational American invention – a technique for dating carbon based on its residual radioactivity. More of that in a moment.

Summers wrote what I regard as the best general primer on the *zimbabwes, Ancient Ruins and Vanished Civilisations of Southern Africa*, that sadly, like all others with the exception of Hall's, is long out of print. Robinson did a particularly useful stratification of part of the Western Enclosure on Zimbabwe hill. Hall had already removed 5 feet of deposits in 1903. Much of the remainder had been shovelled out by the Public Works Department in 1915, fearing wall damage.

Robinson started to dig at an undisturbed point where the remains of a 'modern' circular hut protruded and in the fabric of which he unearthed sherds of pots with well-defined necks and graphited interiors. Beneath this were 8 feet of daga flooring, the floors and disintegrated superstructures of successive huts which appeared once to have been of better construction than the 'modern' remains. Several hundred beads were found and a carbonised wooden pole which gave a Carbon-14 dating of AD 1440, ± 150 years or so. Archaeologists were delighted that this date supported the guesses of their learned predecessors, although they recognised that they were dating huts, not the grand *zimbabwes*. At levels below this Robinson found more burned pole-impressed daga flooring and another carbonised pole which gave a dating of AD 1075, ± 150 years.

Randall-MacIver, you will recall, avowed that the Zimbabwe culture could not possibly be older than the eleventh century. Robinson soon realised that several layers of daga floors lay below his eleventh-century pole. Three more trenches were dug which indicated that daga flooring had once covered the whole enclosure. In what he thought was a midden between base-rock boulders, Robinson found the remains of a further 77 vessels, 29 of which were the same as in the level above. He retrieved 42 beads similar to those found elsewhere, plus a handful of beautiful beads of translucent greyish-green glass with snapped ends. These were definitely alien.

The find which excited the most interest was a number of pottery figurines in this lowest level: animals, phalli, long-horned cattle and humans, plus the remains of thirty-four pottery vessels decorated with stamped impressions, which could be attributed to a well-known Iron Age tradition. If these pottery figures are religious artefacts of a kind – and the consensus opinion is that they are – then they are pointers to an embryonic 'culture' in the making at Great Zimbabwe from much earlier times than had previously been contemplated. This was apparently confirmed by another carbonised wood sample found below the midden on natural earth. It carbon-dated to AD 320, ± 150 years, which takes us back to the early Christian era, a thousand years earlier than any of the early archaeologists had dared suggest. The crucial element here is, however, that it seemingly dates the remains of a *settlement*. It was, moreover, a settlement of quality huts (rather than nomadic bivouacs), whose occupants knew how to fashion ornamented ceramics and icons for their religious practices.

Settlements of that complexity certainly do not arise overnight. We have no way of knowing when the very first walls rose round this settlement or indeed when it was first occupied but it is not unreasonable at least to wonder if its roots were not established well before the start of the Christian millennium. And when did people first stop and trade here? No one has seriously asked that question since Carl Mauch; indeed, it may well be a question – the key question – which is beyond the skills of archaeology to answer, because these founders left all but nothing for the archaeologist to work with.

Robinson's dig provided for the first time a complete stratigraphic map of a Great Zimbabwe settlement from its Iron Age beginnings through to the golden age of mighty stone monuments. In spite of the new and paradoxical carbon datings, however, these local workers chose in the main to follow the party line of their academic predecessors at eminent British universities.

In 1973, the Historical Monuments Commission's Chief Inspector of Monuments from 1964 to 1970, Peter Garlake, wrote a much-admired 'definitive' treatise entitled *Great Zimbabwe* (Thames & Hudson) which assessed Robinson's findings, asserting unequivocally that the Rhodesian research supported the conclusions of Caton-Thompson and Randall-MacIver. From the moment I opened the pages of Garlake's book I experienced a sense of unease, triggered in particular by this sentence where he comes to the defence of his fellow-archaeologist, David Randall-MacIver: 'Randall-MacIver's approach had been faultless, his excavations careful, and his assessment of the basic culture of the occupants of Great Zimbabwe unassailable.' That is very debatable. Randall-MacIver's approach had been hurried, and even Garlake goes on to admit that his dating evidence came from the stratification of a trench from which Hall had earlier removed several layers of deposits. Does this constitute careful excavation and unassailable assessment?

My heart sank further when I read the book's introduction by the eminent British archaeologist, Sir Mortimer Wheeler: 'I welcome this book as a comprehensive and probably final account of Great Zimbabwe as we can now recover it from the depredations of half a century of largely (though not entirely) untutored curiosity.' Oh dear. Not another final account to keep the untutored curious at bay and the lost city safe for archaeology. Not only that, but the *definitive* book which, I have to say, it has remained to this day.

But Garlake's book is doubly fascinating. It contains many new revelations, not only because archaeology, post-1949, has been revolutionised by the Carbon-14 dating technique, but also because it is the first true piece of propaganda reflecting the new political relevance of Great Zimbabwe in a country about to dissolve into internal racial war. For the moment, however, we need to go back to that epoch-making by-product of an earlier war, atomic fusion, and consider how much credence can be placed on this Carbon-14 method of dating.

Ordinary wood, or charcoal, contains a known portion of radioactive carbon (Carbon-14). The radioactivity decays at a known rate from the time the wood ceases to live so its age can be calculated by measuring the amount of extant radioactivity. The technique has a margin of error, a 'standard deviation' averaging ± 100 years. There is also the problem that the level fluctuates. We now know that there were fluctuations after AD 1100, and between AD 1400 and 1800 they were quite violent.

Robinson went on to find another paradoxical piece of ancient wood, this time actually under a massive wall in the Elliptical Building at Great Zimbabwe – the lintels of a drain in fact. This unquestionably had to be an item of building material from the golden age of the monuments – the wall would probably not have still been there without it. Or if we stay loyal to Caton-Thompson and Randall-MacIver, it had to be of the fourteenth century or later.

Robinson's timber was local *ubande* (*Spirostachys africanus*), probably the same as Mauch took for cedar and caused him to speculate about cedars of Lebanon, and Solomon and Sheba. The younger of the two timber samples dated AD 700 ± 95, the older AD 590 ± 120. That makes it possibly as old as AD 470, and that is all but a thousand years earlier than the scientific guesses. Let us also not forget that this is a relic from the great days of monument-raising, not a burned hut pole from the Zimbabwe culture's founding time.

More dramatically, the lintels are earlier than some expert opinion believed the Bantu entered the country. The implications of this particular point electrified everyone, not least Peter Garlake, who immediately engaged in damage control on behalf of the archaeological establishment. He proposed: 'These dates (for the *ubande*) were earlier than both MacIver and Caton-Thompson's estimates of the building's age but they did not in fact date the building. They only showed that the wall must have been constructed at some indefinite time after the fifth century. *Spirostachys* is a tree which lives for up to 500 years so if the samples were taken from the heart of the tree then the radiocarbon dates could be that much earlier than the dates the poles were cut.'

Garlake also suggests that the poles could have been reused from earlier buildings. This is pure supposition. He has no way of knowing whether the wood was old or new, or recycled, and by the rules of his trade, adjusting findings speculatively is disallowed. Garlake would further have us believe that skilled ancient carpenters went hunting for the oldest *ubande* in living memory. My information and experience is that very few live anything like 500 years, especially in an area where good wood would have been in great demand for buildings and as a cooking fuel. Is it at all reasonable to suggest that masons about to build Great Zimbabwe's most spectacular wall would have chosen a truly ancient tree or recycled a piece of old timber?

At no time does Peter Garlake even contemplate that the dating could be correct and there were carpenters/masons here long before anyone previously suspected, craftsmen experienced in the construction of massive dry-stone walls, on level foundations, properly battered and with efficient drains. These drains would, of course, have needed to be calculated for flow and structural stress before the stonework commenced. The walls above the drain rise 10 metres.

Why is this avenue of possibility not pursued? Presumably because the dating conflicts with the accepted archaeology and plays into the hands of the Romantics. Instead, Garlake focuses on the extensive pottery finds and decides they demonstrate 'a gradual internal evolutionary process within a single tradition', ending at Great Zimbabwe with 'luxurious glazed ceramics'. There is, he admits, 'a single abrupt change' around AD 1000. Garlake also concedes that one of the designs – guilloche – is foreign and 'a pattern probably too complex to have been developed independently by a people with apparently no tradition of arabesque design'. He gets round this by suggesting that the pattern could have been copied from an imported article with guilloche decoration. Imported by whom, and when?

A similar strange defence is mounted to explain Chief Mugabe's ignorance of ancestors who slowly evolved a great culture: 'The invasion [of Zimbabwe hill] of an unimportant Karanga chief finally disrupted a continuous historical tradition that can be traced back through the Rodzwi, the Tora, Mwene Mutapa and Mbire to the foundations of Great Zimbabwe. Mugabe's incomprehension of the history, significance or purposes of the buildings allowed him to turn them into cattle kraals and use many of the stones to build the rough walls that block and divide several enclosures.' Garlake adds this rider, giving the first hint that other – political – currents are running beneath the surface here: 'The same ignorance eventually fortified white questioners in their mistaken beliefs that the indigenous people had nothing to do with the building of Great Zimbabwe.' For a man of liberal tendencies who is doing his best to support the Shona school of origin this is a most patronising description of a Karanga chief.

One cannot propose a case for a continuous cultural evolution by Mugabe's ancestors, then reject the chief's testimony because he does not fit into this scheme of things or have any recollection of it. Chief Mugabe would have worshipped his ancestors as much as most Shona do and his ancestors would have been revered in oral tradition. The right conclusion here is surely that Mugabe's people had no oral traditions of elite ancestors. Why? Perhaps the only reasonable answer is because they had gone elsewhere or 'died out' too long ago even for Chief Mugabe's ancestors to have remembered them.

Garlake is maligning the 'white questioners' as well. I know of no 'white questioner' (with the possible exception of Richard Hall) who has said that the indigenous people had nothing to do with the building of Great Zimbabwe. Who gathered up those millions of tons of stone; indeed, who raised them? It is the level and the nature of indigenous involvement in the conception and the sophistication of the construction that has been questioned.

To resist, as Garlake does, the very idea of alien influence seems to me to create an artificial barrier to discovery. In fact the only 'gradual internal evolutionary process' at Great Zimbabwe for which we have incontrovertible evidence in the form of artefacts is trade with aliens. Remember that the point of all this is that Garlake's *Great Zimbabwe*, endorsed by Sir Mortimer Wheeler, is still widely regarded as the defining text on the Zimbabwe culture. Nothing remotely as comprehensive has been published in the thirty years since it appeared. It still has pride of place in Zimbabwe academic establishments.

Imagine my surprise, therefore, when I found proof that Garlake was also laundering his evidence to support his case. He quotes Rhodes' scout, Frederick Courtenay Selous, in support of his theory of an entirely indigenous origin: 'Selous was a man who had spent many years travelling throughout Mashonaland and who, because of an unparalleled knowledge of the country and the people, had been employed to guide the B.S.A. Co's occupation forces into the country. He consistently said he knew no reasons of organisation, skill, technology or opportunity, why the Karanga should not have built Great Zimbabwe.' Does this not give the impression that Selous, who was probably the most expert observer we have, supported the indigenous Bantu theory of origin?

I had done quite a lot of work on Selous by the time I read *Great Zimbabwe*, being fortunate enough to have access to a first edition of his wonderful *Travels and Adventures in South Central Africa* through the Travellers Club in London. I was, however, at that time studying Garlake from a first edition found in Cape Town. Where might I find another first edition of Selous's book? It occurred to me that Rhodes was certain to have acquired a first edition of his scout's famous journal and a quick call to Groote Schuur produced not just a confirmation but another invitation to work in Rhodes' library.

Here is what Selous actually said about the Karanga and the Zimbabwe culture:

Let us suppose, then, that two or perhaps three thousand years ago a commercial people penetrated from Southern Arabia to Mashonaland. They were acquainted with the requirements of the civilised nations of Asia at that period and understood the value of gold. This metal they discovered amongst the hills and the streams of Mashonaland.

In time these Arabian merchants gained a footing in the land and taught the black aborigines to mine for them. Their principal station was at Zimbabwi, where they built with the forced labour of the aborigines, a temple for the worship of Baal and a strongly built and well-situated fortress.

But I take it that, like the Arabs in Central Africa at the present day, these ancient Arabians brought few or no women with them, but took a very handsome allowance of wives from amongst the aboriginal blacks.

For a long period intercourse was kept up with Arabia, and during this period the gold seekers spread over the whole of south-eastern Africa from the Zambesi to the Limpopo, everywhere mixing with the people and teaching them their own rude arts of wall-building and gold-mining.

In course of time we will suppose that events happened in Arabia which put an end to all the intercourse with the distant colony in Mashonaland, and as time went on, as the alien race were still in small numbers compared with the aboriginal blacks, and as they had none of their own women with them, they gradually became completely fused and nationally lost amongst the aborigines . . . at any rate I am absolutely convinced that the blood of the ancient builders of Zimbabwe still runs (in a very diluted form, if you like) in the veins of the Bantu races, and more especially so among the Barotosi of the Upper Zambesi, who are, there is little doubt, a branch of the Barotsi tribe who were destroyed by the Matibili in Mashonaland, though the separation took place long prior to this event.

I make this suggestion after much thought, a study of the relics unearthed at Zimbabwe, and a knowledge of the natives of South-Eastern Africa gained during many years of travel.

Selous is actually the star witness for the school of alien influence – very ancient influence – not as Garlake implies, the other way around! Or am I doing Garlake an injustice? Did he secretly believe – he certainly never admits to it – that the Karanga were a mixed race descended in part from the ancient Moors?

Then another bizarre thought crossed my mind. With so much evidence to suggest that there had been alien influence, why was Garlake trying to hold a line he was frankly too intelligent to have believed in so absolutely? Were other forces at work? I have no particular axe to grind with Peter Garlake because as we will see in a moment he did have other reasons for being parsimonious with the truth. Nor am I that qualified to question his presentation of what is undoubtedly the most powerful case ever put for a spontaneous Karanga authorship of Great Zimbabwe. Garlake had by then, however, attracted stern criticism from a number of academics who were suitably qualified.

'In order to escape from the conclusive Carbon-14 evidence,' says Professor Gayre of Edinburgh, 'those among the later archaeologists who have constituted themselves the exponents of the pro-Bantu school have been forced to ludicrous shifts to explain the evidence away.' He turns his attention on the two pieces of wood supporting the drain. The Carbon-14 dates are, you will recall, AD 615 and AD 727 with a margin of about 100 years. 'We are therefore justified in taking the average date as between AD 615 and AD 727 which gives us AD 671 as the approximate date for the erections of which they were a part. . . . The timber was taken from that part of Zimbabwe where the quality of the stone and craftsmanship is of the best. . . . We are, because of this, forced to conclude that the seventh century AD is about the central point in time when the most advanced and skilled builders were at work. Basing his estimates on W.T. Libby [the American who did the Carbon-14 tests], Professor R.A. Dart gives terminal dates of AD 377 and AD 941.'

Professor Gayre accuses Garlake of a 'complete misrepresentation of the evidence to fit a Bantu-origin theory', and reminds Garlake of graves at a *zimbabwe* near the Zambesi river which Garlake himself had admitted are 'not African', yet have been positively dated from

AD 680 to AD 800–900. These human remains were buried with, or wearing, fine pottery, gold and ivory ornaments. Gayle fulminates:

Here we have a whole jumble of unproven, and in some cases disproved, assumptions, all designed to maintain the myth of Bantu origins. There is no evidence that the Bantu had settled in large numbers in Rhodesia at this time . . . any stray Negroids can be explained by the possibility of scattered and small settlements having been established from the Congo to the coast in the Zambesi valley. But such Negroids were not the occupants of the land, which at this time was in the hands of the Cappoid Bushmen and Hottentots. Therefore the erection of Zimbabwe, as established by Carbon-14 dating, is prior to the large-scale arrival of the Negroid-Bantu in Rhodesia.

Peter Garlake, surprisingly, survived this hot debate. No one seems to have noticed his manipulation of Selous's testimony. His boss, the long-serving Dr Roger Summers, while remaining a card-carrying member of the Shona school, had admittedly started to question some enigmatic features of the building techniques at Great Zimbabwe, but these were never voiced loudly enough to prevent Garlake's thesis becoming the contemporary theory of the Zimbabwe culture that the archaeologists and the Shona most liked.

Here then is a summary of his view of the Karanga Zimbabwe culture:

EARLY IRON AGE

A period when the Karanga ancestors lived in huts in the rocks and raised cattle and grain. In the west there was a separate culture called the Leopard Rock people. The Zimbabwe culture may have been an offshoot of it.

TWELFTH TO THIRTEENTH CENTURY AD

Pottery shows a 'single abrupt change'. Early walls of poor quality are built, also improved solid-daga walled huts. A Karanga elite begins to emerge. The early wall on the hill may have initially been for defence, later for show/status. Religion, bringing cohesion, develops.

FOURTEENTH TO FIFTEENTH CENTURY

Great Zimbabwe mostly built. The Leopard Rock people flourish on the gold trade. Entrepot towns grow on the east coast. Valley settlements expand, work gold, copper, bronze, and engage in spinning and weaving. Eastern ceramics are imported as are glass beads. Great outer wall built. Extensive trade ensues with communities like the Ingombe Ilede in the north-west and on the Zambesi; 'Swahili' middlemen run this trade. The period sees the growth of provincial centres with populations of between 1,000 and 2,500 adults. Trained (Bantu) masons travel to the provincial sites and undertake the building.

EARLY FIFTEENTH CENTURY

Building at Great Zimbabwe climaxes with the construction of the temple, the tower, platforms and monoliths. The Western Enclosure acquires special sanctity, evidenced by soapstone artistry.

MID-FIFTEENTH CENTURY

The social structure is a rich elite ruling country peasants. The Zimbabwe culture starts to lose control of the provinces and its population uses up too many resources. The Ingombe Ilede prosper through direct access to the Zambesi river. Shortage of salt obliges Karanga King Mutota to move north where the Mwene Mutapa empire is founded. The Mazoe river, a tributary of the Zambesi, may still have been controlled by Mutota. Mwene Mutapa gains control of trade, particularly gold, and overuns the Ingombe Ilede.

SIXTEENTH, SEVENTEENTH AND EIGHTEENTH CENTURIES

Mwene Mutapa kingdom is short-lived and by the end of the century is gone. Great Zimbabwe is now the provincial residence of

Mweni Mutapa's wives. The southern Rozwi kingdom arises from breakaway southern provinces, ruling in the south from their own stone courts. It continues to flourish until the eighteenth century, trading by then with the Portuguese.

NINETEENTH CENTURY

In the 1830s these southern provinces are invaded by a series of Ngoni armies from the south and the Rodzwi suffer defeat and destruction so complete that the only material evidence of their former greatness is their ruined stone buildings.

My view of all this is that had Peter Garlake simply allowed the possibility that the grand *zimbabwes* had enjoyed foreign input I would have had no argument with an otherwise scholarly thesis. Similarly, I would expect him at least to allow for the idea that 'old Moors' had sought gold in these parts, possibly for thousands of years.

But Garlake will have none of that and, in spite of hundreds of contradictory alien artefacts, prefers to keep his theory of a home-grown Karanga craft-culture pristine. In my view that reduces the thesis to a politically inspired myth. It also places it outside the real origin debate because it continues to sidestep the seminal question – how did these cattle-herders learn how to raise the largest stone city south of the Pyramids?

Although I have never met Peter Garlake I have great sympathy for his predicament and believe I understand the pressures he was under because at the time I, too, was caught up in the strange political currents produced by the end of colonialism in central Africa. Ian Smith's party, the Rhodesia Front, introduced ever more draconian laws to ensure that published or broadcast 'information' toed the party line or, more specifically, did nothing to support black nationalism. In time Smith's parliament would pass the Law and Maintenance Amendment Act which proscribed dissemination of any information likely to cause 'alarm and/or despondency', under threat of two-year prison sentences. As Controller of Rhodesia

Television in Bulawayo fronting my own evening news show this put me right in the front line. We were once banned from broadcasting the Maize Marketing Board's crop forecast because it was judged bad enough to cause alarm and/or despondency. In the end it made my job untenable and within two years I would decide it was safer to leave the country.

The evidence that Peter Garlake got caught up in this farce is there, if you know where to look for it. There is, as a start, his enigmatic book dedication: 'For John and all who share his beliefs and therefore his present circumstances.' We are not told who John is but I think it is safe to assume that he is somewhat persecuted. Then the foreword, which starts out innocently enough: 'From July 1964 to December 1970, I was the Senior Inspector of Monuments of the Historical Monuments Commission of Southern Rhodesia', and he thanks all those he worked with. He signs the foreword with the simple initials 'P.S.G.' but then one realises that he is writing not from Rhodesia but from the Institute of African Studies, University of Ife, Ile Ife, Ife, Nigeria. In a kind of exile, I suspect.

Peter Garlake's suggestion that the Zimbabwe culture was black through and through would certainly have alarmed the last Rhodesian white government; indeed, the thesis had already provoked angry outbursts in their parliament. In 1969, G.H. Hartley, the Rhodesian Front member for Fort Victoria, complained to the legislative assembly:

There is one trend running through the whole of the presentation of the image of the ruins which is apparently being directed to promoting the notion that . . . these buildings were originally erected by the indigenous people of Rhodesia. This may be a very popular notion for adherents to the Zimbabwe African People's Union and Zimbabwe African National Union and the Organisation of African Unity but I wish to make the suggestion that this notion is nothing but sheer conjecture.

I feel that it is quite wrong that this trend should be allowed to continue to develop . . . this trend among people, particularly among members of the staff of the National Historical

179

Monuments Commission to portray the ruins in one light only, should be corrected. . . .

The Minister of Internal Affairs as recorded in Hansard agrees: 'I have intimated to those concerned . . . that it would be more correct that, as yet, no irrefutable evidence is available as to the origins of the ruins . . . it would be wrong to allow particularly visitors to this country to be influenced unduly by one train of thought. There is a great deal of evidence, which I personally have studied a good deal myself, to indicate that what I have said is correct: there is no irrefutable evidence of the origins of the ruins at the present time. I have made this point to the persons likely to be concerned.'

A year later Parliament heard that: 'The [Honourable Member for Victoria's] remarks . . . on Zimbabwe have certainly borne fruit. There was something of a storm in a teacup over them but the results have been satisfactory and a new guide book is being prepared on behalf of the Historical Monuments Commission in which all theories relating to Zimbabwe will be presented absolutely impartially.' This was confirmed in a government White Paper of *c.* 1970 which formally ordered that no official publication could state unequivocally that Great Zimbabwe had been created by Africans.

I can only deduce that Garlake became caught up in this whirlpool but it is to a degree supported by a cryptic comment that is the last line in his book. He records that shortly after these exchanges in parliament, the director of the Rhodesian Ancient Monuments Commission gave a press interview in which he avowed: 'The Commission holds no view of Zimbabwe's origins – that is for the museum to argue.' 'A particularly ironic conclusion,' Garlake observes, 'for the Rhodesian museums no longer employ an archaeologist.'

Thankfully by then Ian Smith's government and white supremacy in Africa was on its last legs. Robert Mugabe successfully led his troops in a war of independence under a 'Zimbabwe' banner, but his victory, understandably, also ended serious research into alternative authorship theories. Subsequently, a whole pack of sleeping dogs have been left to lie.

More than a century after the first Royal Geographical Society expedition sought to resolve the origins of the lost city, none of the seminal riddles have been answered and the Zimbabwe culture has instead been parked in a politically correct cul-de-sac.

The official record is now one of listless guesses. The geometrical conical tower, for example, is relegated to a 'symbolic Karanga grain bin'. The mysterious soapstone columns 'may well have served as reminders or tallies of the individual dead'. The unique Great Zimbabwe birds are dismissed as 'stiff, crude diagrams; conventional statements of a generalised avian theme'. I have even seen a suggestion that the very early pottery figurines were toys.

Is it any wonder that this lost marvel of the southern hemisphere becomes less well known with every passing day? Rather more dangerous is that politically correct but observably questionable interpretations of events have now become the official record taught to children. You will recall my quoting from a recent (1998) primer by Harvard University's Dean, Mark Bessire, which borrows Garlake's title, *Great Zimbabwe*. It concluded with the following timeline:

c. AD 1000, Ancestors of the Shona arrive on the Zimbabwe plateau.
c. 1250–1300, Mapungubwe becomes important trading centre.
c. 1270–90, First major building projects at Great Zimbabwe.
c. 1300–1450, Great Zimbabwe reaches the height of its power.

Can you spot what has happened here? This children's primer should say that the first major building could have started in AD 671 which is the mean Carbon-14 date of that piece of *ubande* wood under one of Great Zimbabwe's most massive walls. However, it has been corrected by almost exactly the 500 years Peter Garlake said was the lifespan of the tree even though nobody knows its real age. Time has made gospel of a dubious guess.

So from here on I propose to abandon the argument – it is going to run a while yet – as to exactly when the grand *zimbabwes* were constructed and concentrate instead on the ancestors of the people who built the first stone buildings and on the people who started formal trade in the precious metal that paid for them. Who were the first blacks to enter these lands from across the Zambesi, what skills did they bring with them, and were they gold traders? Or were there other people with them with special skills and did they deal their gold through others? So far as I am aware no one has backtracked to any of these original settlers with a view to establishing what knowledge they could have brought with them.

Then one morning at Groote Schuur, Alta Kriel, the ever-helpful curator, put on her white gloves and pulled down from the shelves of Rhodes' study a pristine first edition of a book called *The Sacred Cities of Ethiopia* – by Theodore Bent! This is such a rare book (the author was dead of malaria by the time it went into circulation) and of so little general interest I could not escape the feeling that the last hands to turn its pages might have been those of Rhodes himself. Indeed, the only reference I had ever even seen to the book was in the Royal Geographical Society's obituary to Bent:

In the winter of 1892 Mr and Mrs Bent set out for Africa, this time to investigate the extensive ruins in the north of Abyssinia. This journey threw much new light on the early connections between the people of Abyssinia and those of south-west Arabia, whence both the writing and the language of the old Abyssinians must have been derived.

It is described in Mr Bent's volume, *The Sacred City of the Ethiopians*. In the winter of 1893–4, Southern Arabia, the mother country of both the peoples whose antiquities had been examined in the two preceding years, was visited and a considerable addition made to our knowledge of the little-known Hadramut country.

This was revisited during the succeeding winter, while that of 1895–6 was devoted to exploration of the African coast of the Red Sea. The last fatal journey is said to have resulted in the discovery of fresh archaeological matter in Sokotra and Southern Arabia, in the latter of which some new ground was broken.

This makes no mention of Great Zimbabwe, so what new ground is being referred to? Within minutes of opening Rhodes' copy of *The Sacred Cities of Ethiopia*, however, that became obvious. Theodore and Agnes Bent had never stopped tracking the people he had termed the 'authors' of the Zimbabwe culture; indeed, Bent had given his life to that very Grail.

NINE

The Road to Ophir

Even by African standards Ethiopia has been a rumbling volcano of humanity since the dawn of recorded time. Politics and religion have produced repeated magma flows of displaced people, mostly in a southerly direction. Before I studied its history I had always assumed that these troubles were of recent origin, but this is not the case and if we are looking for a source of refugees, Ethiopia, more than anywhere else in Africa, has to be a prime choice. Evidently, although admittedly almost secretly, the Bents felt the same.

During the last century, Ethiopia, once known as Abyssinia, has experienced all the typical African traumas of hunger, disease, a particularly evil brand of colonialism, a communist coup, almost ceaseless drought and starvation, inept government and self-serving politicians. It was the first African country to be used as a test ground for modern war machines, the place where Mussolini practised aerial warfare and the effects of poison gas. But go back a few thousand years to the times that we have been researching, and the excesses above seem just a natural part of the national tradition.

The earliest Arabian geographers like Ibn Hawkal saw Ethiopia as 'an immense country with indefinite borders and solitudes', protected by its desert and mountains. In the *Periplus of the Red Sea* it is recognised as a source of obsidian and ivory (but not yet gold) and Pliny reports that it exported African exotica, like rhino horn, hippopotamus hides, tortoiseshell, monkeys and slaves; but again no gold. There were gold mines in ancient Ethiopia but they do not appear to have been prolific enough to impinge on the record. A Greek explorer 500 years after Pliny opined that the gold displayed in the rich trappings of the monarchy was earned from a profitable trade with the interior. It may well have been Zimbabwe gold in transit.

As the historian Felipe Fernandez-Armesto (who draws an immediate comparison between Ethiopia and Zimbabwe) writes in *Civilisations*, Ethiopia's isolation produced a singular culture: 'Even at the time of her most intense contacts with the Romans, her clergy had to be appointed from Alexandria [hence the wide use of Greek], at a crucial time of Monophysite heresy, which erred in underestimating the humanity of Christ and making him uncompromisingly divine. When Monophysite worthies from the Roman Empire fled orthodox persecution in the second and fifth centuries, Ethiopia received some of the most celebrated of them, and the future of the Ethiopian church as a splinter group of the Christian world became inescapable.'

Solomon, as the father of the nation, featured large for more than a thousand years. He was recognised by the Agawa Dynasty, and by the people from whom they sprang, the Awga who spoke a Cushitic language. The Amhara, speakers of the Ge'ez dialect (another exclusive cultural feature of the area) regarded the Agawa as foreign intruders. There were also rivals for the mantle of Solomon among the worshippers of Sheba and the refugee communities who espoused 'the new Israel', which will become pivotal to our story. In terms of the likely movement of people south it is also worth keeping an eye on the believed dates of some of these upheavals, especially in relation to seminal dates at Zimbabwe.

Solomon seemingly had material influence on the people of Ethiopia a thousand years before Christ and this influence could have provoked migrations south. Whether, indeed, his fabled union with Sheba founded an Ethiopian dynasty is a matter for speculation; it is the strength and durability of the tale that should interest us. In the same way as the description 'King Solomon's Mines' could simply describe the source of his gold rather than a place he actually owned and where Sheba built him a temple, the Ethiopian legends could be describing the ancient influence of Solomon and Sheba on what was then a very primitive Ethiopia. Almost all legends are apocryphal anyway.

A later Ethiopian king, Azana, left boastful and detailed descriptions on stone stelae of the mayhem he caused: the precise numbers of his victims, the brutalities he inflicted (and occasionally his munificence) and the punitive exile of the vanquished to distant parts of the country. One little war was launched against enemies attacking and destroying Ethiopian trade caravans which, true or false, is at least evidence of trade routes north and south and the value the Ethiopians put on them.

In the early centuries of the Christian millennium, the Ethiopian kings converted to Christianity, resulting in yet more major movements of the faithful which are still reflected in Ethiopian society today. 'To become Christian in the fourth century was to become part of the growing common culture of the Near East,' writes Armesto, 'to share the religion of many Greek and Indian traders in the Indian Ocean.' To this we should add 'old Moors', who were observably at least as active. But this was followed by the rise of Islam and by the ninth century, about the time when even the Shona school is happy to acknowledge the arrival of northern cattle-herders, Ethiopia was a beleaguered empire surrounded by enemies other than to the south.

Yet in spite of all this human abuse Ethiopia remains hauntingly lovely and intensely religious. It lays claim to one of the oldest forms of Christianity on the planet. Admittedly, for more than a thousand years this has often been a God in hiding and most of His churches are extraordinary underground bunkers – stone temples of monumental proportions at least as impressive and similar in construction if not always in style to Great Zimbabwe's mortar-free walls. These alone would have been enough to attract Theodore Bent and his photographer wife to Ethiopia if indeed the quest for the authors of the Zimbabwe culture had remained their Holy Grail.

At the beginning of the twentieth century very little was known of these Ethiopian monuments. Visiting them and the wild mountain territory which had offered some protection from the forces of Islam was extremely dangerous. But this was a very determined couple when it came to treading the road to Ophir. They also had a reputation to rebuild. By 1905, the disciplines of the new archaeology were firmly in place, and the Bents' pioneering book on the Zimbabawe culture, *The Ruined Cities of Mashonaland*, had been derided as Romantic and unscientific by the young Turk from Oxford, David Randall-MacIver.

The Bents were termed 'antiquarians' by this scientific establishment. The fact that they were very widely travelled and extremely knowledgeable, and that their book and its conclusions displayed considerable scholarship, counted for nothing. This in spite of the fact that thanks to Rhodes and the Royal Geographical Society the Bents had been the first western scholars to visit Great Zimbabwe solely for the purpose of science, and as a result had made the most intriguing finds.

But literally everything they unearthed was rejected as inadmissible to the origin debate because their methods had not followed the new rules of archaeology. When, for example, they dared to suggest that Zimbabwe's unique conical tower was probably a religious symbol because it so closely resembled other towers known to be symbols of phallic worship, it was rejected as speculative. Time has shown the Zimbabwe tower to be the most interesting geometrically. Today, such draconian rules on speculation have been considerably relaxed, perhaps because pictorial images can so readily be produced in support of speculative observations. The evidence of one's own eyes must have some value. There is even some new evidence to give force to Bent's theory about the Zimbabwe tower being a religious artefact. Recent excavation of a 'workers town' adjoining the Gîza Pyramids has revealed that mini-pyramids – stone towers – apparently of religious significance, complemented most of these workers' compounds.

A similar case might now be made for the validity of the Bents' comparison of the Zimbabwe tower with the tower on a coin of known Phoenician origin. This features a religious tower sited at Byblos remarkably similar in shape to the Zimbabwe tower. Close examination of this coin, which for some reason the Bents do not mention, reveals that it is located behind a wall bearing a hatched pattern like the one round the top of the Elliptical Building's outer wall, and inside an open-roofed stone-walled monument. The

A coin from Phoenician Byblos showing a tower in a temple remarkably similar to Great Zimbabwe's enigmatic conical tower.

raised-stud pattern round the rim of the coin is also identical to a distinctive pattern on one of the Zimbabwe birds. But this, along with all the other intriguing artefacts in the Bents' Pandora's box of finds was emphatically rejected. For the coin to be admissible as an indication of the date of the Zimbabwe tower it would have had to be found in the tower's foundations when Ms Caton-Thompson dug there, and of course it was not.

Contributors to the Zimbabwe story have been plagued for a century by political rectitude of one kind or another and by these arcane disciplines, but none so mercilessly as Theodore Bent who was in fact a serious scholar. For him the rigid application of the new rules for archaeological finds amounted not just to the death of

188

his reputation as an investigative historian, but also to his actual death. After his book was dismissed as Romantic speculation he went to Ethiopia to find physical evidence to support his theories and was there bitten by the malaria-infected mosquito that killed him.

Ethiopia is ideally placed if you are looking for stepping stones from ancient Egypt to Great Zimbabwe. The shortest crossing point on the Red Sea, Bab el Mandeb, separates Ethiopia from Yemen, the Sabaean kingdom of ancient times. Directly north of Ethiopia is the old Negro kingdom of Nubia, which adjoined Egypt and shared a cultural heritage with Egypt. To the south-east is Somalia, peopled by fierce warrior tribes who fit the descriptions of the savage Zindj and whose Indian Ocean coast hooks back to face the Hadramat region of Arabia. To the west, Uganda, and the territory which later became Rwanda, was ruled for most of the past by the tall, elitist Tutsi, a people who look like the Somalis and the Ethiopian highlanders and who once kept a slave-tribe, the Hutu. Due south is Kenya, and south-east of Kenya, Tanganyika (now joined with Zanzibar island as Tanzania), both dominated in olden times by tall war-like nomads, the ancestors of the modern Turkhana and Masai.

Unlike any of these African neighbours (with the notable exception of the old Nubians) Ethiopia has a long, classical and religious tradition which produced a monolithic stone-building culture. For the Europeans of the old world, Ethiopia was always an alluring and mysterious 'lost civilisation' in the heart of Africa, a cultural oasis of an ancient Christian sect led by 'Prester John'. The rumour was that this was the last resting place of the Ark of the Covenant and it could be said that our story begins with Prester John because it was a search for him by the intrepid Portuguese mariner, Batholomew Diaz, which would produce in time the first eye-witness accounts of our lost city deep in the African hinterland.

I join the road here, too. If, as I suspect, the proto-Karanga followed a path down Africa that a millennium later became roughly the route of the Great North Road, then that was the road my family would take south from Tanganyika in 1947. But, with Mr and Mrs Bent, we need to step back a pace or two before we can join that long walk of the Karanga migration.

There were two ways to find your way to Great Zimbabwe in ancient times. You could sail south aboard one of the new Phoenician ships, then walk inland, or you could trek down Africa. It is possible, indeed likely, that both methods were used at different times. How strong is the case for the first alien influence at Great Zimbabwe having been imported by explorer-merchants from ships? The earliest indications that a voyage rather than a march might have fuelled the evolution of the Zimbabwe culture are those famous biblical references. The King James version of the Bible gives chapter and verse on King Solomon's shopping lists to his Phoenician mariner-merchants. Top of that list is gold: 'Now the weight of the gold that came to Solomon in one year was six hundred and three score and six talents of gold. . . . Beside [that which] chapmen and merchants bought. And all the kings of Arabia and the governors of the country bought gold and silver to Solomon . . . and King Solomon made two hundred targets [of] beaten gold; six hundred [shekels] of beaten gold went to one target.' There are fifteen references in II Chronicles 9 alone. The most specific records that every three years 'the servants also of Hurram, and the servants of Solomon, which brought gold from Ophir, brought almug trees and precious stones'.

There has been considerable speculation about the three years it took Hiram's fleet to bring Solomon his gold from Ophir. One theory promotes a voyage to India, another that the Phoenician fleet took a year travelling to an east African port, a year trekking inland trading for gold and gathering, perhaps growing, sufficient food for the long return journey. Sea journeys of several years were not uncommon in those days and these maritime traders could easily have taken a year visiting the various settlements in the interior where gold, ivory and perhaps hardwoods were traded.

We know a good deal more about Solomon and Sheba than they did in Theodore Bent's day and this new information is quite revealing if we are indeed looking for a king whose fortune depended on colonial, or at least colonial trading, connections. Solomon's name means 'sun' (although in no account I have read to date has this association been mentioned). Many Zimbabwe artefacts, including the birds and the stelae, carry sun-symbol discs. The early sun-gods of Solomon's homeland were hawk-headed and these self-same gods had responsibility for the protection of ancient mines. It surely does not go beyond the bounds of reasonable speculation to suggest that these birds (whose inscribed symbols have thus far not been translated), who were found guarding Great Zimbabwe's most sacred stone keep, are icons of a sun-god. To my mind the only question is: a sun-god to which cult?

No one has seriously suggested that Solomon had great ambitions outside his own borders but there are a number of stories confirming his skill as a diplomat and an adept of trading partnerships. Soon after Solomon became king he made an important political marriage – thus securing future diplomatic relations – to the daughter of an Egyptian pharaoh. Her dowry is said to have included 1,000 musical instruments! But more relevant to this story, 80,000 Egyptian builders. Solomon has remained famous throughout history for his opulent palace and temple. The scriptures say he sent 10,000 workers a month to Lebanon to fell and transport over land and sea the tall cedars of Lebanon. It is this legend which so excited Carl Mauch when he found at Great Zimbabwe a wooden beam he thought was the same wood as the cedar of his pencil.

Stories as old as this must, however, be interpreted with caution. What we can reasonably conclude from the Scriptures is that Solomon was in the market for quality hardwood and that he possessed a skilled labour force that could build monumental stone temples and palaces. It is also not commonly acknowledged that Phoenician craftsmen were the architects of Solomon's palace and temple. The temple consisted of three large rooms of richly carved cedar, cyprus and marble with a huge bronze altar and bronze columns 40 feet high.

Solomon's abiding reputation for wisdom comes from the alleged conversation he had with God when, invited to name his heart's desires, instead of choosing riches and power, he said 'Give thy servant therefore an understanding heart to judge Thy people, that I may discern between good and evil.' Pleased with this request, God apparently also endowed him with more material gains. Although Israel was at this time a pocket-kingdom of some 30,000 square miles sandwiched between Assyria and Egypt, Solomon's much-vaunted wisdom and his ability to run the treasury attracted considerable interest, including that of his neighbour, the Queen of Sheba. By then he had already concluded a number of lucrative trading partnerships with neighbouring kings, most notably with the Phoenician King, Hiram of Tyre.

Solomon commissioned Hiram's large fleet, or was a major investor in the expedition which sailed from Esyon-Geber or Eilat on the Red Sea to unknown Ophir. But did they really sail off 'into the blue' as the legend suggests? I find it hard to believe that the notoriously secretive Phoenicians would put in so huge an invest-ment without some strong expectation of riches at the end of it.

Sheba may also have shared with Solomon some of the trade secrets of her successful entrepot kingdom when she made her fabled visit and, if one is to momentarily join the Romantic school, produced the royal house of the Ethiopians. Certainly the young Queen was attracted by Solomon's wisdom, affluence and good looks. He was reportedly dark-haired, tanned, lean and with a gracious smile and a lively spirit. He wore elegant tunics dyed royal purple, golden collars and chains and a golden circlet inset with sea-green stones.

Sheba was duly impressed with Solomon's palace which boasted '40,000 horse stalls and 1,400 chariots', which sounds excessive but the archaeologists have in fact since unearthed some 450 horse stalls and 150 sheds for chariots at Megiddo alone. There were vineyards, gardens, pools, singers, and musicians with exotic instruments. Solomon received the young Sheba seated on an ivory throne with gold armrests and golden embroidery. She was understandably seduced, but there is considerable documentation to support the idea that Solomon won Sheba's respect, love and an intimate partnership as much by intense, extended conversations on all manner of topics, as by his wealth. Sheba was, after all, a very wealthy young woman in her own right and it is unlikely that these two would not have talked about how it was to be made.

On this one trip she brought Solomon a tribute of 'a hundred and twenty talents of gold [about 6 tons!], and spices in great abundance and precious stones'. One of the ancient Jewish encyclopaedias, the *Kebra Negast*, suggests that this really was a meeting of kindred spirits. Apparently the pair roamed Jerusalem together as she questioned Solomon and watched him at his work: 'The Queen used to go to Solomon and return continually, and hearken unto his wisdom, and keep it in her heart. And Solomon used to go and visit her, and answer all the questions which she put to him . . . and he informed her concerning every matter that she wished to enquire about.'

Like where to go for gold?

Which brings us back to Ethiopia. Their ancient Christian church believes to this day that the union of Solomon and Sheba produced Menelik I, father of the Ethiopian Solomonic Dynasty whose last earthly representative was Ras Tafri or the Emperor, Haile Selassie. The worldwide Rastafarian cult still worships Ras Tafari, not least because his famous ancestor, Menelik, is also credited with rescuing the Ark of the Covenant from apostate Jerusalem. However, before getting lost in this labyrinth of religions and myths, we should review the evidence which could support the idea that Solomon's Phoenicians might have sailed down Africa, beached their ships somewhere and marched inland in search of the source of the alluvial gold being offered for sale at the coast.

It should perhaps be noted here that the best way of getting to India from the Red Sea ports in ships, which could only properly run before the wind, was to sail south before the north-east monsoon between November and May, land to reprovision and take on water, then ride the south-west monsoon across the Indian Ocean between May and November. The initial run south would need to be at least as far as the equator, but these ancient mariners would more likely have gone further south to more verdant coastlines where water and better food supplies would have been more readily available.

The Phoenicians confirmed that they had made such voyages when, in the 1920s, a French scholar, Ernest Renan, led an expedition to investigate the site of ancient Byblos. Renan was particularly interested in the linguistic history of Byblos, which is also the Greek word for papyrus, leading to 'biblion' or book, and in turn, to bible.

Renan found several stelae – granite slabs – covered with Egyptian hieroglyphics, and a bas relief of a goddess he believed to be Hathor, with a hawk's head. More extensive excavations latr produced a series of semi-intact royal tombs that yielded gold, silver and jewellery, and an elaborate sarcophagus, confirming that this was the last resting place of Ahiram (Hiram), King of Byblos and Solomon's business partner. Theodore Bent's suspicion that Great Zimbabwe was the product of Phoenician ancient influence was enhanced, you will recall, by a comparison he made between the lost city's conical tower and a tower pictured on a coin from Byblos. The inscribed tablets recorded that the Phoenicians were the descendants of two groups, the early Canaanites, who inhabited the coast of Lebanon, and the Sea People, who invaded Lebanon about 1200 BC. Thus this new nation had an established maritime tradition which they enhanced by the development of ships with hulls fit to sail the open seas.

Along the coast of Lebanon they established a loose federation of city-states built on islands or rocky promontories that provided natural harbours for ship-building and trade. Byblos, Tyre, Sidon and Arqad became fabulously wealthy as the Phoenicians expanded their sphere of trade. In time it would encompass all of Europe and, almost certainly, much of Africa. The wrecks of two wooden ships believed to be Phoenician have been found on the Indian Ocean coast, one of which is thought to have circumnavigated the Cape.

At home the Phoenicians were literate, fine craftsmen who evolved an alphabet of twenty-two consonants, which is the foundation of the English alphabet and is the core of Hebrew, Arabic and Syriac script. They raised glass-making to a fine art and made delicate terracotta pots and votive statues. They worshipped Baal and a powerful mother-goddess, Astarte, both as earth-mother and heavenly mother. Cult statues of Astarte in many different forms, including clay and stone figurines, were left as votive offerings in shrines and sanctuaries as prayers for good harvest, for children, and for protection and tranquillity in the home. The figurines found at the lowest levels at Great Zimbabwe and at David Randall-MacIver's altar site near Umtali more closely resemble some of the Phoenician anthropomorphic votive offerings than any other artefact in the historical record.

The Phoenician gods were incorporated in varying degrees by their neighbours, and Baal and Astarte eventually took on the look of Greek gods. The Babylonian King, Nebuchadnezzar, sacked Tyre in 573 BC and in 332 BC Alexander the Great took over this and the remains of Phoenician culture, embodying it into the Hellenistic culture. But had hardy seeds from these ancient religions already been sown abroad by 'ancient Moors'? The early Greeks, as we shall see in a moment, were seminally influential in ancient Ethiopia. The ancient Egyptians also knew of Ethiopia as the fabulously wealthy 'Land of Punt'.

The weight of all this information from several sources, albeit mostly anecdotal, indicates that from time immemorial there was an established sea route down the Red Sea to the gateway to black Africa, Ethiopia. Moreover, modern Moors still ply the route in wooden dhows that closely resemble the sailing ships of yore. So it is inarguable that cultures who knew how to build in stone could, indeed did, make extended journeys south in search of gold, precious stones and other valuable trade goods, including all the items listed in the tribute the Queen of Sheba took to Solomon. The Phoenicians even left written records – stelae again – of journeys to exploit the riches of the lower Arabian peninsula, where mining colonies became so settled they had their own temples for hawk-headed gods.

The Egyptians were also on their way down Africa. Directly south of Egypt was the Negro kingdom of Nubia. Among other ties these Nubians worshipped Gods also found in Egypt, the most powerful of whom was Horus, representing the sun in the guise of a hawk. There is nothing to have prevented these early, cultured Nubians (Group A Nubians as they are called) influencing, through trade and conquest, societies to the south. Moreover, there is good archaeological evidence to indicate that Egyptian colonists, now backed by a mighty dynastic empire on the lower Nile, took over Nubia.

As the Egyptian tribes coalesced, their colonies became stronger, in particular the kingdom of Hierakapolis on the Upper Nile. The old gods metamorphosed into the winged deities we have already met. Hathor even took on special colonial duties as the god-protector of natural resources brought back to Egypt from far-off places. His enforcer was the hawk-god Eye of Ra.

The bead which Dr Sauer found at the Dholo Dholo *zimbabwe* was dated by Flinders Petrie to the later part of this era of Egyptian colonial expansion.

The archaeologists also tell us that the Nubian A group were farmers who practised irrigation and maintained large herds of animals. They had a governing elite who apparently monopolised foreign trade, exchanging Nubian goods like valuable jewel stones, incense, copper and gold for Egyptian crafted items, metals and grain. They were also the middlemen for the produce, like ivory, of the less developed cultures to the south.

This is not just speculation. A 'royal' cemetery of the Nubian A group has been carefully excavated at Qustul. The tombs of the elite are of a size equal to or greater than the contemporaneous 'royal' tombs of Hierakopolis. The goods in them are also richer and feature iconography, which suggest that these are the remains of a king in his own right, not an Egyptian subject. These Nubian kings wore a tall white 'crown', symbolising Horus the hawk.

One of the comparisons which has been made with these Nubian royal tombs is the so-called Treasury of Atreus, a Mycenaean tomb of the fabulously wealthy tribe which ruled the shores of the Greek mainland 1,300 years before Christ. The tomb yielded surprising contents. Alongside the royal dead and masks of gold and silver there was a considerable amount of equipment, as in the Nubian royal burials. This included jewellery, weapons, and beaten gold and silver drinking vessels, one representing a bull with forward-facing horns like those of Nubian cattle and exactly like the horns on soapstone bowls found at Great Zimbabwe. Moreover, the tomb was a tower, or 'beehive tomb' comprising concentric layers of precisely cut stone.

What happened to the Nubian A group is unclear, but they certainly sustain the idea of a southern movement with the knowledge required to build monumental stone structures or, if you prefer, the first stepping stone of cultural diffusion south out of Egypt.

There are written records of King Aha-Menes, King of the 1st Egyptian Dynasty established at Memphis, planning an invasion of Lower Nubia, and at about this time all the royal tombs in Qustal cemetery were looted and burned. The current consensus is that in the face of aggressive Egyptian expansion, the cultured Nubian A group were driven south into Upper Nubia, which was then the territory of a group called the Pre-Kerma culture (developed in the region of the town of Kerma) some 2,500 years before Christ. Little is known of this Pre-Kerma culture other than it was Negroid African, that it was settled, and that its domestic dwellings were mostly circular – rondavels – as they are today in much of rural Zimbabwe. These settlements each had 'pits', lined with clay, which were used as silos and grain stores.

One of the remaining riddles at Great Zimbabwe, at the foot of the hill on which stands the fortress (or citadel), are two immense pits, and similar pits have been found at other *zimbabwes*. The current view is that from these pits came the 'daga' for the hut floors and walls, but the idea seems dubious, if only from the point of view of flooding.

If you combine the Pre-Kerma culture with the refugee Group A Nubians – an amalgam which the archaeological record says happened – you have an uncanny model for one interpretation of the origins of the Zimbabwe culture: a Negroid (Kerma) people living in round huts who were transformed by an influx of refugees of their own, or a similar, race (Nubian A) who had superior knowledge of gold production, trade with northern cultures, expert architects and stone-builders, and a religion dominated by a hawk-god. This model would also illuminate one of the most intransigent of the Great Zimbabwe enigmas – the absence of any inscriptions or other forms of writing. The Group A Nubians, while cultured, also lacked literacy and certainly never developed it once they were subsumed into the Pre-Kerma hegemony.

Could the ever-expanding Egyptian Empire have turned this Nubian mixture – or dissatisfied elements of it – into a migrant population? Most cattle-dependent African tribes have nomadic inclinations anyway. If refugee nomads did flee Nubia to escape colonial oppression from Egypt their next stops south would have had to be either Uganda to the south-west or Ethiopia to the south-east. Could this explain the very distinctive features of the mountain people of both regions?

Until the middle of the nineteenth century Uganda was ruled by a people who are black, have woolly hair, but are otherwise not typically Negroid; indeed, a lot of them are so tall – 7 feet is not uncommon – they are typical of no other race on earth. They also have thin, aquiline facial features. They are elitist by nature and they kept a local tribe, the Hutu, who are entirely African in appearance and of normal stature, virtually as their slaves. The traditions of the Hutu, not denied by the Tutsi, say the Tutsi immigrated here from the north. (This tradition was used by the Hutu in Rwanda, where they are now in the majority, to justify the genocide of more than a million Tutsi in the late 1990s.)

The Tutsi are by tradition cattle-herders and they live in compounds of round huts. The cattle they raise are semi-wild and have distinctive forward-pointing horns that are featured on bas-reliefs all over ancient Egypt and in even older Mycenaean tombs. There are also horns of this style carved on a Zimbabwe bird and on soapstone bowls. The native people in this area of north-central Africa who most resemble the Tutsi are the highland cattle-herders of Ethiopia. This comparison was drawn to my attention by Dr Henry Atkinson, who was on holiday in Cape Town when I was working there. Henry lives an interesting life in the remote outback of Ethiopia, searching out and reopening ancient gold mines. Until I spoke to him I was not aware that there were ancient gold workings in Ethiopia.

Ethiopia, adjoining Arabia, was an even more volatile melting pot than Nubia. If human waves did diffuse south away from imperial pressures in the north then their contact with the complex cultural mix that was Ethiopia would have been seminal and we should be able to find evidence of their presence. That, I am sure, is why Theodore Bent went there. I do not think there is an explicit case to be made for a single uninterrupted exodus flowing down Africa like a trickle of army ants. If, however, a diaspora over centuries is considered, each migration soaking up new knowledge and experience before fresh conflicts provoked further movement into the relative safety of the southern wilderness, the concept becomes more credible. There is even a good model for just such a migration in the Matabele. After General Msilikaze fell out with the Zulu king, Chaka, the general's impis fought their way north until they had crossed the Limpopo and could safely settle in Karanga country. Once settled they learned something of the gold trade from alien entrepreneurs and, later, compliments of Rhodes, of the effectiveness of the Martini-Henry rifle.

We know that Lobengula actively considered moving on when another pressure group – the British South Africa Company – disturbed his comfortable conquest of the Shona. Had the chief set up a new Matabele kingdom on the Zambesi it would – in terms of its skills, economics, dress, armaments and in the case of its ruler, a taste for champagne – have been very different culturally to the impi who fled Zululand just a century previously. Was this how it happened in the black kingdoms bordering the ancient civilisations of the Phoenicians, the Egyptians, and the Sabaeans?

There is good evidence that the Queen of Sheba's Sabaeans cast acquisitive eyes on Ethiopia and, as mentioned, a large part of the populace still regard Sheba as the mother of the nation, her union with Solomon having produced the first emperor of Ethiopia, Menelik I. Visit the old capital, Aksum, today and you will be shown Sheba's swimming pool, a rock-hewn reservoir where villagers gather water and small children splash and play. The Queen is known locally as Makeda and is said to have made Aksum the centre of her empire, and built a 52-room palace complete with Romanesque plumbing, whose unremarkable ruins lie on the outskirts of town. Across the way, they say, is Sheba's actual grave.

The archaeologists dispute all this, claiming some eight centuries separate the Aksum culture from that of Solomon and Sheba, but a majority of Ethiopians do not regard it as a myth and the religion which has grown up around it continues to thrive.

There is no doubting that Ethiopia has been a powder keg of religious and political conflict since the dawn of recorded time. There are, for example, more than eighty languages spoken, while the religious spectrum encompasses ancient Christianity, a segregated neo-Jewish community, Islam in all its shapes and forms, Protestants, Roman Catholics and followers of local animist sects. Ethiopia has been a religious battleground for Christians and Muslims for longer than anyone can remember, fuel enough for countless refugee migrations.

It was this clash with Islam that first excited European interest in Ethiopia. In 1145 when the Second Crusade was being prepared, a fantastic rumour swept through western Europe that a priest-king named Prester John was ruling a Christian kingdom of the Nestorian faith 'behind the lines', so to speak, of the Muslim 'horde' of Persians and Medes. It was said that Prester John desired to join forces against Islam with western Christendom and had been triumphant in a number of battles. His advance had been stopped at the Tigris river in Mesopotamia for want of boats. Prester John himself was said to descend from the Magi – the wise men who followed the star to Bethlehem.

Then in 1170 a letter purporting to come from Prester John himself, addressed to the Byzantine Emperor Comenus, was circulated to Pope Alexander III and the Holy Roman Emperor Barbarossa. Calling himself 'King of Kings' over the 'Three Indias' the letter described the fabulous wealth of this realm and gave a bizarre list of its fauna, including elephants, panthers and several species unknown to man before lapsing into a fantasy of 'horned men, one-eyed giants, men with eyes back and front, cyclops' and other freaks. The Byzantines, not unnaturally, decided the letter was a hoax and the only follow-up was an attempt by the pope to make contact with Prester John. He sent a message with his personal physician but the man was never heard of again.

Even so, the legend of Prester John proved durable because it was known from travellers' tales, among them Marco Polo, that there were definitely elements of ancient Christianity lost among the Islamic and Mongol hordes of the East. If the Nestorians had been prepared to mount flank attacks in support of any one of the six bloody Crusades between 1095 and 1229 the Templars might have prevailed a lot sooner.

The shifting allegiances of the followers of Islam and of the Nestorian Christian god divided parts of Asia and the Middle East for centuries. There were once Christians in Mecca. The most definite evidence we have that ancient Christianity prevailed in Ethiopia as far back as the fourth century BC (it may have been first established much earlier), is one of those inscribed stone stelae erected by King Azana (sometimes spelt Ezana), inscribed in Greek, Ge'ez and Sabaean. It reads: 'I conquered the Arab people. If you remove this stone from its proper place I will kill your families as punishment.' It is particularly significant that this warning should have been addressed to Sabaeans. Saba was Sheba's kingdom, the closest part of Arabia to Ethiopia. King Azana's warning to the Sabaeans indicated that there had been centuries of conflict and this, coupled with religious differences, could well have provoked refugee movements south.

That the Sabaeans had the wealth to sustain wars of acquisition is not in question. There are Assyrian inscriptions on stelae in which King Tiglath Pileser II (733 BC) records tribute from Saba of gold, silver and incense. Eratosthenes (276–194 BC) refers to the Sabaean capital as 'Mariab' and calls it one of the four great nations of the area, a view supported by Agatharchides (120 BC) who applauds the wealth of Saba. By then the Sabaeans must have been getting their large imports of gold from countries outside Arabia and North Africa. Mashonaland is much the closest source.

Almost anywhere you look in the histories, among the artefacts, and at the ruined buildings of Saba, one finds uncanny links with Great Zimbabwe. Writing for the *Encyclopaedia Britannica*, Sir T.H. Holdich points out: 'In the Wadi Sher which leads northwards from the head of the Haramat into the central districts, there exists the remains of at least one great Himyaritic [Sabaean] town, with traces of megalithic buildings and rock exhibiting Himyaritic inscriptions. . . . Large unhewn stones of the dolmen type [are to be found] similar to those found in Mashonaland.'

The most startling comparison of all is, of course, the temple of Awwam, buried in the desert at the ancient Sabaean capital of Marib in Yemen. It is a great stone ellipse, of a size, shape, system of curved walls, and orientation practically indistinguishable from Great Zimbabwe's Elliptical Building or temple. Great Zimbabwe has two rows of chevron patterns round a fourth part of the main wall. A pattern in the stone on the Marib wall is identically positioned. Inscribed walls at both sites are well built, while the reverse faces are rough. The two temples are both the product of gold-rich societies.

The *Periplus of the Red Sea* records that much of the East African coast, including the district of Azania (modern Tanzania), was, by the first century AD, ruled by Sabaeans through local governors. Gold-hungry Sabaeans, working their way down the east coast, must have surmised from the evidence of alluvial ingots and gold dust offered for sale at the coast that there was an eldorado in the hinterland, and I cannot believe that they would not have gone looking for it. Everyone else did. Again, it adds weight to the idea that Sheba, keen to establish good relations with Solomon (to whatever level we feel inclined to interpret the word), and who arrived on his doorstep with 6 tons of gold, surely would have said something about where it came from.

The critics who deride such Romantic ideas have always based their case on the absence of artefacts of *proven* Phoenician origin at Great Zimbabwe or any material evidence that it was an Egyptian or Arabian trading outpost, provided you turn a blind eye to the fact that the Zimbabwe birds appear to be icons to Hathor. There is also unequivocal evidence from later times indicating that Great Zimbabwe had a trading area, with workshops used by aliens. In the period under discussion – Zimbabwe's earliest beginnings – the ivory and gold traders would have been little more than mobile caravans on very occasional visits: every three years the Bible says of Hiram and Solomon. These old Moor traders remained like this until David Livingstone's time; indeed, a great deal of his exploration was based on information from Arab traders, particularly slave-traders he came across deep in the African hinterland. One such gave him a map that allowed him to make his famous journey, 'discovering' the mighty Congo river.

Every effort would have been made by these journeymen to travel as light as possible. Valuable possessions – such as weapons, a drinking cup or a knife – would have been cared for as a matter of life or death. The only excess baggage would have trade goods, mainly cloth and beads. Even the Shona school acknowledges that the grand *zimbabwes* spilled ancient beads. One, says William Flinders Petrie, is of the most ancient times. Mr Robinson's snap-ended glass beads could be also, as could those found at Mapungubwe. Cloth, of course, would have rotted. But this is just not good enough to convince the archaeologists, even though Sauer's bead was washed from the floor of a *zimbabwe*. Comparable artefacts of known antiquity must be found with it for it to have any value as a dating tool.

So what about Adam Renders? By this rule no artefacts mean no Adam Renders! This is patently nonsense because we have at least two written references, not only to the fact that this skilled alien existed, but that he took to wife two daughters of the chief of Great Zimbabwe and must therefore have had considerable local influence.

Adam Renders is one of the reasons I have grown ever more convinced that anecdotal evidence, of which there is a great deal, must be carefully reconsidered in this more liberal age of historical investigation. We should certainly be reviewing the judgements that have been made of Great Zimbabwe's hawk-headed stone birds, towers of phallic shape, inscribed stelae, and monumental stone circles, all of which at least echo Phoenician and Ethiopian artefacts of proven date.

To return to our hypothetical migrants from the troubled north that found refuge in Ethiopia, were processes still in train which could have impelled them to move on into the unknown wildernesses to the south? By all accounts both Saba at the lower end of the Red Sea and Ethiopia opposite were torn apart by religious and political conflicts for all of the 1,000 years under investigation. The Sabaeans converted from heathenism to Christianity. Then in the fifth century they were conquered and became officially Jews, part of the hegemony of Judaism. At the end of that century the Christian Ethiopians invaded Saba to rescue Sabaean Christians from the notorious persecutions of King Du Nawas.

At the end of the sixth century, just about the time when the Great Zimbabwe Carbon-14 datings suggest we should start looking for an architect with a knowledge of the mathematics of monumental stone structures, the Persians overthrew the Christian Ethiopian government and made possible Islam's bloody proselytism of the whole region. One can only guess at the waves of refugees this created. Fernandez-Armesto observes: 'By the ninth century AD [when Nilotic people were settling in numbers in Mashonaland], pressure caused by infiltration of nomadic peoples from the north seems to have driven families to resettle southwards. We read of shadowy and diabolic female rulers . . . images of unnatural and scandalous chaos of implicitly demonic origin.' These religious wars would certainly have created many refugees; indeed, we know they did because a group of Judaised Arabs ended up in a remote part of Ethiopia where they are known today as the Falashas. These 'black Jews' have an important part to play in our story.

Edward Ullendorf in his respected book *The Ethiopians* (Oxford University Press) describes the Falasha cult as a mixture of Judaism, paganism and some Christian elements. They know the Pentateuch but not the Talmud. They worship the Sabbath as a deity and practise circumcision and clitoridectomy. 'Like their Christian fellow Ethiopians, the Falashas are stubborn adherents to formalised Hebraic-Jewish beliefs, practices and customs, which were transplanted from South Arabia into the Horn of Africa.' The Falashas also claim to be derived from King Solomon and the Queen of Sheba!

My migration theory is becoming somewhat less hypothetical.

It is time to take a breath and rejoin Mr and Mrs Theodore Bent who, in 1904, stepped ashore in Ethiopia. From the beginning it was a considerably more difficult exploration than their trip to Mashonaland. Ethiopian factions were, as ever, at each others' throats in several regions. Many of the monuments they wanted to inspect were controlled by misogynist monks. Theodore thought he had lost his intrepid wife on one occasion when he went alone to a male-only monastery. Monks coming up behind him found Mrs Bent waiting on the trail, decided even that was too close, and escorted her roughly down the mountain without leaving word of her removal.

Then, as now, a visit to Ethiopia is to step back in time. The scenery, especially in the mountain regions where the natural monoliths of the Great Rift are jagged teeth across an eternal skyline, is stupendous. Fast-flowing rivers plunge into great lakes through arid canyons which, lower down, fade into a shifting haze of semi- and absolute desert. It is a bird-watchers' paradise with twenty-eight endemic species, including magnificent birds of prey as tough and as merciless as the mountain people. This step back in time is actual rather than whimsical. The Ethiopians never took to the Gregorian calendar, and have their own that runs about seven years and eight months behind ours, with leap-year days creating what amounts to a thirteenth month each year. They also have their own clock, with two twelve-hour cycles beginning at 6 a.m. and 6 p.m., and their own indigenous script, the Ge'ez alphabet.

Even so, the Bents noticed 'striking points of comparison' with Mashonaland as soon as they entered the mountains and mixed with the people in the villages. Here were wooden head pillows all but identical to those found in ancient Egypt and at Great Zimbabwe, game-boards with many holes, millet beer, iron being smelted using clay blow pipes found all over the Shona ruins, inscribed standing stones, and much more. 'They cannot all be accidental but point either to a common origin or a common influence,' Theodore states.

As they travel on Bent reviews Ethiopia's more contemporary history, reminding us that Greek influence spread and established itself here after the conquests of Alexander the Great, hence the joint use of Greek on inscribed stones. One of these, copied by the

Greek monk, Cosmas, refers to a conquest of Abyssinia (Ethiopia) by Ptolemy Indicoplenstes when Sabaeans were still worshipping Baal-Ava.

The Bents manage to reach the ancient village of Yeha (old Ava) near Adoua, where they saw echoes of the hundreds of miles of Inyanga stonework: 'An enormous extent of terraced mountains. Hundreds of thousands of acres must have been cultivated but is now all ruined.' Here also they come across their first stelae – two stone monoliths bearing what Bent describes as Himyaritic (Sabaean) inscriptions. Eventually they arrive at their destination, the ancient city of Aksum, and are greeted by a sight to gladden their hearts – a line of stone columns which they are told were once topped with statues, just as the important Zimbabwe stelae are topped with bird statues. 'Here there are for miles traces of buildings with large stone foundations at the edge of the plain', Bent observes. There are also 'a mass of Himyaritic inscriptions which absolutely prove that the Ethiopians descend from an ancient Arabian colony which gradually lost its identity and merged with the negroid races around it'.

Bent was not to know that these 'traces of buildings with large stone foundations' were just the tip of an iceberg. Across the country in the century following Bent's visit, the world would slowly gain access to the stone monoliths of Lalibela. There are eleven of these extraordinary 'buried' churches. According to the legend, King Lalibela was instructed by God to build his veritable maze of temples, some cut 50 feet into the rock, connected by tunnels, secret passageways, stairs and little wooden bridges. The temples are separated from the surrounding rock by deep trenches. Some of them represent huge crosses. King Lalibela was also instructed to build a 'River Jordan' and a 'Mount of Olives'. Two local geographical features were duly landscaped. The extraordinary eleventh-century *Beit Giorgis* was built by the King after a fully armoured Saint George appeared and censored Lalibela for not dedicating a church to him.

This is about the time when the very grand *zimbabwes* were being planned and started in Mashonaland.

Why these Ethiopian Christian temples were so carefully concealed, or more accurately, designed for concealment, has been much debated, the general assumption being that it was to protect them from Islamic incursions. All are decorated to a greater or lesser degree: *Medhane Alem* (Saviour of the World) resembles a Greek temple, others are more primitive. *Beit Golgotha* (House of Cavalry) features fine figurative reliefs. *Beit Mariam* (House of the Virgin Mary) has massive pillars and beautifully sculptured arches. Inside this structure is a distinctive stela which the priests keep covered with a cloth, believing it to be inscribed with the past and the future of the world. Human beings, they warn, are too weak to accept its truths. A similar protective custody is maintained by the monks at Aksum's *Mariam-Tsion* (St Mary of Zion) church where the Ark of the Covenant is said to be hidden away. Its 'fearsome light' kills mere mortals, especially women, so they are kept out of the church altogether.

All the way into Aksum, the Bents are literally tripping over tall stelae, some plain spikes of stone like those which originally crowned the Zimbabwe hill ruins, some inscribed like the soapstone stelae the Bents found and gave to Rhodes. Three-quarters of a mile outside the city they come across a 20 foot high column still standing. Others lay on the ground around it. The standing stone has Greek and Sabaean inscriptions. It is King 'Aizane's' (as Bent calls him) death-threat of 1,300 years ago to the Arabs. Evidently the warning against its removal has worked.

Since Bent's time hundreds of stelae have been found around Aksum. Many of them are similar to the columns raised at Great Zimbabwe. The largest, broken into four pieces, is more than 100 feet long and weighs more than 500 tons. They continue to baffle scholars.

The Bents follow a line of stelae into the ancient city which they are told were once crowned with statues, 'one of gold, one of silver and three of brass'. Here Theodore Bent is also introduced to the translations which the monk, Cosmas, made from inscriptions on an Adulitan stela. So far as I am aware the following description has never been published since it appeared in Bent's obscure book. He wrote: 'It described how every two years the King of Aksum sends an expedition to a place called Sasov very rich in gold mines. The traders stop at a certain point, make a hedge of thorns piled together, and establish themselves there. Then they kill their oxen and expose pieces on the thorns, also salt and iron. Then the natives approach bringing ingots of gold called "tanchara" and each one gives gold for the pieces of meat, the salt, the iron – one, two or three ingots.'

This fascinatingly detailed account of the technique employed by the earliest 'ancient Moors' to barter for gold with the primitive Africans of the south literally stunned me. Not so much because it fits the alien influence thesis so well but because I had this uncanny, surely impossible, feeling that I had *seen* it happening somewhere!

TEN

First Footsteps

The traders stop at a certain point, make a hedge of thorns piled together, and establish themselves there. Then they kill their oxen and expose pieces on the thorns, also salt and iron. Then the natives approach bringing ingots of gold called 'tanchara' and each one gives gold for the pieces of meat, the salt, the iron – one, two or three ingots. (Cosmas)

Probably the best ethnographic documentary maker of my generation, Adrian Cowell, spent years making a film in the Brazilian Matto Grosso entitled *The Tribe That Hides from Man*.

The Tribe was a remarkable film with an extraordinary ring of authenticity, largely because Adrian spent five years in appalling conditions failing to find the tribe. He and Chris Menges walked for days, weeks, months and finally years, through the dark green forest, following in the footsteps of two Brazilian conservationists who were determined to make contact with the tribe and move it to safety before it came into conflict with new white settler-farmers from the slums of Rio. These conflicts resulted, almost inevitably, in the death of the naïve Indians. If they attacked with their lethal blowpipes the settlers destroying the forests on which their entire livelihoods depended, they were shot. If they tried to integrate with the settlers they caught diseases to which they had no natural resistance. They also had little resistance to the flashy goods of settler-traders, especially alcohol, and they had no understanding whatsoever of prostitution.

Thinking back on those miles of film I realised that I had seen re-enacted the process of contacting aboriginal people as described by the Greek monk, Cosmas, in the translations quoted by Theodore

Bent. In Indian clearings in the Amazon delta, Menges filmed the Villas Boas brothers hanging out food, bright new pots and tools to entice the Indians. They arrayed their lures, moved out of the clearing, then climbed into their hammocks and waited. Even in the cases of successful contacts, several of these baiting sessions were required and the waiting could be interminable. In this case the lures vanished without trace. Nobody ever saw an Indian, just fleeting shadows of human forms in the thick foliage. It was tremendously dangerous work because the little darts fired with great accuracy by invisible blowpipes really were lethal.

The poignant thesis of the film was that here was a cheerful, happy, independent race who lived with nature, valued it and had determined to stay that way. The truth of the matter was that if you put out enough trade goods and hung around long enough you would make contact in the end. There are no tribes hiding from man in the Matto Grosso today, although Adrian and his associates did live to see the creation of a huge Indian sanctuary now protecting some of those who took the bait.

There are certainly no tribes hiding from man in Mashonaland, presumably because those ancient Moorish traders described by Cosmas learned the same lesson. The proto-Karanga or the San (if, indeed, they were the people who picked up the Arab barter goods) needed salt and iron for weapons. Swapping such valuable commodities for useless gold ingots would have been irresistible.

Cosmas's description of the initiation of the trade process via barter is fortunately quite detailed and for me, a reporter, detail has always proved the most reliable guide to the authenticity of an account. For example, barter, rather than trade via a currency, seems to have been the favoured exchange of the Zimbabwe culture throughout the long centuries of its tenure. Certainly no evidence of a mutually acceptable currency, with the possible exception of some cowrie shells, has ever come to light.

There are several other details in the Cosmas translation, which can be read for clues. The Ethiopian (or traders in partnership with Ethiopians) expeditions were not random explorations of territory where the natives were still 'wild', but dedicated sorties every two years to barter with people the traders knew had gold. They must have been there before to know that there was gold on offer and they must have known the kind of goods the natives would swap it for.

The use of oxen feels like a system worked out from experience. Beef would have been a very succulent food to a Boskop people used only to tough game meat. As we shall see in a moment, it is also thought that the first Karanga migrants to Mashonaland did not possess cattle so they too would have liked tender meat. The ergonomics of a system whereby you use oxen to pack in your heavy trade goods like iron and bags of salt, butcher the oxen to enhance the display and only have to carry home bags of gold nuggets, is sophisticated. The traders even established a rough rate of exchange – one, two or three ingots for meat, salt or iron, says Cosmas.

The reference to a hedge of thorns could be another pointer. They are used protectively all over east and south-central Africa. The cattle-dependent people who live on the fringes of the Tsavo East National Park in Kenya build thorn *bomas* for their cattle, strong enough to be lion-proof. These hedges are invariably made of an acacia with a long white thorn that I have seen used for drying beef to 'biltong'. 'Butcher-bird' shrikes hang grasshoppers on these aptly named 'wait-a-minute' thorns until they are ripe for eating.

Then there is the reference to 'iron' that the natives crave as much as the salt and tender meat. This surely indicates that the natives have no iron of their own, or are dealing with superior ironsmiths; that is, that they are Stone Age people.

Reading between Cosmas's lines also reveals a rough clue to the date of these expeditions. Although they are undertaken to a schedule – every two years – they do not appear to be dealing with settled communities. The proto-Karanga would have lived in settlements of sorts from the time of their arrival. Cosmas's description more closely suggests contact with the tough little San hunter-bowmen of the Stone and early Iron Age who lived nomadic lives, surviving mostly in primitive bush bivouacs. The Boers have many a salutary tale to tell of how fierce the Hottentots and bushmen could be; indeed, in the early days in the Cape they hunted them as vermin. You certainly needed caution to approach them.

211

The expeditions were apparently dedicated to the acquisition of gold. There is no mention in Cosmas's account of ivory, precious stones, slaves or even almug trees. Most significantly the gold came in ingots and this detail really does suggest that Aksum's expeditions took place long before any form of deep mining and gold processing had been implemented. Remember also Dr Sauer's description of how gold ingots of an ounce in weight, along with ancient Egyptian beads, could be garnered from the floors of *zimbabwes* simply by washing them. On the down side, the land of Sasov rings no bells with anyone so there is no way of positively identifying the country described in the Ethiopian account. But we do have some more clues.

Other than the badlands of Ethiopia, no significant source of gold exists in Arabia or north-east Africa and it is unlikely that the Ethiopians would have taken two years to come and go from their own up-country gold fields. Mashonaland is indubitably the nearest large goldfield. If we assume that expeditions mounted every two years equated to expeditions lasting two years then Mashonaland is about the right distance away whether you choose to do the journey on foot, by sea, or a combination of both. It took David Livingstone years to travel across half of Africa on foot and by boat.

Perhaps most intriguingly, Cosmas's account goes some way, as no other account ever has, to eliminating the only other prime candidate for the actual builders of the Zimbabwe culture being entirely alien, in this case Indians. Because throughout the ages India has always produced gold, and Indians have an observable passion for the precious metal, there has always been a potent school of thought that India was the gold-producing nation that sustained the dreams of avarice of Solomon, Sheba and Hiram – especially as the Phoenicians are known to have sailed as far as India.

The subject has been widely broadcast in a documentary by Anthony Irving, that he called *Behind the African Mask*. His thesis is based on the work of the Slovak-American historian, Dr Cyril Hromik, who in addition to exploring the Indian connection has compiled an impressive set of statistics on the extent of the Zimbabwe culture. Some 18,000 *zimbabwes* or stone ruins have now been plotted in southern-central Africa. One conurbation covers 36 square kilometres. There are 100 kilometres of ancient canals, terracing covering 5,000 square kilometres, 2,000 stone pits and 2,000 known ancient mines. It is the largest collection of ancient ruins in Africa outside Egypt. And it is Dr Hromik's passionate conviction that he has the physical evidence to prove that this was all built by Indians who came here for the gold, beginning so far back in historical times that any trade with Solomon is of comparatively recent origin. Moreover, this was not a creative partnership between Indians and the Bantu (the Bantu were not in southern Africa then), but initiated by ancient Indians who sailed here in catamarans, the earliest form of ocean-going boat.

All manner of ethnographic and physical evidence has been collected by the industrious Dr Hromik to support this radical idea, and is somewhat impressive, especially when supported by the pictures in Anthony Irving's film. Dr Hromik starts with a good number of linguistic connections. In southern India 2,000 years ago, for example, the word that Buddhist monks used for gold was *shona*. The same root word for the precious metal exists in a number of other Indian languages. Perhaps more intriguing is his observation that in Indian Dravidian weddings the bride, called *bali*, was ritually mutilated by having a joint of her finger removed. Some Khosa tribes in South Africa used to employ a marriage priest known as Mama Bali to carry out the same operation. The word 'Bantu' is echoed in the Tamil language as 'brother' or 'kinsman' and there are Indian words for cotton-cloth and medicine very like Bantu words. 'Manica', as in Manicaland where some of the most impressive *zimbabwes* are located, is an Indian word meaning 'precious stones'. Without questioning any of the above we should not forget (as Dr Hromik has the grace to remind his audience in Irving's documentary) that India has 400 languages, including 94 forms of Hindi.

More focused is the work done by Oxford and Princeton University which shows a connection between the blood groups of the Quena (bushmen) and Bantu people and Indians, which does not show in West Africans.

Very old Indian maps show the Cape province separated from the African continent, and label it 'Diab', an Indian word for 'two waters'. The boats which plied these two waters were, according to Dr Hromik, the ancient marine-going 'catamarans', a word which in India means 'tied logs'.

But Dr Hromik is at his best when he turns to the religions, monuments and icons of India, going back 6,000 years to when gold mining and processing started in India and introduced a love of the precious metal which has been sustained since. Indians still dress themselves and their temples in as much gold as they can afford to lay their hands on. Some 450 tons of it are used cosmetically every year. In the old days it was crushed with stone rollers in rock mortars, which can still be found today. Mine props have been found that carbon-date back to the time of Christ. Two hundred and fifty years before the birth of Christ the Indian King, Ashoka, is recorded on a rock stela as having issued instructions to his missionaries to go out into the world, spread the Buddhist religion – and find gold. In the gold-bearing districts of India, stone-workers to this day cut symmetrical tiles of granite, as in Mashonaland, and build them into temples and village houses.

Ancient temples, of course, are India's pride and joy but Dr Hromik draws us away from the magnificent structures to a variety of lesser-known shrines with distinct echoes in Africa. He visits Indian temples hand-carved into the bedrock, as in Ethiopia. On some sites upwards of 200,000 tons of stones have been sculptured by the monks to create a monolithic temple complex. In the mountains are more simple places of worship: 'Sky' cells without roofs for prayer, rings of rocks with great religious significance, lingams (rounded rocks very like miniature Zimbabwe towers), dolmans (three-cornered shrines containing round religious stones), Yoni stones representing Shiva's female aspect which have holes bored through the middle and are very like the round stone 'drums' and 'spinning whorls' the Bents found at Great Zimbabwe, and game boards using stone pieces like the Bents discovered both at Great Zimbabwe and in Ethiopia. Recent research into San agriculture has recorded that they actually weighted their digging sticks with stones shaped just like this.

Dr Hromik makes much of the alignment of significant rocks, paths, arches in caves, and other geographical features that he suggests were used to predict the solstices and act as celestial clocks. The alignment of these features and of some of the *zimbabwes* imply to him that they were Indian holy places, as all Indian temples have an alignment which is religiously meaningful. But so many complex measurements on so many different locations are a little speculative for my taste. The one thing that you can virtually guarantee in the granite kopje country of southern Africa is that rocks of interesting shape will line up with a hill behind which the sun will obligingly rise or set. Theodore Bent's cartographer, R.M.W. Swan, speculated about this to his cost. Dr Hromik also traces stone-walled paths in Africa leading to stone circles where he has, more convincingly, found anachronistic round stones echoing significant religious markers in many primitive Indian temples.

For me this all rather peters out somewhat when Dr Hromik, like so many historians, antiquarians and archaeologists before him, tries to fit all this fascinating collection into a single homogeneous theory. His theory requires a very substantial *Indian* labour force to cut and raise all that stone. Why have they left so few incontrovertible signs of their extended presence? Indians revere monuments, especially religious monuments, and their country boasts some of the most magnificent in the world. The *zimbabwes*, even the grand *zimbabwes*, are very plain by comparison and show few of the features, not least the very intricate wall carving, of Indian monuments. So far as I am aware no statues or definable icons of the ubiquitous Indian deities, like Shiva, have been found. Given that the grandest of the African monuments, Great Zimbabwe, does feature very clear-cut icons – the Zimbabwe birds – this absence is surely strange.

Dr Hromik says the Indians lost interest in southern African gold when it became more difficult to produce using the techniques available at the time. They abandoned the trade to the Arabs now firmly settling on the east coast. Why was this, if it was still a viable trade for Arabs, and India's appetite for gold has remained consistent? Dr Hromik's general thesis that there could have been an ancient Indian trading presence in southern Africa from very ancient times is an acceptable one. If, as he says, it was linked with the San then he may have made an invaluable contribution to the enigma of the bodies in the Mapungubwe graves and even to the idea, so far unresolved, that the great southern *zimbabwes* and the Zimbabwe culture as a whole owes more to various San–alien partnerships than has previously been acknowledged. Moreover, Dr Hromik is not alone in suspecting a significant Indian contribution to the evolution of the gold trade in southern Africa that was after all the springboard for the Zimbabwe culture.

The Scottish academic Professor Gayre devoted a good part of his book, *The Origin of the Zimbabwean Civilisation* (Galaxie Press, 1972), to proving how the monsoon wind systems would have carried ancient ships from the Middle East to India from November to May, then reversed to allow return trips, resulting in landfalls in the region of Madagascar, from May to November. Theoretically these ancient mariners could have done the round trip in a year but that would have allowed little time for trade so they probably took longer. Professor Gayre suggests that for the navies of Tyre, Israel and Saba the route was first southwards on the north-east monsoon, taking in Punt until they reached Madagascar for refitting and provisioning ahead of the long journey across the Indian ocean. They may even have had to spend a season there growing a food crop. The following year they would take the south-west monsoon to India, a voyage of three months, followed by a trading period. In the third year they crossed back across the Indian Ocean on the north-east monsoon, refitted and provisioned again and caught the next south-west monsoon home through the Gulf of Aqaba. These winds are predictably regular and this neatly fits the biblical accounts of three-year gold-collecting voyages for Solomon.

There would also have been time for the traders to acquire gold in Africa during the refit periods. Says Professor Gayre: 'The location of Ophir as a place in India becomes almost a certainty, but only as the entrepot – the trading port – where African gold was traded for the other items that appear on Solomon's exotic shopping list, like peacocks and spices. . . . Since India was always an importer of gold not an exporter, it means that these passages had to include a gold-rich country. The only one of consequence along these sailing routes was Mozambique with its hinterland of Rhodesia.'

Gayre's sailing plan has always struck me as an ingenious but a somewhat expedient explanation of those enigmatic three-year voyages by Solomon's fleet, although it has to be said that other scholars have noted how secretive the Phoenicians were. 'They gave no thought to proclaiming discoveries,' comments Constance Irwin in her book on the Phoenicians (W.H. Allen, 1964), 'being less concerned with their public image than private profits. Theirs was in fact a conspiracy of silence. Although they disseminated culture along with the more profitable items of trade, they never shared information regarding trade routes, markets or winds and currents. The routes were their roads to riches, and as such were shielded from prying potential competitors.'

So the Greek monk, Cosmas's, account that Theodore Bent unearthed, remains for me the only description of early African trading expeditions with sufficient detail to be plausible. But again, if we read a little deeper between its lines there are a number of indications that both Ophir the entrepot, and Havilah, the source of the gold, were in Africa, not India. Dr Hromik's excellent descriptions of the age and nature of the Indian gold industry have also convinced me that Cosmas's translation describes African trading expeditions. If, as he insists, the Indian gold industry has a 6,000-year history of supplying the Indian ruling classes and its affluent religions with a precious metal which demonstrated status, it is hardly likely that this elite would have allowed what amounted to Arab pirates to land and bribe the peasants into trading ingots of the national gold supply for scraps of meat, iron and salt. Nor indeed do Indian peasants fit Cosmas's description of wild natives gullible enough to trade in this way.

But Dr Hromik's observations do make it more likely that ancient trading forays did go south from Ethiopia and find gold, and this eldorado would not have remained a secret forever. In any event a southern exodus of settler-migrants was inevitable, as people sought peace and religious freedom away from the interminable conflicts in the states around the horn of Africa.

Each new piece of information entering the origin debate is now beginning to render untenable the Shona school's seminal belief that the Zimbabwe culture was built without alien influence.

Regrettably Cosmas's translation, while otherwise very explicit, does not provide a location for the place where ingots of gold could be traded for tender meat and iron tools. It seems likely, however, that he would not have bothered to record the expeditions if they were no more than trading outings to other parts of Ethiopia. But can we at least give the southern ethnic gold producers a name and could it be the aforementioned 'Zeng' (sometimes referred to as Zang or Zindj)? Were they a black diaspora?

There is unfortunately a 'Dark Age' shadow across south-central Africa at the start of the Christian millennium, a veil as impenetrable as that over Britain after the departure of the Romans. Even the Shona school, which claims to be able to define a continuity of African evolution through kingdoms, with names like Karanga B, Mwene Mutapa, and Rodzvi (of which more in a moment), admits a 200-year gap in the record.

Professor A.H. Keane, Vice-President of the Anthropological Institute of Great Britain, researched the ancient records of the enigmatic Zeng and quotes from several accounts of them controlling the African east coast from the Somal horn to dominions as far south as Sofala: 'From them the seaboard itself took the name Zanguebar [Zanzibar], the Balid-ez-Zeng or "Land of the Zeng".' The *Periplus of the Red Sea*, a seaman's guide to these waters, *c.* AD 110, warns mariners that Zeng lands extend down the east coast as far as a land called Azania. When in 1964 Julius Nyerere made Tanganyika and Zanzibar island independent of colonial control he called the new state Tanzania.

Tanzania, or if we go back to its earlier name Azania, bordered several countries which must have been involved in any southern migration: Zambia, Congo, Burundi and Rwanda are to the west; Mozambique and Malawi to the south; Uganda and Kenya to the north. Kenya shares a boundary with Ethiopia and Tanzania. Zambia, to the north of Mashonaland, is Tanzania's neighbour.

Any southern diaspora from Arabia/Ethiopia would most likely have called at Zanzibar island. When I came to Africa in 1947, docking at the port of Mombasa, the adjoining island of Zanzibar was still ruled by Arabs, and their ocean-going dhows, which appeared to have sailed straight out of history, still plied these harbours. We followed the traditional route south, first inland to Tanganyika and then down the still-unpaved Great North Road to northern Rhodesia and finally southern Rhodesia, settling in Mashonaland. It is patently a much older road than ever I imagined, and almost certainly, as we shall see, the route of the Bantu migration to Mashonaland. I retraced part of the journey for this book two years ago. There are still dhows coming down the coast to Zanzibar and, a further indication of how slow change can be in Africa, the Great North Road is in worse shape now than it was half a century ago.

Professor Keane's research revealed that Claudius Ptolemy, writing in the second century AD, supports the Greek *Periplus* and describes dark-skinned people as far south as Mozambique. His account has been used to support the claim that there were Bantu in the Great Zimbabwe region much earlier than some would put them there. Others have suggested that the Zeng were a mix of Negroes and Arabians whose dominion was confined to coastal lands. These people came to be called Swahilis and the Shona school has decided that these are the people who traded and transported the gold of the hinterland. Writing in the tenth century the Arab traveller, Masoudi, gives the most detailed description of the Zeng living near Sofala. They were ruled by an elected king called Waqlimi, the name meaning 'the Son of the Supreme Lord' and they worshipped a God by the name of Moklandjalou.

And did this black diaspora keep on the move? A Zimbabwe ethnologist, James Mullan, points out that *Waqlimi* is phonetically surprisingly close to the Sesotho term *Morwa wa ka Limi*. The Sotho, who today live in Botswana, Basutoland and elsewhere, call their god *mulimi*. The coastal blacks encountered by later explorers called themselves by a name which has been phonetically recorded as 'Wak Waks'. It is at least probable that the people Masoudi

219

describes as worshipping Waqlimi were Waks; their god-king being *Wak-limi*. Travelling further south to the Zulu nation, the word for god is *Mkulunkulu*, which is not a million miles removed from the Zeng god *Moklandjalou*, bearing in mind that Masoudi reported everything phonetically.

Are these the first faint footprints of a Nilotic diaspora spreading right down Africa, accompanied, or certainly serviced, by Arab traders? The archaeologists can help somewhat. Dr Garlake says that in about the ninth or tenth century (at about the time Masoudi was describing a Zeng presence) new immigrants entered south-western Matabeleland to create what is known as the Leopard Rock culture: 'Their pottery shows such a marked typological break with early Iron Age wares that, in this instance, there can be little doubt that these people were immigrants who had no direct cultural relationships with the previous inhabitants . . . they were a pastoral people for whom cattle, for the first time in south-central Africa, played important cultural and economic roles.' Garlake goes on to acknowledge the 'rather risky' supposition that these people came from Botswana; that is, they were the early Sotho Bantu. They are possibly the ancestors of the people who built Mapungubwe, the gold-rich, artistic settlement south of the Limpopo which pre-dates Great Zimbabwe. They may indeed have founded the dynasty which went on to build Great Zimbabwe. Garlake prefers the idea that two groups developed 'in the same direction at much the same time'. The word 'Zang' may also simply have been a generic term (like 'Kaffir' was a century ago) for central African black tribes about whom little was known.

The pottery record tends to support the idea of a two-pronged Bantu migration that already had trading contacts with foreigners. One style of ceramics prevails in Iron Age sites along the whole of the Zambian watershed. Another type is found in Malawi and Zimbabwe – the route of the Great North Road. The people who made the Malawi/Zimbabwe pots could not have come down through Katanga and across the inhabited Zambian watershed without their ceramics being influenced by the Zambian style. This pottery evidence dates from very old communities. Ceramic sherds of the Malawi/Zimbabwe style at Great Zimbabwe were associated with Robinson's burnt posts that carbon-dated to AD 320 ± 150. Moreover, every one of these early Iron Age sites in the south contains evidence of trade with foreigners, mainly glass beads and pierced cowrie shells.

It is, however, from a Stone Age cave in the Zambian watershed that we have, so far as I am aware, the earliest apparent evidence of contact between the ancient black inhabitants of central Africa and ancient Moors. My discovery of it was a piece of extraordinary luck. Lodged as a bookmark in an expensive volume on the life of Rhodes, in a Cape Town bookshop, I found a battered paper on the northern Rhodesian Stone Age by Dr J. Desmond Clark, who in the 1950s worked at the Rhodes–Livingstone Museum. Two diagrams caught my eye.

One is from a cave in the Mpika district north of the Zambesi and is a typical bushman painting of the type found all over southern Africa. (These artists have been named the Nachikufu culture and the earth floors of their caves have revealed many kinds of Stone Age implements.) Another cave from the same site displayed, in faded red pigment, a very strange drawing. The pigmentation appears to be the same as the bushman painting and implements for grinding pigments were among the Stone Age implements found. 'There is,' observes Dr Desmond Clark, 'a sudden change to entirely stylised drawing – circles, ladders, strokes, capital Us and Is, crescents, tectiform designs and combinations of lines, dots and circles.' The second drawing is alien and – he was told by expert Orientalists he consulted – represented: 'a debased form of some kind of Arabic writing, drawn by illiterate or semi-literate persons, in imitation of some ornamental piece of decoration or writing. As yet it is impossible to date this art style but it has been tentatively suggested that [it] may be a debased version of the Cufic word for Allah. . . . In addition to the paintings there are engravings in the same style. They are known from one rock-shelter, but more usually are found on flat, exposed rock surfaces near the banks of streams or rivers. . . . A significant fact is that the distribution of the schematic art style appears to coincide

221

with the known areas of Arab penetration of the sub-continent. Similar paintings occur in Tanganyika superimposed on the naturalistic art group.'

Subsequent excavations by Desmond Clark revealed that these Stone Age deposits were overlaid by a Bantu occupation layer. Moreover, the Stone Age deposits here contained artefacts resembling those from the Tanganyika plateau and stone tools found in late Stone Age middens on the shores of Lake Tanganyika. Clark's work provides an important missing link in the genesis of alien influence in south-central Africa, and if there were old Moors trading, possibly semi-resident on the Zambesi in the Stone Age, then this is much earlier than most experts had previously conceded. It also has a dramatic bearing on the race of those traders, as we will discover shortly.

The significant elements of our 'Time Line' of alien influence now read like this:

950 BC Solomon makes an alliance with the Phoenician Hiram of Tyre and they share the wealth of foreign expeditions, returning with distinctly African goods, particularly gold.

611 BC Neku II circumnavigates Africa.

470 BC Phoenicians sail to the Azores and Madeira. Himilco, to the British Isles.

110 BC Eudoxos of Cysicus is sent by Cleopatra to India. Blown off course returning home he lands on the east coast of Africa where he finds a wrecked Phoenician ship from Gades mounting a distinctive horse-head prow.

24 BC Aelius Gallus, Roman Prefect of Egypt, invades Yemen with an army of 10,000 Roman infantry seeking to take over the Sabaean colonial trade. Illness among the troops forces a retreat.

AD 35 The Greek *Periplus* records that the Sabaean King Kharabit controls East Africa to 'an indefinite extent'.

AD 100 (or earlier) Ancient Moors leave their trade markers (or Stone Age artists copy Arab markers) north of the Zambesi in south-central Africa.

AD 150 Ptolemy's map of the world records accurate details of East Africa, including the correct positions of Mashonaland and Mozambique, which are shown south of 'The Mountains of the Moon'.

AD 700–1000 The Bantu migrate into Mashonaland.

AD 943 Masoudi reports that the Muslims of Oman sailed on the Zang Sea as far south as Madagascar and 'Sufalah' where they meet the 'Wak Wak'.

AD 1140 Idris enlarges on these Wak Wak of Sufalah, describing them as horrible aboriginals whose speech resembles whistling. Hottentots ('Chinese' Hottentots) were later reported as using the name Quae Quae. The San are today mostly known by the generic 'Khoi Khoi'.

AD 1220 Yakut records in his geographia that Sofala is the furthest south city in the country of 'Zang'.

AD 1250 Marco Polo reports (by hearsay, but from Arab sources) that goods are brought by ships to the African side of the Red Sea, then shipped by camel on a thirty-day overland journey to the Nile, then on to Cairo and Alexandria. He also describes the Negroid features of the Zeng. He is cognisant of the powerful current (the Agulhas) between Madagascar and Mozambique, warning that in places it runs so fast that sailing vessels would make no headway even with favourable winds. He must have been told this by Moorish mariners with whom he voyaged to India.

AD 1487 Captain Bartolomeu Dias de Novaes finds the African coast north of Walvis Bay, then rounds the Cape and sails north to Bushman's River. Vasco da Gama follows him, also rounding the Cape. He encounters large groups of San and has to shoot one to get safely back to his ship.

AD 1502 Portuguese explorers visit Sofala and, from old Moors, hear of a 'wonderful rich mine'. They decide this is King Solomon's mines.

AD 1505 The start of Portuguese colonialism with the annexation of Sofala leading, by 1609, to many descriptions of the hinterland. Trade is in the hands of ancient Moors; there are

300 mosques in Sofala. A detailed report by the reliable Dominican missionary, Joao dos Santos, who lived and worked among the Karanga, produces the first detailed testimony of an ancient trade: 'The people of these lands, and especially some old Moors who have preserved a tradition of their ancestors, say these houses were in olden times the trading depots of the Queen of Saba and that from these depots they used to bring to her much gold, following the rivers of Cuama [Zambesi] down to the Ethiopian coast up to the Red Sea. They entered the Red Sea and sailed to the shores which touch Egypt and there they used to off load all this gold which was brought by land to the Queen of Sheba.'

'MODERN' TIMES

1800s

Adventurous western treasure seekers like the American, Adam Renders, find spectacular ruins in the hinterland. They certainly trade and intermarry with the natives.

The first eyewitness account of Great Zimbabwe is that of Carl Mauch who 'finds' the lost city. Land-grabbers, some like Cecil Rhodes, whose appetites aspire to whole continents, turn their eyes north.

Mashonaland, the homeland of a race called the Karanga, part of a black diaspora from the north, *c.* 700–800, becomes Rhodesia where, *c.* 1947, I become an alien settler as part of a post-Second World War white diaspora.

An acrimonious debate between the Romantic school and the Shona school fuelled by the conclusions of (alien) archaeologists rages for the first quarter of the twentieth century, neither side giving ground till this day.

The earliest scientifically authenticated artefact is an Egyptian bead found by Dr Hans Sauer among gold ingots.

Some time earlier the Zimbabwe chief of the time, Mugabe, is photographed by the wife of the leader of the Royal Geographical Society's expedition to Great Zimbabwe,

Chief Mugabe sports a necklace of valuable Venetian pearls, although seemingly he had no appreciation of the value of gold? This picture, by Mrs Bent, was actually taken to show that the Karanga did not have typically African facial features.

> Mrs Bent, wearing what her husband identifies as a necklace of Venetian origin.

Returning us to the present, I have become convinced that this necklace is one of the great undetected clues to several unresolved enigmas in the origin debate. It is certainly the most important photograph Mrs Bent ever took, even though the Bents were interested in the facial features of these Shona, not their alien accoutrements.

The picture casts grave doubts on the critical comments made of Chief Mugabe. He was disparaged as a minor rural chief and maligned for knowing nothing about his ancestors and/or the authors and craftsmen who raised the stone monoliths and in whose shadow he raised cattle from a makeshift village of pole-and-daga huts. Indeed, he was accused of fuelling Romantic arguments by recounting legends of a 'white' origin. I would suggest that Chief Mugabe is exactly what he appears to be, an authoritative-looking

African elder statesman, obviously familiar with traders from the outside world; indeed, he is rather magnificently adorned with their trade goods, as are his indunas.

How much of all the evidence, I wonder, have we failed to take at its obvious 'face value'? Chief Mugabe's photograph is not the only instance where answers to some of Great Zimbabwe's intractable riddles may have been staring everyone in the face for the last century. The researcher who spent more time than any other puzzling over the origins of the grand *zimbabwes*, Dr Roger Summers, was, throughout the latter part of his term as Director of the Historical Monuments Commission, troubled by similar thoughts about certain singular features of the walls of Great Zimbabwe. Could it be, he pondered, that the evidence of alien influence was literally written in these stones?

ELEVEN

Ophir Writ Large

Roger Summers was not immediately rewarded with an answer. Only after gazing hard at the huge walls of Great Zimbabwe for a good many years did he realise that something was inexplicably 'wrong' with them: 'The Zimbabwe ruins are very complex and contain a great variety of details which are *very hard to explain* by a complete acceptance of MacIver's hypothesis,' was his opening gambit in a dangerous game.

Summers was trained at the University of London's Institute of Archaeology. He worked on the ancient ruins of the Zimbabwe culture from his post at the National Museum, Bulawayo, from 1947 until 1970, and served as Chairman of the Rhodesian Historical Monuments Commission for five years. His qualifications are impeccable. In his book, *Ancient Ruins and Vanished Civilisations of Southern Africa* (T.V. Bulpin, Cape Town, 1971), he lays down his 'rules of logic' for archaeological research: (1) All available factual evidence must be taken into account; (2) Evidence must be weighed critically, but personal prejudice must be avoided; (3) Simple explanations and proximate causes are always preferable to complicated or remote ones.

Professor Summers is no Romantic. In the main his beliefs fall within the framework of those of the Shona school and Summers is at one with 'most recent commentators, [who] after careful re-examination of the evidence have accepted the view that Great Zimbabwe is a local phenomenon built by native peoples'.

So what is so *'very hard to explain'* about the walls? What did others miss? Summers' carefully chosen words were expressed at a time (1971) when the authorship of the ruins was a very hot topic politically. From personal experience of how dangerous any

227

utterances about the origin of Great Zimbabwe could be, I am surprised to find Summers stepping into this ring at all. But step he did, and I am thankful for his courage, because the 'wrongness' writ large in these walls offers the best indication yet of those responsible for the lost city's distinctive architecture. Summers believed he had found what amounted to a 'third force', a craftsman clan within Zimbabwe society which was either alien or alien-taught.

Down the years several attempts have been made to date-categorise the different wall types. Today there are four agreed 'stages', varying from irregular blocks piled in chaotic style with no evidence of courses, to equal-sized blocks with the blocks coursed in horizontal layers that form a very regular pattern. The first are believed to date back to the Iron Age at about the start of the Christian millennium and the last, of which Great Zimbabwe is the best example, to medieval times.

The start of this 'best-built' stage, especially in the case of the Great Outer Wall of the Elliptical Building, exhibit, as Summers puts it, 'new and vastly improved techniques'.

He identifies six distinct improved techniques in the Great Wall:

1. Foundation trench with levelled floor, implying some form of levelling instrument.
2. Laying of first course as an even pavement over the whole of the foundation trench.
3. Careful trimming of foundation stones and very strict selection of all stones for thickness.
4. Levelling of all courses (see 1. above).
5. Thick walls with inward-sloped faces, the slope (batter) being even, implying the use of a plumb line.
6. Construction of wall patterns.

'At least two and probably three [of the improved techniques],' Summers adds, *'never appear again in any ancient ruin.'* I have emphasised this statement because I believe it is as close as we can ever get to material evidence, writ in stone, of alien architectural influence in the Zimbabwe culture. Indeed, I would personally go a step further and propose that this, the moment when stone enclosures became works of art, might also be the moment when the Karanga moved from being a hard-working aboriginal society to becoming a culture.

What brought this about? 'One may postulate the appearance of a genius among local architects, but it may involve less of a strain on credibility if one suggests the arrival of someone who was conversant with building techniques elsewhere, since the level and the plumb line have been known as building instruments for many centuries.' Summers thinks this knowledgeable mason arrived and made his contribution some time between 1450 and 1600, the most favoured dates for the best period of Zimbabwe building. But what if this 'best period' started several centuries earlier? We still have that contentious carbon dating of AD 670 for the *ubande* drain supports under one of Great Zimbabwe's most massive walls.

It emerges that Summers is plagued by similar thoughts. An earlier date for the building of the temple (Elliptical Building) would, he admits, 'open all sorts of exciting possibilities such as MacIver could not have foreseen,' and 'it is not entirely stretching possibility to suggest that some Portuguese stonemason may have reached Zimbabwe and entered the service of the great chief living there. . . . Equally probable, although rather less plausible, is that some travelling Arab craftsman may have been responsible.' Given the fact that we have now traced alien influence, most likely by ancient Moors, all the way back to the central African Stone Age we are entitled at least to consider that Arab craftsmen, or Arab-taught craftsmen, were influential in the raising of *zimbabwes* long before their work became so distinctive. Professor Summers was able to see evidence of it in the massive walls of Great Zimbabwe, before there were Bantu here perhaps?

Politically, Summers is now treading on very thin ice and, I presume in recognition of this, he follows the example of respected peers and leaves the country. In 1971 we find him not in Bulawayo but at the South African Museum, working on his book with a Cape Town publisher. It was a wise move, however, because Summers was actually harbouring a theory much more destructive to the Shona idyll of a home-grown Zimbabwe culture than anything he had expressed thus far. He had become convinced that the alien mason was neither Portuguese nor Arab, but a member of a subculture of artistic black craftsmen. On the face of it this should have put him right back in favour, but he had also decided that this subculture was not Shona and might possibly be alien. Remember, we are here reviewing the findings of a quiet, studious academic whose work reflects his great love of Africa and its people. What could he possibly have found that was causing him to wander so far off the safe, beaten track?

The Summers paradox, if we may call it that, starts with his observations that the mighty walls depend on level foundations, implying some form of levelling instrument. The walls, moreover, have inward-facing slopes, the slope (batter) being even, implying the use of a plumb line. But – and this is the paradox – Summers also observed that the use of other instruments vital to the sophisticated mason's trade, particularly the square, were nowhere in evidence. Virtually nothing is square at Great Zimbabwe and there is literally no squaring of walls and corridors as are found in classic Arab and Portuguese architecture. The opposite is in fact true. Zimbabwe is a place of sensuous curves, even the doorways. It is, I think, the true appeal of the place. The architecture is, if you like, whimsical.

Summers thought this too and set out to try and prove it by a close study of the rationale of the architecture of the elliptical temple. All the doorways through its Great Outer Wall are rounded and particular care has been taken to make them very solid. They have even withstood destruction during collapses of other walls which, being all of granite, are immensely heavy. The main entrance to the northern section of the Great Wall has particularly complex and unusual curves for which Summers could find no architectural reason. The minimum section of the entrance narrows to 50 cm, curving out to 2.35 metres on the outer face and 3.30 metres on the inside. As a design for a doorway, says Summers, it is 'fantastic'. As a design for providing a way through a thick, high, heavy wall it has no practical or utilitarian purpose whatsoever.

Summers then considered the problems this shape made for the designer – 'who was manifestly a very clever and practical man' – in particular the lintels, which would have been required to support another 6 feet of granite wall some 3 metres thick. Huge wooden lintels estimated at 600 kg would have had to be raised 3.5 metres above the floor because no stone lintels of this length were available. Extremely sophisticated masonry work was then designed for the wall above the doorway. The slope (battering) of the wall fades slowly and perfectly above the lintels, from 5° from the perpendicular to about 10° at the top. Leaving air spaces in the fill between the dressed faces also reduced the weighting on the wood beams. Perhaps I did feel a strange wind blowing through the walls all those years ago.

Doorways of this complexity create so many problems for the architect – a square one would have been infinitely easier and stronger. Summers presumes that the imperative was purely aesthetic. In other words – and important to other imperatives considered in a moment – it was conceived artistically and imposed on the architect. 'Improvisation of this order can only be undertaken if normal method and underlying theory are understood, so they cannot be attributed to local people,' says Summers. 'Hence the suggestion that the architects obtained a very sound training in the sophisticated and civilised arts of the Arab communities on the East Coast.'

However, this still does not explain why our alien mason never used a square. 'A third possibility has been suggested,' Summers continues. 'The external influence visible in the Great Walls was a second-hand one, derived through somebody who had learned his building trade under some Portuguese or Arab master craftsman but who had no contact with building in the outside world.' What's more, Summers believes he has identified an artistic, artisan subculture within the Zimbabwe culture known as the *Mwenye*. The name crops up in a number of ethnographic accounts. The *Mwenye*, Summers goes on, had living descendants who 'still live in the northern Transvaal and the southern parts of Rhodesia, differ physically and culturally from the Bantu with whom they live and keep themselves socially separate, although they have no tribal organisation of their own. Their appearance, customs and traditions all point to their being the descendants of the "Moors" or people of part-Arab descent who were the actual traders sent inland by Arab merchants on the coast.' They now comprise two small tribes living on both sides of the Limpopo river, called the Venda and the Lemba.

It would be unfair to leave Summers out alone on this deadly limb. His colleague, K.S. Robinson, Inspector of Monuments before Dr Garlake, had already suggested something similar. Robinson interpreted his pottery finds as suggesting that there had been two interventions in the cultural flow of the Zimbabwe culture, 'marked by drastic changes and innovations' with 'fresh ideas introduced by immigrants who may have been the predecessors of the present Shona-speaking people'. Elsewhere Robinson spoke of 'new and vital elements . . . the result of fresh and vigorous new blood'.

Dr Garlake himself admits to the appearance of better surface finishes on pottery at Great Zimbabwe and a radical change in hut building. 'Pole-and-daga' walls were sometimes replaced by solid walls of thick clay. Admittedly, he still denies alien influence as the causal factor in all this.

If, as was now being implied, artistic considerations had been a driving force – perhaps *the* driving force – behind the architecture of Great Zimbabwe, then there was just the man to offer a defining opinion – Frank McEwen, once Director of the Rhodesian National Art Gallery. In preparation for his Rhodesian appointment, he had familiarised himself with the Zimbabwean 'winged angels' in the British and Tishman Museum collections and he came out to Africa via Cape Town to inspect the many Zimbabwe works of art still on display there, in particular the Zimbabwe birds. Frank McEwen proposed the unthinkable, that a country with a tradition of carved stone birds and winged angels had to have an indigenous artistic tradition, even though it appeared to have been obliterated by colonialism. It was his ambition to get this phoenix back in the air and he made no secret of it. Within a few years, flouting a great number of laws, he had started a black artistic renaissance which, forty years on, is Africa's most flourishing school of sculpture, its pieces occupying pride of place in institutions like the New York Museum of Modern Art.

What appeared to be McEwen's most eccentric gesture – a giant battleur eagle which he kept on the balcony of his apartment at the gallery and flew in the park behind it – turns out to have considerable relevance to our story.

Things came to a head for Frank when Joseph Mazerika came into his gallery with his latest sculpture, a master work displaying interlocking male and female figures of amethyst quartz; the woman was carved in white quartz, the male in the darker rock. The racial implication did not go unnoticed in Rhodesia where it was illegal for a black man to have relations with a white woman. Frank was told to destroy the sculpture, but instead quit the country, taking the piece with him. Many years later, when I realised that a hundred years of research had thrown no new light on the role and function of the Zimbabwe birds and the importance of art to the Zimbabwe culture, I thought of Frank McEwen, finding him and his wife in a remote cottage in the south-west of England. The famous amethyst 'loving couple' still had pride of place in his house.

After listening to the progression of my research, culminating in the revelations of Roger Summers that Great Zimbabwe had been shaped aesthetically, Frank suddenly said: 'You've tapped in to the hidden river.' He agreed that there must have been artistic alien influence and pointed out that all the world's great art schools had needed their promoters: Prince Philip IV of Spain behind Velasquez, Van Gogh's famous brother, Theo, and the pharaoh, Akhenaton, whose patronage produced new styles of naturalistic art and literature, including the famous painted limestone bust of Nefertiti, Akhenaton's queen. Frank seemed to find Akhenaton, who became pharaoh in 1379 BC, a particularly good model for the Zimbabwe culture. He was one of the first of the Egyptian pharaohs to worship one god, Aten the god of the sun, who later, of course, became the hawk-god Horus whose icons obviously attract comparison with the Zimbabwe birds. Moreover, Akhenaton was worshipped in a new kind of roofless temple. His reforms, however, were too radical and when he died in 1362 BC his temples were

233

demolished. The followers of his reforms were persecuted and many fled this oppression.

McEwen saw himself as one such promoter, or patron, in the art vacuum he found in Mashonaland. Equally he was at great pains to stress that there is a world of difference between promoting and influencing artists. This is perhaps the world of difference which separates the Romantic (and often racist) theory of Semite aliens using natives to build megalithic stone cities with temples and art reflecting their own old religious beliefs, and the alternative – that a receptive, newly affluent Karanga accepted alien advice and art patronage to help with the creation of the Zimbabwe culture. 'I couldn't teach my people anything about the creation of the work,' McEwen insisted. 'They were teaching me.'

But these fledgling black artists he encouraged could easily have been seduced into what he called 'airport art' – mass-produced soapstone tourist souvenirs ranging from simple busts to napkin rings – so he took the school into hiding. McEwen found a valley in the eastern mountains near where the first *zimbabwes* had been built. This 1,200-acre sanctuary had no road to it and could only be accessed through a narrow opening between massive rocks. The artists asked that spirit-mediums first visit the valley to ensure it was 'favourable', confirming for McEwen that the ability to carve the mysterious images his artists were producing had a direct link with native traditions. These shamans also reported that they had found the remains of *zimbabwes*, ancient pots and grave sites, and that the area had caves containing the icons of ancestor-spirits, but McEwen was never shown any.

An access to the valley, just wide enough for a truck with building materials and food plants sufficient to sustain a community in traditional huts, was cut using the old Karanga practice of heat exfoliation. McEwen remembers his sense of awe as he stood and watched the creation of rock slabs identical to those of which Great Zimbabwe is built. 'As soon as the artists settled in they were extremely happy,' he recalls. 'We ate nothing but home-grown vegetables and wild fruits together with fresh-killed meats.' McEwen, who had stalked stag in his native Scotland, did the hunting. Speaking of the artists' work, he says: 'The results were immediately, well, extraordinary. . . . I knew Picasso rather well, and Matisse, Carot and Leger but I have never seen anything like this. I watched them very closely hoping to work out where the inspiration was coming from. They would go into a kind of dream-state seemingly staying that way until they could see the work in absolutely perfect three dimensions then quickly, before they lost the dream, execute it – execute it in a frenzy.'

McEwen took the works of his secret school – abstract sculptures, large and small – to France and an exhibition at the Musée Rodin. Reviewers enthused: 'These Shona artists have taken up their tools where the fifteenth-century artists laid them down.'

Frank urged me also not to forget the winged angels anonymously tucked away in London and New York. The piece in the Tishman Collection was his particular favourite: 'It is an absolute miracle. As great as any Egyptian sculpture and proves that these people understood the principles of advanced sculpture, the principles of three-dimensional art.' McEwen also regarded this figure as artistic proof of a formal religion within the Zimbabwe culture. 'Winged figures exist in all religions,' he pointed out. The same was almost certainly true of the other soapstone carvings from Great Zimbabwe, especially the Zimbabwe birds, and of the more ornately carved columns and bowls unique to Great Zimbabwe. 'Few religions function without sacred vessels.'

McEwen was, moreover, in general agreement with my conclusion that alien influence was a flickering flame playing across the whole history of the Zimbabwe culture. Perhaps a more accurate word for this influence is *promotion* of the latent talents of the indigenous people. 'An artistic class would have grown up within the culture,' Frank remarked, coming very close to the conclusions of Roger Summers. 'Just as we have now with sons following in the footsteps of their fathers. It would have been closely connected with the indigenous religion, indeed many of the pieces carved today still represent ancient spirits from the old animist days.' Then he too said that he thought the ancestors of this ancient artistic class could be traced to the Venda/Lemba. He was convinced that the hidden river had continued to flow, albeit sluggishly, with the Venda/Lemba who had remained known for their carvings, particularly of fish. Their work still attracts the higher prices in Cape Town's smart African art shops.

Prior to my reunion with Frank McEwen I had always assumed that the Lemba people were all but extinct, a little like the Kalahari San, too few in number to retain any individual identity. I have also been wary of the proposition (made by almost every observer from Selous onwards) that certain Shona display non-characteristic facial features. Mrs Bent's photograph of Chief Mugabe and his indunas, you will recall, was actually taken to illustrate the proposition. There is little in this photograph, and in the others I have seen, to indicate that among some Shona are to be found the more aquiline facial features of northern tribes like the Tutsi or those of Ethiopia, nor have I changed this view. It is in a line of enquiry too often tinged with racial prejudice to be worth pursuing. The more I studied material about the Lemba, however, there was no denying that they certainly shared a strange, quite detailed, legend of their origins which set them apart from other Bantu people, not least because it held that the Lemba were descended from North African or Arabian Semitic races. Or to put that more bluntly, most believed they were descended from a 'white' tribe.

Sadly I only ever interviewed one Lemba. He had applied for a job as a security guard at the television station I ran in Bulawayo and had been mistakenly listed by my secretary as 'Bemba', a large tribe to the north. The only reason I remember him is because, on his application form, he listed his religion as Jewish – and insisted Bemba be corrected to Lemba. A black Jew was not significantly unusual because for centuries western missionaries had ensured that Africans were exposed to most religions, certainly the established religions. There are flocks of black Catholics, Protestants, Muslims, Jehovah's Witnesses, Seventh Day Adventists – and Jews. But none of us (or hardly any of us) knew that Rhodesia housed remnants of a lost tribe claiming Jewish antecedents and the authorship of the Great Zimbabwe ruins nor that there was a tribal-sized group of them south of the Limpopo river in a very rural area of South Africa called Vendaland.

A South African ethnologist, Dr N.J. van Warmelo, who began his work in the early part of the last century and would become Chief Ethnologist to the Department of Native Affairs and the acknowledged expert on the Lemba, had in fact studied the Venda intensively. Moreover, his testimony is especially valuable because he had the advantage of working with the Lemba long before western influences had materially altered the remote rural areas of South Africa and, it has to be said, before being a Lemba set you apart and of interest to (in Lemba terms) well-heeled academics and, nowadays, tourists. Hopefully, I am not being gratuitously critical of modern Lemba but these factors could have an important bearing on the veracity and durability of their singular beliefs about themselves. What needs to be recognised right away is that essentially the Lemba core beliefs of their unique, frankly bizarre, origins have not changed since van Warmelo first went among them in the 1930s. From the beginning van Warmelo acknowledges this: 'It cannot be assumed, even if some tales from the Old Testament have often been told to the natives, that these tales should have taken such a hold on their fancy as to cause them to be woven into the traditions of the tribe.' What *is* 'woven' very tightly into these traditions runs as follows.

The original Lemba were made up of ten tribes like the Lost Tribes of Israel. The tribes diffused south from a place called 'Sena' in the Middle East whose exact location has been entirely lost to the Lemba. They settled first on the Zambesi then travelled to the Shona plateau and built Great Zimbabwe where they were known as the '*Mwenye*'. They were driven out of the lost city after an act of apostasy – they ate mice! Throughout their wandering the proto-Lemba carried with them a ceremonial drum, the *ngoma lungunda*. Van Warmelo described this as 'the sacred drum which was borne along on their wanderings like the Ark of the Covenant'. Some Lemba believe that their wandering Jewish ancestors paused for a time among the Ethiopians who, of course, have their own myth of the rescue from Egypt of the Ark of the Covenant.

If we now step forward several decades to the second half of the twentieth century, Professor Gayre, the Scottish anthropologist, also engaged on a field trip to investigate Venda/Lemba legends of origin. He returns with stories told to him by the Lemba essentially supporting van Warmelo's, but even more astonishing. The Venda/Lemba, Gayre claims, believe their *male* ancestors were white. 'The Lemba do not eat rabbit, hare, pork, carrion or meat with the blood in it,' Gayre wrote in *Mankind Quarterly*. 'In addition the Lembas not only practice circumcision but are essential in the circumcision schools among their neighbors. It is not difficult to see that they adhere to the dietary laws of the Mosaic or Levitical code.' It has been argued that Professor Gayre was a propagandist for white supremacy but his notes have subsequently been essentially confirmed by other researchers, right up to the present day.

The Revd Harald von Sicard, a fine Karanga linguist who spent twenty years studying and recording oral traditions of the Lemba (also B. Schlomann, O.C. Dahl, T. Price, and J. Blake-Thompson), found the same singularities as van Warmelo and Gayre in Venda/ Lemba legends and practices.

> They have facial characteristics usually associated with the Swahili Arabs of the east coast.
> Lemba oral tradition holds that their ancestors came from overseas in a big boat.
> There are similar words for 'sun' in the languages of the Lemba and the natives of Madagascar.
> The Lemba are known as the *Mwenye*, which is also the word used in Mozambique for Indian Muslims.
> The Moorish traders who used the Sabi valley and held regular markets in the interior were known as the *Amwenye Vashava*.

Professor Gayre dates the genesis of the Zimbabwean *Mwenye* to the sixth century AD building which fits well the earliest Carbon-14 dating for *zimbabwe*. Before this time, he correctly points out, the Arabs were Christian or Pagan.

Another jump forward to the middle 1990s finds the British ethnographer, Dr Tudor Parfitt, industriously beating this same trail in an attempt to locate legendary 'Sena'. He finds that the Lemba legend has now started to bring tourists to Vendaland and there are established support groups with their own flag: a blue cloth embroidered in gold with the Star of David. He spends enough time with the Lemba for them to invite him to traditional gatherings, and is told essentially the same core story, but also hears revelations – tribal secrets – that embroider the fabric. A Lemba tribal headman, Solomon Sadiki, vice-chairman of the Lemba Cultural Association, tells him that he had been told by his father that the tribe came from Sena, which was in Egypt or Yemen, went to Ethiopia where they were called Falasha, then moved on south again: 'Our forefathers reached the east coast of Africa. When they left the coast they went and built the great stone city of Zimbabwe. But the Lemba broke the law and the people thought Mwali [god] was cross with them and they went and lived among the nations.' Another elder disagrees. He points out that in the Bible, Nehemiah lists the ten Lost Tribes of Israel and that one of them was from 'Sena' – 'the sons of Sena, three thousand, nine hundred and thirty'. Sena, he affirms, was a town in Israel, north of Jericho.

So is there any bedrock to this legend? Dr Parfitt does not much like Professor Gayre (very reminiscent, in fact, of Dr Randall-MacIver's dislike of Theodore Bent), describing him as 'the editor of a racist journal called the *Mankind Quarterly*, in which in 1967 he had written a short article on the Lemba'. Dr Parfitt notes that Gayre went on to write a book, *The Origins of the Great Zimbabwe Civilization*, at the behest of the Rhodesian government, with the clear objective of showing 'that black people had never been capable of building in stone or of governing themselves'. (Dr Parfitt later interviews the last Rhodesian Prime Minister, Ian Smith, who derides this as ridiculous and points out that he had better things to do with his time, and that it was not 'in keeping with Government policy'. I knew Ian Smith quite well. He was politically deluded but rarely dishonest.) The ironic point of all this, however, is that Dr Parfitt apparently overlooks the fact that it was Professor Gayre's book, *The Origins of the Great Zimbabwe Civilization*, which first confirmed the Lemba belief that its *male* line was once white.

239

It was the following-up of this bizarre lead by scientists, including Dr Parfitt, that has subsequently introduced an astounding new possibility into the Zimbabwe origin debate. It was also Professor Gayre who suggested another much-needed link in the proposed southern exodus of the people who may have been the Lemba.

It seems that there is another group of black Jews, even less well known than the Ethiopian Falashas, resident on the tiny Comoros islands in the Indian Ocean. (The word Falasha is Amharic for 'stranger'.) Like the sect in Ethiopia these Comoran neo-Jews follow a truncated Hebrew tradition that reflects the knowledge of the people in south-west Asia at roughly the time of King Solomon. The Comoros are situated between the island of Madagascar and the Indian Ocean coast. Following the meridian west from the middle of Madagascar it passes just south of the Comoros and then hits both Sofala and Great Zimbabwe virtually on the nose. It is hardly surprising that Professor Gayre was drawn to conclude: 'It would seem that the Falashas of Ethiopia and the Black Jews of the Comoros Islands derive their cultural descent from the Hebrew trading people in or about the region of Saba at the time of King Solomon and Hiram, King of Tyre.'

Very reluctantly, even the arch-sceptics of the Shona school have in recent times been obliged to acknowledge the singular skills of Venda/Lemba, although in this context no mention is made of their apparent Jewishness. 'Similar sets of iron-working tools to those found by Bent and Hall,' admits Dr Garlake, 'were used in recent times by the Venda.' He also lets slip that the Venda/Lemba 'are known for their stone chiefs' dwellings and their metal working skills'. More simply (and unbeknown to Theodore Bent who placed so much importance on the fact that all the natives lived in mud huts) there was, indeed is, a group of Africans in this region who traditionally built in stone.

We even have a contemporary description of the Venda/Lemba at this work. In 1931, Professor Percival Kirby, a musician from the University of the Witwatersrand, went to Vendaland to record the tribe's distinctive music. En route he came across a *kraal* being built for the newly appointed Chief Tshivase, men from all over

Vendaland having assembled for building operations which included (as Kirby told Dr Summers): 'Huge retaining walls . . . to keep a series of terraces in position on the mountain side. Staircases of stone were constructed . . . and these, together with several connected passages were enclosed by walls which were furnished with loopholes. . . . Several of the walls were furnished with vertical stones [stelae] . . . some of the walls were at least 14 feet high and 5 feet thick.'

'Even more recently,' says Professor Summers, 'Dr Revil Mason has visited Vendaland and seen not just the ruin of the building Kirby saw being built – but a new one being built for yet another Chief Tshivase.' Dr Summers observes somewhat wryly that it seems the Venda could turn them out at the rate of six buildings to the century.

Finally, there is the testimony of the contemporary Zimbabwe archaeologist, Ken Mufuka:

> The second tribe associated with the Dzimbahwe culture are the WaRemba [Lemba]. The WaRemba can definitely trace their history to the Mwene-Mutapa [Monomatapa]. Today they live among the BaVenda and are known for their custom of removing blood from a dead carcase. They were the adventurers of southern Africa: they travelled widely between the East Coast and Dzimbahwe. They lived by their wits; they were merchants and seemed only to have settled down after the demise of Dzimbahwe confederation. They were known particularly for their skill in stretching copper wire into fine bracelets. . . . Future research on Great Zimbabwe should move to the BaVenda and WaRemba rather than concentrate on the monument itself.

I agree, and it would have suited me well to have closed this book with the considered words of a Zimbabwean academic. But, by the time that was written, other scientists were already on the trail and had focused the most modern of tracing techniques on the possibility that there was an incredibly ancient answer to the origins of the lost city.

Just as everything to do with the science of archaeology changed dramatically in the middle of the twentieth century, with the invention of Carbon-14 dating, another new science – DNA 'fingerprinting' – has in the last few years resulted in a similar, even more startling, breakthrough with the Lemba. At the heart of the Venda/Lemba Jewish legend is the belief that a priest named Buba led the tribe out of Judea.

Orthodox Jews believe that their priests are a hereditary caste, the *cohanim*, the descendants of Aaron, the older brother of Moses. As the millennium closed the use of DNA sequences as a positive method of identifying individuals and their ancestors became commonplace and encouraged a group of geneticists to apply it to the Aaron–*cohanim* tradition. Dr Karl Skorecki – who is also a priest – of the Technicon-Israel Institute put the idea to Dr Michael F. Hammer of the University of Arizona, who studies the genetics of human populations and is a specialist in the Y, or male, chromosome. Y chromosomes are passed, mostly unaltered, from father to son. Where mutations have occurred they remain distinctive fingerprints in male lineages. In 1997, the Hammer–Skorecki team announced that their study of the Y chromosomes of Jewish priests (who are not the same as rabbis) and lay Jews had shown that a particular pattern of DNA changes were much more common among the priests than among laymen.

This work was taken up by Neil Bradman at the Centre for Genetic Anthropology at University College, London, who recruited an Oxford geneticist, David Goldstein. Could the Y chromosome technique be used to link and perhaps confirm obscure elements of the Jewish diaspora as well as any priestly links? The study confirmed that many Jewish priests do have a particular set of genetic mutations in common. Some 45 per cent of Ashkenazi priests and 56 per cent of Sephardic priests had the *cohanim* genetic signature, even though these two branches of the Jewish priesthood live geographically apart. In the whole Jewish population the frequency of this genetic signature is reduced to 3 to 5 per cent.

Goldstein was even able to make a calculation of when the owners of the *cohanim* genetic signature last shared a common ancestor. Depending on calculations of 25 and 30 years per generation he nominated 2,650 or 3,180 years ago. As legend has it that Moses assigned the priesthood to the male descendants of his brother, Aaron, after the Jewish exodus from Egypt 3,000 years ago these dates are, to put it mildly, intriguing. Even more intriguing for me, however, were the results of genetic tests Goldstein made from the Lemba; 9 per cent – twice the Jewish lay norm – of Lemba men displayed the *cohanim* genetic signature!

Lemba society is split into twelve 'clans' (some say ten) of which the most senior is named after Buba, the priest who they believe led the tribe out of Judaea and upon whose orders in their new African homeland they practised circumcision, kept one day a week holy, and followed Jewish dietary laws. Some 53 per cent of the Buba Lemba whose Y chromosomes David Goldstein studied displayed the *cohanim* genetic signature. Unless the whole science of genetic fingerprinting is somehow fatally flawed, the Buba clan of the Lemba must once have had descendants in the Jewish priest caste founded at the time of Solomon or earlier.

Postscript

History, not just this history, will be rewritten using the new tools of genetic mutations. Nothing even remotely as powerful has previously come to the aid of archaeologists, in particular origin theorists. Dramatic, sometimes shocking, home truths about who we all are and where we come from are just over the horizon. One such by Bryan Sykes, Professor of Human Genetics at the University of Oxford, using genetic fingerprints from mitochondrial DNA, claims that everyone of native European descent, wherever they live in the world, can trace their ancestry back to one of seven women.

But the most exciting aspect of this new science is that it can with great accuracy make quantum leaps back in time. Back before human time in fact, and the genetic scientists have already cast new light on the seminal debate of the origins of our species, and whether Homo sapiens, the so-called 'thinking apes' of modern Europe, are the descendants of Neanderthal or Cro-Magnon ape-men. The informed opinion, now virtually a consensus, is that we all began in Africa and, intriguingly for this story, that cultural awareness, particularly cave-art, began in Ethiopia at sites like Omo-Kibbish that are well over 100,000 years old. Personally I cannot wait for the revelations about the San People that must come in the near future from refinements of the techniques of genetic dating.

At the beginning of this book I declared my brief to be that of an investigation of the origins of the Zimbabwe culture, not of the temple-cities like Great Zimbabwe, and I feel I have shown beyond reasonable doubt that the temple-cities are the more recent, eclectic window-dressing of a much older society. If now, however, we throw off the time constraints suggesting that this was a culture which came and went in a single millennium, the lid is lifted on a period of history that has never been properly considered in the Zimbabwe context other than by very old, much-derided Romantics. With genetic fingerprinting still in its infancy it is still, admittedly, only possible to peep into this Pandora's box.

Is there *anything* in the myths and legends, the Bible's layered apocryphal tales, the oral traditions and peculiar practices of singular tribes like the Lemba, to add flesh to these vague shadows of truly ancient priests whose genetic fingerprints have travelled down Africa? Could the Lemba be the descendants of one of the Lost Tribes of Israel? There is a considerable amount of documentation from various sources of the expulsion of ten tribes from Israel by the Assyrian King, Shalmaneser V, after his conquest of their country in 722–721 BC. But no one knows what happened to them, although the few ancient accounts we have indicate that they were driven south.

The Apocrypha, a set of Hebrew books (or parts of books) included the Septuagint translation of the Old Testament (into Greek), reputedly made by seventy Jewish scholars in Alexandria around 200 BC. Remarkably the Septuagint turns out to be a very accurate record. As a result of comparisons made with the Dead Sea Scrolls that include a fragmented copy of Isaiah, we know that the old Jewish scholar-scribes applied rigorous checks to their copies. They would total up the number of letters, then find the middle letter of the book. If the copy was not the same as the original they would start again. For example, a comparison of Isaiah 53 from the Dead Sea Scrolls with a later (Massoretic) text shows only seventeen differing letters, and ten of these are mere differences of spelling like, say, 'Honour' as opposed to its US form, 'Honor'.

Nowadays the word 'apocryphal' is used to warn of texts that need to be taken with a pinch of salt. But is the original Apocrypha a rather more reliable record than we thought? Does it offer any clues to a refugee tribe, or remnants of that tribe, which worked its way down to south-central Africa and there made a seminal contribution to the creation of a unique culture which would go on to build monumental temple-cities, one of which, Great Zimbabwe, is, dimensionably, a mirror image of Marib, the temple of the Queen of Sheba, in the deserts of modern Yemen?

All the ancient translations aver that the Assyrians did drive out ten of the twelve Hebrew tribes which, under Joshua, had taken possession of Canaan, the 'Promised Land', after the death of Moses. By then, after the death of Solomon, the Jewish kingdom had split in two. Two tribes set up the kingdom of Judah in the south and the remaining ten ruled Israel. These ten tribes of Israel then vanish from the face of the earth. They remain arguably the greatest missing persons (or mass murder) mystery of history and the search for them has never stopped; indeed, it goes on at this very moment via the Internet. The Apocrypha (IV Ezra) says the lost tribes were forced into arid lands beyond the 'Mountains of Darkness', uninhabited by human beings. The Zeng, remember, were even in much more recent times regarded by Arabians as subhuman. A later, more detailed, account describes them as vanishing into a country of great mountains and rivers where they were trapped behind a river, the Sambatyon, with magical properties. It defied anyone crossing it during the week but calmed down on the Sabbath, a most effective trap for Israelites immobilised by their holy day of rest!

Be that as it may, I think we have finally reached the end of the road. I strongly suspect that it is a road that can now only be retraced by the genetic scientists and they alone may some day give the answer to a question that I would never have dreamed of asking when I began this enquiry: did the Shona plateau become the promised land of a lost tribe of Israel?

Whatever the truth, these Semitic refugees did not build the Zimbabwe culture alone; indeed, by the time the great *zimbabwes* were built they would, as Frederick Courtney Selous first suggested, have been indistinguishable from the local people, just as now they are but genetic traces.

This is Zimbabwe's matchless heritage. I pray that before too long Zimbabweans may be in a position to rejoin the commonwealth of nations, spearhead the research into their exotic past, and promote lucrative access to the ancient architectural treasures they alone possess.

Bibliography

Ardrey, R. *African Genesis*, London, Collins, 1961

Baines, T. *The Gold Regions of South East Africa*, London, Stanford, 1882

Barnard, A. *Hunters and Herders of South Africa; a Comparative Ethnography of the Khoisan People*, Cambridge University Press, 1922

Barros, J. de. *De Asia*, Lisbon, 1552

Beach, D.T. *The Shona and Zimbabwe*, London, Heinemann, 1980

Beckingham, C.F.W. and Huntingford, G.W.B. (eds). *The Prester John of the Indies*, Cambridge ,Hakluyt Society, 1961

Bent, J.T. *The Ruined Cities of Mashonaland*, London, Green & Co., 1893

Berhard, F.O. *Karl Mauch, African Explorer*, Cape Town, Struik, 1971

Bishop, W.W. and Clark J.D. (eds). *Background to Evolution in Africa*, Chicago and London, University of Chicago Press, 1967

Boozair, E., Malherbe, C., Smith, A. and Berens, P. *A History of the Khoi Khoi of Southern Africa*, Cape Town, David Phillip, 1966

Brentjes, R. *African Rock Art*, London, Dents, 1969

Bruwer, A.J. *Zimbabwe: Rhodesia's Ancient Greatness*, Johannesburg, Hugh Keartland, 1965

Burke, E.E. *The Journals of Carl Mauch, 1869–1872*, National Archives of Rhodesia, 1969

Cann, R.L., Stoneking, M. and Wilson, A.C. 'Mitochondrial DNA and Human Evolution', *Nature* (1987)

Carroll, S.T. 'Solomonic Legend: The Muslims and Great Zimbabwe', *International Journal of African Historical Studies* (1998)

Caton-Thompson, G. *The Zimbabwe Culture; Ruins and Reactions*, Oxford, Clarendon Press, 1931

Coupland, R. *East Africa and its Invaders*, London, Oxford University Press, 1938

Dart, R.A. *Foreign Influences of the Zimbabwe and pre-Zimbabwe eras*, Salisbury, NADA, 1965

Deacon, H.J. and Deacon, Janet. *Human Beginnings in South Africa*, Cape Town, David Philips, 2002

Dunn, E.J. *The Bushmen*, London, Collins, 1931

247

Bibliography

Fagan, B.M. *Southern Africa During the Iron Age*, London, Thames & Hudson, 1965

Fouche, L. (ed.), *Mapungubwe*, Cambridge University Press, 1937

Gardner, G.A. *Mapungubwe, Vol. 2*, Van Schaik, 1963

Garlake, P.S. *Great Zimbabwe*, London, Thames & Hudson, 1973. See also *Journal of African History* 9, 11 (1968 and 1970)

Gayre, R. *The Origin of the Zimbabwe Civilisation*, Salisbury, Galaxie Press, 1972. See also *Mankind Quarterly* 4 (1964)

Goedicke, H. (ed.). *The Report of Weenamun*, Baltimore, John Hopkins University Press, 1975

Grenville-Freeman, G.S.P. *The Medieval History of the Coast of Tanganyika*, Oxford University Press, 1962

Hall, R.N. *Great Zimbabwe*, London, Methuen, 1905

——. *Prehistoric Rhodesia*, London, Unwin, 1909

—— and Neal, W.G. *The Ancient Ruins of Rhodesia*, London, Methuen, 1902

Harden, D. *The Phoenicians*, London, Thames & Hudson, 1962

Hourani, G. *Arab Seafaring in the Indian Ocean in Ancient and Mediaeval Times*, Princeton, Princeton University Press, 1995

Huffman, T.N. 'The Rise and Fall of Great Zimbabwe', *Journal of African History* (1972)

Huntingford G. (ed.). *The Periplus of the Erythraean Sea*, Cambridge, Hakluyt Society, 1980. Also known as *The Periplus of the Red Sea*

Keppel-Jones, A. *Rhodes and Rhodesia. The White Conquest of Zimbabwe*, Montreal, McGill-Queen's, 1987

Kessler, D. *The Forgotten Jews of Ethiopia*, New York, Simon & Schuster, 1958

Kirby, P. *The Musical Instruments of the Native Races of Africa*, London, Oxford University Press, 1934

Leakey, L.S.B. 'New Finds at Oldevai Gorge', *Nature* (1961)

Lewis-Williams, J.D. *Discovering South African Rock Art*, Cape Town, David Philips, 1990

Libby, W.T. 'Chicago Radio-Carbon Dates III', *Science* (1952)

Livingstone, D. *Missionary Travels and Researches in Southern Africa*, London, 1857

MacIver, D.R. *Medieval Rhodesia*, London, Macmillan, 1906

MacKenrick, P. *The Northern Stones Speak*, London, Chapel Hill, 1980

Marinatos, S. *Crete and the Mycenae*, London, Thames & Hudson, 1960

Mathers, E.P. *Zambesia: England's El Dorado in Africa*, Rhodesiana Reprint Library, 1891

Maund, J.E. *On Matabele and Mashona Lands*, Proceedings of the Royal Geographical Society, 1891

Mayer, A. *The Archaeological Sites of Greefswald: Mapungubwe Hill*, University of Pretoria, 1996

Bibliography

Menoll, R.P. *The Zimbabwe Ruins near Fort Victoria*, Rhodesian Scientific Association, 1902

Mphelo, M.N. 'The BaLemba of the Northern Transvaal', *Native Teachers' Journal* (1936)

Mufaka, K. *Dzimbabwe: Life and Politics in the Golden Age*, Harare, 1983

Murray, M.A. *The Splendour that was Egypt*, London, Sidgwick & Jackson, 1949

Pankhurst, R.K.P. (ed.). *The Ethiopian Royal Chronicles*, Addis Ababa, Oxford University Press, 1961

Parfitt, T. *Journey to the Vanished City*, London, Hodder & Stoughton, 1992

Peters, C. *The Eldorado of the Ancients*, London, Pearson, 1902

Potts, D.T. *The Arabian Gulf in Antiquity*, Oxford, Clarendon Press, 1990

Phillipson, D.S. 'The Excavations at Axsum', *Antiquities Journal* (1995)

Price, T. 'The "Arabs" of the Zambesi', *Muslim World* (1954)

Rightmire, R.J. *The Evolution of Homo Erectus*, Cambridge University Press, 1990

Robinson, K.R. 'Excavations on the Acropolis Hill', in Summers, Robinson and Whitty (eds), 1961, pp. 159–92

Schofield, J.F. 'Zimbabwe: A critical examination of the building methods applied', *South African Journal of Science* 38, 81–111

Shinie, M. *Ancient African Kingdoms*, Edward Arnold, 1965

Sicard, H. von. *Lemba Clans*, NADA 39 (1972)

——. 'Shaka and the North', *African Studies* (1955)

——. 'The Lemba Ancestor Baramina', *African Studies* (1953)

——. *Lemba Initiation Chants*, Ethnos, 1963

Stayt, H.A. (ed.). *The Bavenda*, London, 1931

Summers, R. *Inyanga: Prehistoric Settlements in Southern Rhodesia*, Cambridge University Press, 1958

——. *Excavations in the Great Enclosure*, in Summers, Robinson and Whitty (eds), National Museums of Southern Rhodesia, 1963, pp. 236–88

——. *Zimbabwe; a Rhodesian Mystery*, Johannesburg, Nelson, 1963

——. *Ancient Ruins and Vanished Civilsations of Southern Rhodesia*, Cape Town, T.V. Bulpin, 1971

Theal, G.M. *Records of South Eastern Africa*, vols I–IX, Cape Town, C.J. Rhodes, 1893–1903

Ullendorff, E. *The Ethiopians*, Oxford University Press, 1960

Van Warmelo, N.J. *The Copper Mines of Musina and the Early History of the Zoutspanberg*, Pretoria, 1940

Walker, E.A. *Arabs and East Coast Africa*, London, Longmans Green, 1957

Walton, J. 'The Soapstone Birds of Rhodesia', *South African Archaeological Bulletin* (1955)

Whiteway, R.S. *The Portuguese Expedition to Abyssinia in 1541–3*, London, Haklut Society, 1902

Bibliography

Whitty, A. *A Classification of Prehistoric Stone Buildings in Mashonaland and the Origin of Stone Architecture at Zimbabwe*, National Museums of Southern Rhodesia, 1957 and 1959

Willoughby, J. *A Narrative of Further Excavations at Zimbabwe*, London, George Phillip, 1893

Wilmot, A. *Monomatapa-Rhodesia*, London, 1896

Index

Index

Index

Index